ISBN 978-1-333-35835-8
PIBN 10494758

This book is a reproduction of an important historical work. Forgotten Books uses state-of-the-art technology to digitally reconstruct the work, preserving the original format whilst repairing imperfections present in the aged copy. In rare cases, an imperfection in the original, such as a blemish or missing page, may be replicated in our edition. We do, however, repair the vast majority of imperfections successfully; any imperfections that remain are intentionally left to preserve the state of such historical works.

English
Français
Deutsche
Italiano
Español
Português

www.forgottenbooks.com

Mythology Photography **Fiction**
Fishing Christianity **Art** Cooking
Essays Buddhism Freemasonry
Medicine **Biology** Music **Ancient**
Egypt Evolution Carpentry Physics
Dance Geology **Mathematics** Fitness
Shakespeare **Folklore** Yoga Marketing
Confidence Immortality Biographies
Poetry **Psychology** Witchcraft
Electronics Chemistry History **Law**
Accounting **Philosophy** Anthropology
Alchemy Drama Quantum Mechanics
Atheism Sexual Health **Ancient History**
Entrepreneurship Languages Sport
Paleontology Needlework Islam
Metaphysics Investment Archaeology
Parenting Statistics Criminology
Motivational

STUDIES IN ECONOMICS AND POLITICAL SCIENCE

EDITED BY PROFESSOR W. A. S. HEWINS, M.A.

THE REFERENDUM IN
SWITZERLAND

THE LONDON SCHOOL OF ECONOMICS AND POLITICAL SCIENCE

10 ADELPHI TERRACE, STRAND, LONDON, W.C.

The special aim of THE LONDON SCHOOL OF ECONOMICS AND POLITICAL SCIENCE is the study and investigation of Economic and Political Institutions. Many of the Lectures and Classes are designed to promote a wider knowledge of modern commercial conditions, and to meet the needs of those engaged in the Civil Service, municipal employment, journalism, teaching, and public work. The School provides training in methods of investigation, and affords facilities for original work in Economics and Political Science.

PUBLIC LECTURES AND CLASSES are held on Economics, Statistics, Commercial History and Geography, Commercial and Industrial Law, Railway Economics, Banking and Currency, Finance and Taxation, Muncipal History and Administration, and Political Science.

SPECIAL CLASSES, only open to full students of the School, arranged as a three years' course of study, are held in each subject. Students carry on their studies under the DIRECT PERSONAL SUPERVISION of the Lecturer.

THE LECTURES are usually given between 6 and 9 P.M. THE CLASSES are held both in the evening, between 6 and 9 P.M., and during the daytime.

THE SCHOOL IS OPEN TO MEN AND WOMEN.

THE SCHOOL YEAR commences in October. There are THREE TERMS, each about ten weeks in duration, viz.: (1) October to December; (2) January to March; (3) April to July. STUDENTS MAY JOIN THE SCHOOL AT ANY TIME.

THE FEES FOR FULL STUDENTS ARE £3 A YEAR, OR £1 A TERM. Students may also be admitted to one or more Courses of Lectures on payment of fees varying in amount with the length of the course.

SCHOLARSHIPS, varying from £25 to £100, are given to enable students of ability to pursue their studies at the School.

STUDIES IN ECONOMICS AND POLITICAL SCIENCE are in course of publication under the Editorship of the Director of the School.

All communications should be addrsssed to the Director, W. A. S. HEWINS, M.A., The London School of Economics and Political Science, 10 Adelphi Terrace, London, W.C.

THE REFERENDUM IN SWITZERLAND

By SIMON DEPLOIGE

ADVOCATE

With a Letter on the

REFERENDUM IN BELGIUM

By M. J. VAN DEN HEUVEL

PROFESSOR OF INTERNATIONAL LAW AT THE
UNIVERSITY OF LOUVAIN

Translated into English

By C. P. TREVELYAN, M.A.

TRINITY COLLEGE, CAMBRIDGE

Edited with Notes, Introduction, and Appendices

By LILIAN TOMN

GIRTON COLLEGE, CAMBRIDGE

LONGMANS, GREEN, AND CO.

39 PATERNOSTER ROW, LONDON

NEW YORK AND BOMBAY

1898

STUDIES IN ECONOMICS AND POLITICAL SCIENCE

Published under the auspices of the London School of Economics and Political Science, and Edited by Professor W. A. S. HEWINS, M.A., *Director of the School.*

1. THE HISTORY OF LOCAL RATES IN ENGLAND. By EDWIN CANNAN, M.A., Balliol College, Oxford. Crown 8vo, 2s. 6d.

   "An interesting summary of the development of one element of taxation. It is still more interesting as the first publication of the newly-established London School of Economics and Political Science, which is attempting to do, though on different lines, a work analogous to that which has been for some years carried on by M. Boutmy's well-known Ecole des Sciences Politiques in Paris."—*Times.*

2. SELECT DOCUMENTS ILLUSTRATING THE HISTORY OF TRADE UNIONISM. 1. THE TAILORING TRADE. Edited by F. W. GALTON. With a Preface by SIDNEY WEBB, LL.B.

   "What Professor Brentano failed to find when he collected the materials for his memorable essay 'On the History and Development of Guilds and the Origin of Trade Unions,' Mr. Galton has discovered in great abundance, setting forth in his introduction the historical sequence and the economic significance of the documents themselves, and the movements they illustrate, with no little skill and insight."—*Times.*

3. GERMAN SOCIAL DEMOCRACY. By the Hon. BERTRAND RUSSELL, B.A., Fellow of Trinity College, Cambridge.

   "A history of the movement during the last thirty years, and of the abortive efforts to retard its growth, leads up to the consideration of its present position, which is approached in a fair-minded spirit and discussed with insight and judgment."—*Times.*

4. THE REFERENDUM IN SWITZERLAND. By SIMON DEPLOIGE, University of Louvain. Translated by C. P. TREVELYAN, M.A., Trinity College, Cambridge, and Edited with Notes, Introduction, and Appendices, by LILIAN TOMN, Girton College, Cambridge.

5. LOCAL VARIATIONS OF RATES OF WAGES. By F. W. LAURENCE, B.A., Trinity College, Cambridge ; Adam Smith Prizeman, Cambridge, 1896.   [*To be published shortly.*

6. THE ECONOMIC POLICY OF COLBERT. By A. J. SARGENT, B.A., Brazenose College, Oxford ; Hulme Exhibitioner and Whately Prizeman, Trinity College, Dublin, 1897.
                                    [*To be published shortly.*

7. SELECT DOCUMENTS ILLUSTRATING THE STATE REGULATION OF WAGES. Edited, with Introduction and Notes, by W. A. S. HEWINS, M.A., Tooke Professor of Economic Science and Statistics at King's College, London ; Director of the London School of Economics and Political Science.
                                              [*In preparation.*

And other Volumes.

INTRODUCTION

THE Swiss have systematised direct legislation by means of two institutions, the referendum and the popular initiative. The referendum is a popular vote on laws or legislative questions which have already been discussed by the representative body. The popular initiative is a further development of the principle of direct legislation, by which sections of the community are able to draft a law themselves on any subject, or to insist that the Legislature shall do so.

Proposals to establish some kind of direct legislation, and especially the milder form of it, the referendum, have been made in the Belgian and Australasian Parliaments, in the first case as a substitute for the royal veto, and in the second as a way out of deadlocks between the two houses of the Legislature. In the French Parliament various attempts have been made of late years to get certain laws submitted to the people, and to introduce the referendum into the communes.[1] The introduction of a communal referendum has also been proposed in the Italian Parliament.

In the United Kingdom the referendum has been advocated by writers of more or less eminence as a substitute for the House of Lords, and as a corrective

[1] See J. Signorel, *Le Referendum législatif*, pp. 171–181.

for all the evils of party and parliamentary government.[1] The referendum has been extensively used in the British Trade Union world,[2] and has existed for over a century in many of the states of America in the form of a popular vote on constitutional changes.[3] A Direct Legislation League was formed there in 1894 to secure the introduction of the referendum and initiative in the Swiss form, not only in all the American states and municipalities, but also in the Federal Government, as a remedy for the prevalent corruption of political life.[4]

The expediency of direct legislation by the people is therefore more than a question of speculative interest: it has become a question of practical politics.

M. Deploige's objective and impartial study of the historical development and actual working of the referendum and the initiative in Switzerland—the country which has the most extensive experience of direct legislation by the people—will therefore interest not only the student, but the politician and the intelligent citizen. It is, however, most important to bear in mind that direct legislation of the people as practised in Switzerland forms a part of a peculiar and complicated constitution. To study it without considering the people who work it, the system for which it was designed, and the circumstances in which it

---

[1] See *Contemporary Review*, April 1890, "Ought the Referendum to be introduced into England?" A. V. Dicey; also the discussion on the subject in the *National Review*, 1894, by Professor Dicey, Mr. Curzon, Admiral Maxse, Lord Grey, and Mr. St. Looe Strachey.

[2] See *Industrial Democracy*, S. & B. Webb, 1898.

[3] *The Referendum in America*, E. P. Oberholtzer, 1893, and the *Adoption and Amendment of Constitutions*, C. Borgeaud, 1895.

[4] The organ of the League is the *Direct Legislation Record*, published quarterly. Editor, J. Eltweed Pomeroy.

originated, is like examining and criticising a set of wheels without inquiring whether they are intended for a perambulator, a coach, or an engine. For we must remember that in Switzerland the people have an Executive which does not resign when out-voted by the Parliament, a Parliament which does not dissolve when its measures are negatived by the people, and an electorate who, whilst constantly rejecting the laws made by their representatives, nevertheless usually send back those same representatives to serve for the same term of years. Party organisation, as we understand it, seems to be almost unknown in the Swiss Republic. The referendum, in fact, exists in Switzerland under circumstances and amid surroundings that are without parallel in any other country. M. Numa Droz, who has been President of the Confederation, and who is one of the most able of the Swiss constitutional writers, has expressed grave doubts as to the possibility of successfully introducing it into other countries without at the same time accepting other parts of the Swiss Constitution. Indeed, it is only by realising the peculiarities of the Swiss Constitution that the referendum appears in its true light as part and parcel of the Swiss ideal of democracy.

The Swiss Republic, though but a speck on the map of Europe, is composed of twenty-two "sovereign" states united in a Confederation, "in order to ensure the independence of the country against foreign nations, to maintain internal tranquillity, to protect the liberty and rights of the confederated citizens, and to increase their common prosperity." [1]

---

[1] See Swiss Constitution, 1874.

Three of the twenty-two cantons are subdivided into demi-cantons, and each of the twenty-five has its own constitution and special laws, its own legislative, executive, and judicial authority. They differ from each other in race, language, religion, and habits of thought. The French occupy the cantons of Vaud, Geneva, Neuchâtel, and parts of Fribourg, the Valais, and Berne; the Italians spread over Ticino and part of the Grisons, which is inhabited for the greater part by Romance-speaking people, and German is spoken by the majority of the people in fifteen cantons.[1] All official documents, laws, and administrative orders issued by the Federal Government are published in three languages—German, French, and Italian—while in a canton like Berne, where the people are partly French and partly German, the cantonal laws and decrees are published in both languages. The cantons can be classified according to religion just as easily as according to race, but the lines of race and religion do not coincide.[2]

The government of Switzerland could not, under these circumstances, be highly centralised, yet union of some kind is an absolute necessity. The Swiss

[1] According to the last census, 634,613 speak French, 155,130 Italian, and 38,335 Romance, and no less than 2,083,097 German; Zürich, Basle (Rural and Urban), Aargau, Thurgau, Schaffhausen, Appenzell (Inner and Outer Rhodes), Uri, Schwyz, Unterwalden (Obwald and Nidwald), Zug, Glarus, St. Gall, Lucerne, Solothurn, and Vaud are almost entirely German.

[2] Lucerne, Uri, Schwyz, Unterwalden, Zug, Fribourg, Ticino, Valais, Appenzell (Inner Rhodes), and Solothurn are Catholic; Zürich, Berne, Schaffhausen, Appenzell (Outer Rhodes), Vaud, and Neuchâtel are Protestant; Glarus, Basle, Thurgau, and St. Gall have a Protestant majority; while the Grisons, Aargau, and Geneva are equally divided. According to the census of 1888, there are about 1,716,548 Protestants to 1,183,828 Catholics.

cantons are so small that the population in the largest numbers scarcely half a million, and in the smaller ones about 13,000. To avoid absorption in their powerful neighbours and to preserve their independence, they have entered into an alliance, of which the Federal Government is the political expression. Hence we find in Switzerland an intense local patriotism and a very real national patriotism, great jealousy of any encroachment by the Central Government, and also the firm intention of supporting it at all hazards.

The Swiss citizen is first of all a member of a commune, then a member of a canton, and last of all a member of the Federal Government. The three thousand communes into which the country is divided are, in fact, the basis of the Swiss Constitution, for it is only by being a member of a commune that a Swiss becomes a citizen of the republic. The communes vary in size and extent, those that include the large towns being in a different position as regards wealth and population from those in the purely agricultural districts. Each commune, whether large or small, is practically a state in miniature, with an organised government, consisting of a deliberative and an executive body. In the German parts of Switzerland the deliberative body, known as the Communal Assembly, is composed of all the resident male citizens. They meet together at regular intervals, and decide all questions relating to local police, sanitation, the maintenance of highways, the erection of buildings, and the sale of landed property.[1] At

---

[1] The descendants of the original settlers alone have the right of managing the communal lands. They are known as the Bürger or citizens, and the assembly in which they discuss these questions is

these meetings they fix the annual budget, pass the accounts, levy new taxes, and elect the Executive Council and other local officials.

Any member of the Assembly may offer motions or amendments at the meeting, but usually these are brought forward by the Executive, or referred to that body before being finally voted on.

The Executive, which is generally known as the Communal Council, consists of a body of three or four members, one of whom is chosen as president or mayor. Their function is to carry on the current business of the commune.

In the towns of Berne and Zürich it has become impossible for the people to assemble together in a mass meeting, owing to the growth of population, and we therefore get the councils elected by the people. In Berne since 1887 there is a Communal Council of nine members, and a Municipal Council, which supervises the Communal Council. The inhabitants of the commune elect these councils annually, but they do not surrender their powers to them. A communal voting by ballot takes place once a year at least, in which the people decide on all important questions, the town being divided into several districts for the purpose of voting.[1]   In

called the Bürgergemeinde. The difference between this assembly and the Communal Assembly is very slight in practice. When the question of communal lands comes up, the later settlers or "inhabitants" abstain from voting.

[1] At these communal votings the citizens assent to the annual budget, fix the local rates, and decide questions as to the purchase or sale of property the value of which is more than 100,000 francs. On June 28, 1896, the people of Berne rejected a proposal to elect the Communal Council by proportional representation, they rejected

addition to this, any 500 citizens may bring forward any proposal which is submitted by the councils to the people.

The commune of Zürich was reorganised in 1891, and possesses now a council of nine members, which act as the executive, and a "Great Municipal Council," which is the deliberative body. In this case, also, the electors vote finally on all important matters, and on all appropriations over a certain amount.[1]

The right of the people to initiate proposals themselves is also recognised in Zürich, and is vested in any 800 citizens.

In most of the French communes the general body of inhabitants elect a council which attends to the matters ordinarily dealt with by the people in the German communes. There are, therefore, two councils, one dealing with general policy and matters of importance, and a smaller executive body with a mayor at its head.

In the canton of Geneva a communal referendum was established, in 1894, much like that of Berne and Zürich. The difference is, that in Berne and Zürich certain questions must go to the people and be voted on, whereas in Geneva a voting only takes place when a demand to that effect has been presented by a certain number of citizens.. In the

---

a plan to organise a fire brigade, they accepted a proposal to lower the price of gas, and a proposal providing for the maintenance of the cathedral tower.

[1] In December 1894 the people of Zürich decided to buy up the existing tramways. In June 1896 they agreed to lay down three more lines, at an estimated outlay of 2,000,000 francs. They also decided on buying up land to the value of 950,000 francs to build artisan dwellings.

municipality of Geneva any 1200 electors may demand a referendum on any resolution of the council within thirty days after it has been passed. The budget is, however, excepted. This is never laid before the people. In the other communes of Geneva the number is fixed at one-third of the voters, and the demand must be sent in within fourteen days. The people of Geneva also have the right of initiative. Any 1200 citizens can either draw up a scheme, which must be sent to the electorate without alteration, or they may suggest a project to the councils in general terms, leaving them to work it out. In the first case, the council has the right of proposing an alternative scheme to the people, or can merely advise that the popular proposal be accepted or rejected.

Besides these communal assemblies there are parish meetings, which are assemblies of all the members of the same confession living within the boundaries of the commune. The people in every canton decide what form of religion shall be the State religion. In nine cantons they have adopted Roman Catholicism, in six others both Roman Catholicism and Protestantism, while in five others there are three State Churches, and Neuchâtel supports an Israelitish society besides three Christian sects. The State denominations are supported by the public treasury,[1] but local matters concerning the Church are considered in the parish meetings. The questions dealt with in the meetings include the election of pastors, the building and main-

---

[1] The funds are provided by a tax in some states, and in others out of the proceeds of the Church lands taken over by the State. See Vincent, p. 179, and Orelli, *Staatsrecht*, &c., p. 156, for further information on Church matters.

tenance of houses of worship, and the management of Church funds. The members of this assembly also elect the Church officers, who administer the affairs of the society, supervise the work of the pastor, and in some states act as a board of overseers of the poor.

The School District Assembly is another of these local mass-meetings. The members of the commune —or, in the case of the small communes, the members of several communes—meet together to elect a school board, and to exercise a general supervision over all educational matters. The necessary funds are provided partly by the State and partly by a local rate levied by the school assembly when it meets. The amount to which the State subsidises the commune varies according to the wealth of the commune.

It is difficult to exaggerate the importance of these local assemblies upon the development of Swiss democracy. The introduction of the referendum or initiative into the cantonal and federal constitutions is of recent date; but the people have been trained to direct legislation in their local assemblies for half a thousand years. "Democracy in Switzerland," says Mr. Lowell, "is not merely a national or cantonal matter, but has its roots far down in the local bodies, and this gives it a stability and conservatism which it lacks in most other Continental nations."

The connecting link between the canton and the commune is supplied by the district, which is established merely for the convenience of administration, and has no separate political life of its own. The head of the district is the agent of the cantonal government in the territory over which he is placed.

He carries out the laws enacted by the cantonal legislature, and enforces the orders of the cantonal executive. He is usually elected by popular vote and is sometimes assisted by a council.[1]

The Swiss cantons are the democratic workshops of Europe.[2] On their twenty-five anvils are hammered out almost every conceivable experiment in political mechanics; and if a particular experiment proves successful, it is adopted by one canton after another, until it ultimately receives a definite consecration by becoming part of the Federal Constitution, which is, indeed, largely moulded on cantonal experience. The cantons are, so to say, the "seed-trial" grounds of the various forms of popular government, and offer an unrivalled field to those who wish to study the latest phases and expedients of democracy.

The cantons are free to adopt what form of constitution they like, so long as it is republican, and contains nothing contrary to the Federal Constitution. Therefore all the constitutions and constitutional amendments must be "guaranteed," *i.e.* sanctioned by the Federal Assembly.[3]

[1] In several states of small territory the district is dispensed with altogether, the cantons dealing directly with the communes.

[2] The Swiss Confederation is said to consist of twenty-two cantons; but three of these are divided politically, and are to all intents and purposes separate cantons. Basle is divided into Urban Basle and Rural Basle, Appenzell into Inner and Outer Rhodes, and Unterwalden into Obwald and Nidwald. These half cantons only differ from whole cantons in that they send but *one* deputy each to the Council of States, and count only as half a vote when the State votes are counted in the case of a federal referendum on constitutional amendments.

[3] Constitutional changes are very frequent. Between 1891 and 1895 there were twenty-three revisions, four of which were total revisions.

The spirit of the cantonal constitutions is fittingly expressed by the following phrases: "Sovereignty resides in the mass of the people. It is exercised directly by the electors, and indirectly by the authorities and officials" (The Constitution of Berne, 1893). "The people, in virtue of their sovereignty, give themselves the following constitution" (Constitution of Zürich, 1868).

The Swiss cantons fall into two classes—the cantons with elected legislatures, and the cantons with a system of legislation by mass-meeting.

Eighteen of the cantons have a Legislature consisting of a single chamber, called the Great Council (sometimes the Kantonsrath or Landrath), the members of which are chosen by universal suffrage for periods ranging from two to five years. The usual term is, however, three or four years.[1]

---

[1] In Zurich there is one deputy for every 1200 of the population; in Geneva, one to every 666 persons; and the largest proportion in any canton is one member to 2000 people. In Ticino, Geneva, Neuchâtel, Zug, and Solothurn, proportional representation has been introduced since 1891 for the election of the Great Councils. It was also proposed in St. Gall in 1895, and in Berne in 1896, but was vetoed in each case by the people.

For an account of the different systems of proportional representation tried in each canton, see *Les Lois Suisses de la Représentation proportionelle comparées et commentées*, par Alphonse Frey, in *Le Bulletin de la Société Suisse pour la Représentation proportionelle*, Geneva and Basle, Librairie Georg. The system in Geneva is also described in the *Annals of the American Academy*, November 1895, by Professor Wuarin, of Geneva. See also Droz, *Études et portraits politiques; La Suisse Jugée par un Américain*, pp. 500-504. The method of procedure is of a complicated type, as there are usually several parties at Swiss elections. The system varies considerably in the different cantons. It is a subject which would well repay study. The first elections by proportional representation took place in Ticino in 1892.

b

The work of the Legislature is to pass the laws, vote the taxes and appropriations, and supervise the administration. The people are the check on the Legislature, and they act as a check in three ways.

In the first place, they can veto legislation by means of the referendum, and can make an imperative suggestion as to the subject of legislation by means of the initiative. The different forms which these institutions take are considered in detail by M. Deploige. It is sufficient to say here that the referendum is always compulsory in constitutional amendments, *i.e.* no constitutional change can become law without the popular assent expressly given. In the domain of ordinary legislation there is only one canton, Fribourg, in which the referendum is not recognised in some form or other. It is compulsory in the case of every law in nine and a half cantons, it may take place upon demand in six and a half cantons, and in two it is compulsory for financial questions only.

Every canton, except one, recognises the right of the people to demand, by means of the initiative, either a partial or a total revision of the constitution.[1]

Nineteen cantons recognise the right of initiative in ordinary legislation.

The second check on the Assembly is the popular right of bringing about a dissolution, which is, however, only found in six of the German cantons. A petition for a dissolution is signed by the statutory number of citizens and sent in to the Executive, who

---

[1] Geneva, which is the exception, puts the question of revision to the people periodically every fifteen years. Schaffhausen only recognises the initiative in the case of a total revision.

are obliged to put the question to the whole people, "Shall the Great Council be dissolved or no?" If the people reply in the affirmative, the Council is *ipso facto* dissolved, and a new election takes place. "This device," says Mr. Lowell, "has not, however, proved to be of much importance. Formerly it was sometimes used, and in one case, at least, with success; but owing to the shortening of the periods for which the councils are elected, and the general introduction of the referendum, it is practically obsolete."[1]

Another method of getting rid of the Great Council is occasionally tried. In every cantonal constitution, except Geneva, the people have the right of demanding a total revision of the constitution. The law in most cases provides that if the people decide in the affirmative, the Great Council must dissolve, as a sort of penalty for driving the people to extreme measures and not anticipating the general wish. A new Council is then elected to carry out the revision. This exceptional method was last tried in Ticino in 1890. As a rule, however, the life of the Legislature is measured by the constitution, and not by the exigencies of politics. The Executive[2] is usually elected for the same term as the Legislature, and generally consists of five or seven members.[3] It is of the nature of a business committee of the Legislature, and each member has charge of a separate department.

---

[1] Lowell, p. 230.
[2] Called sometimes Conseil d'Etat, sometimes Kleine Rath, and Regierungsrath.
[3] In Berne, of nine.

It is elected directly by the people in eleven of these cantons, so that there are only eight in which the Executive is elected by the Great Council.[1]

The members of the Executive do not sit in the Great Council, but appear there to make reports on the administration, propose measures, and take part freely in debate without voting. They are the motive power in legislation, and yet are quite subordinate.[2]

The absence of party, which we shall notice at greater length when we come to deal with the Federal Government, is very marked in both the cantonal executives and legislatures. The party in the minority usually have seats allotted to them in the Executive Council, and in Berne and Aargau the constitution expressly directs that this shall be done.[3]

It is a curious fact that direct popular election does not produce a homogeneous Executive any more than election by the Legislature. The minority is, in fact, represented in the Executive in every canton except two, and these are two of the cantons which leave the choice to the Great Council.

The members of the Executive do not resign when they come into conflict with the Assembly, but submit, retain their places, and carry out the orders of the larger Council. Both the members of the Executive and Legislature enjoy practically permanent tenure, the people seeing no reason why they should not

[1] The eight are—Neuchâtel, Vaud, Valais, Fribourg, Berne, Lucerne, Schwyz, and Aargau. In Ticino, Geneva, and Zug the executive is elected by proportional representation.

[2] The Council of State in Geneva can, however, send any measure it did not itself introduce back to the Council for reconsideration.

[3] " The minority shall be equitably represented in the Executive Council " (Constitution of Berne, 1893).

continue to re-elect a good man, even though his views may not always coincide with their own.[1]

In three cantons[2] the people have the right of dissolving their Executive by presenting a demand to that effect, which is referred to the whole people, as in the case of the Great Councils.

The second group of cantons have a much more historic and picturesque form of government than those we have just been considering. In six small and very conservative cantons, or rather in two cantons and four half cantons,[3] there is a system of government known as the Landsgemeinde.

These assemblies consist of the whole of the adult male population, who meet once a year, and are the supreme authority of the canton. The power of the Landsgemeinde is set forth in the Constitution of Uri (Art. 51) in the following words: "Whatever the Landsgemeinde within the limits of its constitution ordains, is the law of the land, and as such shall be obeyed."

Then it continues: "The guiding principle of the Landsgemeinde shall be justice and the welfare of the Fatherland, not wilfulness nor the power of the strongest."

It differs from an ordinary mass-meeting, says Mr. Vincent, "in the respect that the voter not only expresses his political opinions, but instantly gives effect to them. The majority does not imply, wish, or demand the passage of a measure, but enacts it

[1] See *Graphisch-statistischer Atlas der Schweiz*, 1897, for the average terms during which the members have sat continuously.

[2] Schaffhausen, Solothurn, and Thurgau.

[3] These are Glarus, Uri, the two Unterwalden, and the two Appenzells. Until 1848 it existed in Schwyz and Zug also.

at once, and the vote is a solemn legal proceeding." [1]

The business to be laid before the Landsgemeinde
is carefully prepared beforehand by a Council. This
Council is generally known as the Landrath or Kantonsrath. Its members are not elected at the mass-
meeting, but by separate electoral districts. It is
described by Mr. Lowell as a sort of subsidiary legislature which attends to all the details that cannot
well be brought before the people. It passes administrative resolutions, votes the smaller appropriations,
examines the accounts, and appoints the minor
officials. [2]

There is also an executive body elected by the
Landsgemeinde known as the *Regierungsrath* or
Standescommission. It is usually composed of
from five to nine members, one of whom is President, and is officially known as the Landamman.

Each state has practically an independent judicial
system of its own, for the Federal Tribunal is not
a regular Court of Appeal. The organisation of the
Judiciary varies in the different states. There is a
Justice of the Peace or Official Mediator, whose duty
it is to try and settle the matter in a friendly way.
Then there is the District Court, consisting of a
bench of judges, and above that the Cantonal Court.
Criminal matters go before special tribunals. In
certain cantons the people elect all the judges from
the highest to the lowest; in others they elect the

---

[1] *State and Federal Government in Switzerland*, p. 109.

[2] Lowell, p. 225, *op. cit.* Mr. Vincent points out that in this body
there is one delegate for every 400 inhabitants in Uri ; in Nidwald,
Appenzell, and Inner Rhodes, one to every 250 ; and in Obwald as
many as one to 187.

Juge de la Paix and the members of the District Court. The tendency is for the people to extend their powers in this direction. The judges are elected for stated periods, generally four or six years, at the end of which they have to be re-elected. In Zug even the judges are elected by the system of proportional representation—a very curious development of the system. The Swiss cantonal tribunals do not, like the American State Courts, try acts of the Legislature. Only in two of the Landsgemeinde cantons, Uri and Nidwald, does the constitution provide that a person injured in his private property or rights by a determination of the Landsgemeinde may protest, and if the meeting disregards the protest, the judge shall decide between the people and the plaintiff.

By the Federal Constitution the Swiss National Government has only power to legislate on a certain number of subjects, and all powers not expressly conferred upon the Federal Government are vested in the States.[1] The constitution provides no special machinery for executing the federal laws or judgments, these are carried out by cantonal authorities; and by cantonal machinery.

The Federal Government consists of a Legislature, an Executive, and a Judiciary. The Federal Legislature or Federal Assembly, as it is called, is composed of two Houses, the National Council and the Council of States. The National Council, consisting of 147 members, is elected for a term of three years by universal suffrage. The Council of States corresponds to the American Senate, and is the final representative of the old Diet of Ambassadors. Each state

[1] See Federal Constitution of 1874 and amendments.

sends two members to the Council, and if the canton be subdivided, each half canton sends one. The Council of States thus numbers forty-four members.[1]

The Federal Assembly meets twice a year, in June and December, for about four weeks; and there is usually an extra session in March, which is even shorter still. The debates are not officially reported, and only meagre accounts of them appear in the papers. The whole of the proceedings are very quiet, business-like, and rather informal. The two Houses are exactly equal as to powers. Any proposition, even those of a financial nature, may be introduced in either House. The motions or bills, when discussed and adopted by one Chamber, are then sent to the other. The rejection of a proposal by the House which first discusses it does not prevent the other House taking it up. In 1883, for instance, a law relating to civil status and marriage was rejected by the National Council, taken up by the Council of States, and finally passed by both Houses. Bills amended in either Chamber pass to and fro until some compromise is arrived at, or until both agree that it shall be dropped. Grave conflicts between the Houses never occur. If one Chamber continues

[1] The deputies to the Council of States are elected directly by the people in some cantons, in others they are appointed by the cantonal legislatures. There is no uniformity either of payment or of the length of period for which they are elected, some being sent for a year, others for four. The growing tendency is for the people to directly elect the members of the second Chamber as well as the popular Chamber. Ten cantons and six half cantons have now adopted the system. It is becoming the custom to elect the members for three years, so that both elections should coincide, and both Houses be renewed at the same time. This is now done in nine cantons and four half cantons.

to energetically oppose a project adopted by the other, the latter submits with a good grace.

The two Houses sit together for three purposes: to elect the Federal Council and the commander-in-chief, to exercise the right of pardon, and to decide conflicts of jurisdiction between the cantonal authorities.

The Executive consists of a Federal Council of seven members, who are elected for the three years by each new Federal Assembly as soon as it meets.[1] Each Councillor presides over a separate department, and for the sake of convenience he usually retains the same one continuously, though the re-allotment is supposed to be made every year. One of the seven Councillors is elected each year to the supreme office of President of the Federal Council, and is officially recognised as "President of the Swiss Confederation." Another Councillor is elected at the same time to the office of Vice-President. Neither the President or the Vice-President may hold office for more than one year, and the custom is for the Vice-President to be elected President, so that the office really passes in rotation through the Council. The President receives a salary of £540 a year, the other Councillors £480, and none of them are allowed to pursue any other profession or business while in office. The President has no special powers. He is merely the annual chairman of the committee and titular head of the State, and has charge of any one of the seven departments. His position is very inferior to that of any

---

[1] The Council cannot contain two men from the same canton, and by tradition certain cantons are entitled to special consideration. Berne and Zürich, for instance, have always been represented.

individual head of any known executive. Apart from his colleagues he has no power, nor has he any power over them. He is, however, one of a body of seven that count for a great deal. The Council has not any direct executive functions, except in the department of foreign affairs, the customs, postal and telegraph services, the polytechnic school, the arsenal, and the alcohol monopoly. It acts by way of inspection and supervision.

The Executive have important legislative as well as administrative functions. The Federal Council as a body have the right of initiating legislation. They also report in practice on all proposals brought forward in the Chambers before these become the subject of serious debate. It is also very common for the Chambers to pass a resolution, called a "*postulat*," requesting the Council to prepare a bill on some subject. Thus the Federal Council can introduce, draft, and report on legislation; but the President has no vote, no power of suspending or annulling laws.

The relations of the Executive and Legislature are peculiar. The members of the Executive are not allowed to sit in the Assembly. They may, however, take an active part in the debates, though, of course, they may not vote. The Executive has no power over the Assembly. It cannot prevent the Assembly meeting, prorogue it or dissolve it, and can only summon it on extraordinary occasions.

The Federal Tribunal, the chief judicial body of the Confederation, does not occupy anything like the position of the American Supreme Court. It is not the guardian of the constitution, and has no power to pronounce any Act passed by the Federal Parliament unconstitutional and therefore void.

So far we have dealt with the dry bones of the Swiss Constitution. Now we have to consider its two unique and distinguishing marks—on the one hand the absence of the party system, and on the other the direct intervention of the people in the work of legislation by the referendum and the initiative.

The Federal Council represents no one body in the Federal Assembly. It is usually composed of members of the left and centre groups—that is to say, of Radicals and Liberal-Conservatives; but in 1891 a member of the extreme right, Dr. Zemp, the clerical representative of Lucerne, was elected Councillor, and in 1894 was promoted by a three-to-one vote of a dominantly Radical Assembly to the office of President. Nor is it even necessary that the majority of the Council should share the opinion of the majority of the Assembly. From 1876–1883 four of the seven members were Liberals and three Radicals, though the majority of the people's representatives were Radicals.

It follows from this non-party character that the Federal Executive is not expected to be unanimous. No measure, it is true, may be brought before the Assembly unless it has received the votes of the other ministers, but it is a mere matter of form, and a Councillor feels himself in no way bound to support a bill of his colleague because he has been obliging enough to give it his vote in order that it may be debated in the Assembly. What is more, he has no hesitation in opposing it openly, and members of the

Council have even been known to argue against each other in the Assembly.

To Englishmen it would seem impossible that an Executive made up of persons of different political views, and unconnected by any ties of party loyalty, should constitute a strong and efficient administrative body. One would expect such a casual coalition to spend its time in quarrels and fruitless discussions. As a matter of fact, however, it works very smoothly. This is partly due to the placid dispositions of the Swiss Councillors and their readiness to accept a compromise. But such a result could not be possible if the Federal Council were in any sense a "responsible Cabinet," obliged themselves to lay before Parliament and the country a distinct policy, and expected to resign collectively or individually if that policy or any part of it were defeated. No idea of responsible leadership enters into the relationship between the Federal Council and the Federal Assembly. Each minister is elected as an executive official to carry out within his own department the will of the Assembly, and ultimately of the whole electorate. The Councillors are not expected to shine as so many stars in the political firmament. Whatever their politics, they are expected to obey the orders of the Assembly.[1]

Thus no minister thinks of resigning if his measure is vetoed either by the Assembly or by the people at a referendum. If either the Legislature, or in the last resort the electorate, show by their vote that they disagree with him, he submits, and prepares another bill more in harmony with the wishes of his em-

[1] See article by M. Numa Droz, "The Election of the Federal Council," in *Études et portraits politiques.*

ployers. Thus a bill on the construction of railways by private enterprise was substituted for a bill in which the Council had proposed that the railways should be a monopoly of the Confederation, and this without any change in the Government. Since 1848 there have been only two cases of resignation on political grounds, and only one of these was caused by a conflict with the Legislature. When M. Welti resigned in 1891 because his project for the purchase of the Central Railway was rejected by a referendum, his resignation created a great sensation, and was even said to be "unconstitutional." To the Swiss democrat it seems irrational for the State to lose a valuable administrator on account of a difference of opinion. No censure is implied by a hostile vote, the servant has merely misunderstood his master's views. The relationship between the Federal Assembly and the Executive is in fact much like that of a man with his old and trusted family solicitor. The solicitor manages his legal business, persuades him for his own good, and is a factor which cannot be neglected although nominally subordinate. The client usually defers to his advice, and takes no important legal action without consulting his lawyer, but he retains full freedom to take his own course without giving offence, and there arises no question of resignation or dismissal on either side. But this analogy from common life hardly does justice to the real power of the Swiss Executive over the Assembly. For whilst a solicitor advises a client how to act, the Federal Council not only advises as to policy, but is itself the only authority charged with carrying out that policy.

Another important outcome of the non-party character of the Government is the tendency for the
Federal Council to become a permanent body. From
1848 to 1895 there have been only thirty-three
Federal Councillors, the average period of service
being over ten years.[1] Only two Councillors who
were willing to serve have failed to be re-elected, one
of whom lost his seat in 1854, and the other in 1872,
when party passions ran high. The Swiss Federal
Council is, in fact, far more akin to a body of *elected
civil servants* than to the responsible ministry which
governs the United Kingdom, or to its analogues in
some European countries or in the self-governing
British colonies.

The same absence of party spirit characterises the
election of members to the Federal Assembly as well
as to the Federal Council. The Swiss have it so
firmly rooted in their minds, that there is no need to
dismiss a good man because you disagree with him,
that the certainty of the result prevents the elections
from being contested. Only forty per cent. of the seats,
for instance, were disputed in 1887. No great effort,
therefore, is needed to retain seats; and as the minority
know they have no chance of controlling the Government, they cease to agitate, and there is an absence
of excitement about elections generally.[2] M. Borgeaud

---

[1] Four have served over twenty years; and Herr Carl Schenk,
who died in office in 1895, was elected in 1863, served, therefore,
thirty-three years, and was six times President. (See *Graphisch-
statistischer Atlas der Schweiz*, 1897).

[2] M. Numa Droz says: "When the people reject a law in virtue
of their sovereign right, there is no entering into a state of conflict.
The craftsman carries out the work to his satisfaction; the employer who gave the order is of a different opinion, and sends it

has described the motives which influence the average Swiss elector: "If the candidate is obliging and affable," he says, " and if he is a neighbour and a decent fellow generally, and if he belongs to the party from which the elector has been in a habit of choosing, then the elector argues thus: Would it not be an undeserved reproach to turn X out? His opinions may be different from my own, well! what of that! If he does it again, one can always say No"[1] The Swiss elector is, on the whole, more interested in the person of his representatives than in his politics. The rejection of laws by the referendum seems, in fact, to take the place of a change of parties. When the Government is unpopular or times have been bad, and people are generally discontented, they do not give vent to their dissatisfaction by turning their representatives out of office, but they promptly vote down the measures their representatives have prepared. Thus the fate of a law depends a great deal more on the immediate popularity of the Government than on its own merits or defects. It is a novel method of rebuking the party in power, but it is not ineffective. It makes them careful not to offend if possible, and it has the merit of avoiding all violent changes.[2]

back to be altered. The legislator is not discredited. He is in the position of a deputy whose bill has not passed ; there is no want of confidence." (See *Contemporary Review*, March 1895.) This is typical of the way in which the Swiss regard the question.

[1] *Revue du Droit Public, Nov.–Dec.* 1896 : "In the elections which took place in October 1896, out of the 160 members in the National Council there were only 25 new ones, and in the Council of States only 8 new ones. Between 1888 and 1896 the National Council has only lost 20 of its members by non-re-election, while 62 retired voluntarily."

[2] There is also an absence of party machinery and organisation outside the houses of the Legislature. "There are in the Con-

Whether an Executive Government elected on these principles is more or less harmful than a Cabinet representing one party or the other is an interesting problem of political science. One thing is certain, both the Council and the Assembly are less susceptible to popular influence in that they do not change with the changing ideas of the people. The Executive Council in particular pursues its own course, guiding and leading the Legislature in virtue of its superior capacity and experience, telling them what they ought to do, producing the necessary documents, and finally seeing that the orders of the Assembly are carried out. The Council has therefore been called the mainspring or balance-wheel of the constitution.

How far the aloofness of the Executive from the popular currents of opinion in the State is responsible for the desire of the people to intervene directly in public affairs, or, on the other hand, how far such a stable and permanent government is rendered possible by the safety-valve of direct legislation; how far, in short, the absence of party government causes direct legislation, or direct legislation contributes to the absence of party government, is a delicate question for political philosophers to decide.[1]

federation," says Mr. Lowell (p. 313), "no national committees, no elaborate system of primary caucuses and general conventions, no men who make a business of arranging nominations and managing campaigns. The Clericals and the Radicals do occasionally hold Congresses, but these are simply intended to prevent disruption by discussing the questions of the day; they take no part in the nomination of candidates." Parties, however, play an important part in getting up demands for the referendum—still more in drafting initiative demands. There are a group of professional politicians, the *neinsager*, who make a business of collecting signatures against federal laws, and raising an opposition.

[1] Mr. Lowell says, " The causes of the peculiar relation of Swiss

With regard to the organisation and actual working of the referendum and the initiative, M. Deploige's careful study will speak for itself. Though the Swiss experiments in direct legislation have, during the last ten years, excited much interest in the United King-

parties to the Government, and of the condition of the parties themselves, may be sought in various directions." He attributes the low development of party to the shortness of the sessions of the Federal Assembly, which give little opportunity for the development of a party policy or the consolidation of party ties ; also to the fact that the Government has little patronage to bestow, and that the deputies to the Federal Legislature are elected on local rather than national issues. In the case of all elected representatives, the Swiss votes for men with whom he is personally acquainted, and this obviates the need of party machinery for the selection of candidates. No doubt the fact that Switzerland is divided internally by race and religion also prevents the growth of strong compact parties. The referendum itself, Mr. Lowell considers, "tends in a variety of ways to lessen the importance and increase the stability of parties." It tends to split up the issues. "The referendum entails a decision only on the special measure under consideration, and hence the people are never called upon either at an election or a referendum to judge the conduct of the party as a whole. It is no doubt largely for this reason that Swiss political parties have no very definite programmes and little organisation."

Again, Mr. Lowell points out that the referendum tends to draw attention to measures instead of men, "and it is the personal admiration or dislike of public men that forms a great deal of the fibre of party allegiance."

Moreover, the referendum weakens the motives for a change of parties. "If a law is unpopular the people simply refuse to sanction it, and this prevents an outcry against the party that enacted it. If, on the other hand, the people ratify it, there is clearly no use in trying to persuade them that the men in power were very wrong in passing it, and ought to be turned out for doing so. Nor is there any chance for an opposition to work on the popular fears by foretelling the bad laws the ruling party is likely to pass if continued in power, because the people can always reject measures they do not like. Hence it is not easy to finds arguments for electing a new set of representatives drawn either from the past or the future."

dom, they have been more often popularly described than precisely studied. In particular the use of the referendum and the initiative in the government of the canton as distinguished from the Federation has received but scanty notice. In M. Deploige's excellent work the English student will find a more precise and detailed account of these remarkable experiments than in any other volume known to me.

Mr. Lowell, after praising the excellence of the Swiss government, points out that Switzerland is free from many of the difficulties that perplex other nations. Her population is, after all, very small, only three millions in all, "and experience proves that the larger the population the harder is the problem of free government."

These three million inhabitants are not recruited from without by a long line of immigrants which have to be absorbed and to be educated into useful citizens. They are not divided by any glaring inequalities of wealth. There are no very rich or very poor, no millionaires and but few paupers. The Swiss are, therefore, not confronted with the great problem of poverty. There are no eager capitalists always seeking new fields for investment with the attendant result of inflation and crashes. They have no great undeveloped countries to be opened up with untold possibilities of mineral wealth, which arouse all the gambling instincts of a nation. Social equality, too, is very marked. There are no " classes " and "masses," and no great class differences. The people are decidedly stationary, not moving about from one part of the country to another, or rising or falling in

the social scale.[1] Two-thirds of the population are
engaged in agriculture, and the manufacturing element is comparatively small. The great industrial
struggles which convulse other countries and paralyse
trade are therefore non-existent.

There are no very large cities. In 1893 the population of Zürich was 130,000, including suburbs;
Geneva, 78,777, including suburbs; Basle, 75,114;
Berne, 47,620; Lausanne, 35,626. There are no others
with a population over 30,000. There are in couse-
quence no great congested and discontented masses
of unemployed with their burden of poverty and vice,
with which most modern governments attempt to
cope in vain.

For the Swiss foreign policy is a negligible quantity. Their neutrality is guaranteed, and they are
not hampered by belonging to the European Con-
cert, and are not obliged to make enormous sacrifices of men and money in order to keep up military
appearances.

" The Swiss Confederation," says Mr. Lowell, " is
on the whole the most successful democracy in the
world. . . . The people are contented ; the Government is patriotic, far-sighted, efficient, and economical,
steady in its policy, not changing its course with party
fluctuations. Corruption in public life is unknown. . . .
Officials are selected on their merits, and retained as
long as they can do their work, and yet the evils of
a bureaucracy scarcely exist. . . . The Swiss statesmen deserve the highest praise for their labours and

[1] *Cf.* New South Wales, which proposes to introduce the referendum. Fifty thousand were disfranchised in 1893 who had voted
in 1892, because they had changed their residence.

the greatest admiration for their success, but we must beware of thinking that their methods would produce the same effects under different conditions. The problem they have had to solve is that of self-government among a small, stable, and frugal people, and this is far simpler than self-government in a great, rich, and ambitious nation." [1]

I have endeavoured in my footnotes to bring up to date the mass of material on the referendum and initiative which M. Deploige has so clearly marshalled, and I have ventured in a few places to add some further references and explanations likely to be of use to the English reader.

L. TOMN.

[1] "Lowell," pp. 335–336.

CONTENTS

CHAPTER I

THE EVOLUTION OF DEMOCRACY IN SWITZERLAND

CHAPTER II

THE MODERN ORGANISATION OF "LEGISLATION BY THE PEOPLE"

CHAPTER III

THE RESULTS

CONCLUSION

AUTHOR'S PREFACE

THE letter published at the commencement of this volume absolves me from the necessity of a long explanation as to my motives for undertaking a study of the Swiss referendum.

The Belgian Chambers are about to discuss the important proposal for a *royal referendum,* and I have thought that it might be useful at this juncture to make the Swiss referendum known in this country. Although they differ in certain respects, yet these institutions have one thing in common—they are both concerned with the direct intervention of the electorate in the legislation of the country.

I have endeavoured to describe the historical origin of the referendum, to demonstrate its mechanism, and to set forth its results, without taking a side, or being actuated by any prejudices.

My book would have been very incomplete had I confined myself to the works on the subject. The referendum has attracted but little attention up to the present, and has not hitherto been examined as a whole. I have therefore prosecuted my inquiries in Switzerland in person, in order to become initiated into the working of the institution. I now offer the fruits of this twofold investigation to the public.

I must not omit to express my gratitude to those Swiss gentlemen who have given me both useful advice and valuable information.   My thanks are especially due to MM. Ruchonnet and Droz, Federal Councillors; to MM. Naville and Respini, National Councillors; and to Professors Hilty of Berne, Pedrazzini of Fribourg, and Wuarin of Geneva.

S. DEPLOIGE.

TONGRES, *8th March* 1892.

A LETTER ON

THE REFERENDUM IN BELGIUM

BY

M. J. VAN DEN HEUVEL

DEAR SIR,—Your book is most opportune. Yesterday no one spoke of the referendum without a smile.
The direct intervention of the people in legislation
was looked upon as a democratic dream, which could
only be realised under exceptional and transitory
circumstances, or in countries where legislation was
in a primitive stage. It was clearly understood that
a permanent system of popular consultations was
quite a different thing from those unfortunate plebiscites which have taken place from time to time in
France, and from those solemn ratifications of constitutional reforms which are prescribed by the
constitutions of the American States. But quite
suddenly one fine morning, in the midst of the din
of party strife over electoral reform in Belgium, a
powerful voice was heard above the rest, demanding
the immediate introduction of the referendum for a
reason which had not occurred to any one up to that
time, namely, in order to strengthen the royal authority.[1] There was a pause for the moment out of sheer

[1] [On the 27th November 1890, six Liberal members proposed that
there should be a revision of the constitution, and the idea was to

surprise. Then the controversy broke out, and discussion began to rage.

Those who are not enamoured of sudden and untried political reforms have had recourse to the legislation of other countries for guidance and instruction. In spite of a thorough and searching examination, however, they have not been able to find a single country with a monarchical government in which any one has thought of establishing the referendum for the sake of strengthening the influence of the sovereign. And, indeed, in no country have they discovered any attempt to combine the rights of a constitutionally limited head with so democratic an institution as the referendum. The only country which afforded a suitable field of observation was

introduce universal suffrage for the election of members of the two Chambers. M. Beernaert, one of the ministers, suggested instead, in March 1891, that the suffrage should be extended, but that it should not be universal, and also that the Executive should be invested with power to consult the electorate on a law which had been proposed but not yet passed, or on a law which had passed but to which the King had not yet given his assent. The idea was that the referendum would strengthen the royal power, and compensate for the practically obsolete veto of the Crown. The proposal was adopted in the two Houses, with the proviso that the conditions under which the King should directly consult the electorate should be afterwards determined by a law. The Belgian constitution directs that the Parliament, after having voted for a revision, should dissolve, and the question be taken up by a new Parliament. When the next Parliament met, a commission to revise the constitution was appointed; but on the 26th of November 1892 the Minister of the Interior declared that, in view of the unfavourable reception which the referendum had met with both in Parliament and in the country, the Government would officially withdraw its proposals. Three members took the referendum proposal up, but the commission of revision rejected it by 15 votes to 3. The question of electoral reform still remained to be solved, and the discussions seemed so inter-

Switzerland, a federation of a group of republican cantons. The referendum has existed there for centuries, in the seclusion of a few cantons, like some rare alpine plant, and needed the atmosphere of modern ideas and the aid of special circumstances to revivify it, develop it, and make it spread over the whole country.

Your work has a twofold merit. It portrays the referendum for us as a living, working institution, with its almost invariable accompaniment and younger sister, the popular initiative. Your observations have been made on the spot, and are taken from life, and every page of your description irresistibly leads our thoughts back to our own country in order to compare the situations, and to prophesy the results of

minable that the people of Brussels determined to undertake a referendum on the subject. They applied to the municipal authorities to organise it, and a referendum was taken in four communes on the five different propositions of electoral reform. There were many protests as to the unconstitutionality of the proceeding, and finally, on the 14th February 1893, the King annulled the proceedings, and commanded the authorities not to interfere. The Liberal Association then took the matter up, and summoned 111,837 citizens of Brussels, over twenty-one years of age, to vote; 60,732 voted, and 56,338 were in favour of universal suffrage, but as the opponents of universal suffrage had recommended their party not to vote, and as 50 per cent. of those summoned did not vote at all, the result cannot be said to be decisive one way or the other.

For a history of the proposed introduction of the referendum, and a discussion of the principles involved, see Arnaud, *La Révision belge*, Paris, 1893; Fuld, *Die versuchte Einführung des Referendums in Belgien*, in the *Archiv für öffentliches Recht*, 1893, pp. 558–567; De Gamond, *De la Révision constitutionelle en Belgique*, Belgique Judiciaire, 1893; the *Revue générale d'Administration*, November 1893; Wuarin, *Le Referendum belge*, in the *Revue des deux Mondes*, 1st August 1891; Lorand, *Le Referendum*, Brussels, 1890; Deploige, *Le Referendum en Belgique*, *Revue générale*, December 1891; Hauleville, *Le Referendum royal*, Brussels, 1892.—Ed.]

a referendum in Belgium by the habitual results of
the referendum in Switzerland.   Your book is a book
of living politics, and one which is very suggestive.

Three forms of the referendum are discussed in
Belgium.   To distinguish them I have ventured to
term them—

> The Initiative Referendum (*Le Referendum
> d'Initiative*).
> The Referendum of Appeal (*Le Referendum de
> Partage*).
> The Corrective Referendum (*Le Referendum de
> Correction*).

All these three forms seem to me equally bad,
because they all proceed from the same principle, the
direct intervention of the people in legislation, which
in Belgium at the present day could not but result in
a state of things directly opposed to political progress.

Public opinion, however adverse it may be to the
referendum in itself, seems to me to vary in its degree
of opposition.   It is entirely hostile to the referendum
of initiative ; it regards the referendum of appeal
with more or less indifference, but rather unfavour-
ably on the whole; it dislikes and almost fears the
corrective referendum.

I. THE INITIATIVE REFERENDUM.

This referendum, according to its supporters, ought
to take place before every deliberation of the Chambers.
It is an attempt to engraft the popular initiative on
to the parliamentary system.   What a combination !
The people are to be consulted on principles which

are likely to be more vague and dubious than usual, since they are drawn up in general terms, and not elucidated previously by any public discussion between those interested on different sides. The Parliament will moreover be bound to take a certain course without having been first heard. It will be obliged to submit to and accept the vote, however brutally bald and laconic may have been its expression. Such a referendum would resemble an imperative mandate. It would be the immediate ruin of parliamentary government. Popular opinion has been so unanimous, and has opposed the proposal for an initiative referendum with so much energy, that it now seems to be definitely abandoned.

II. THE REFERENDUM OF APPEAL.

Many worthy people then bethought themselves of a compromise, and proposed to utilise the referendum in the case of a conflict between the two Chambers.

"A serious disagreement between the Senate and the Chamber of Representatives," they say, "is a crisis to be regretted, for it prevents the regular and normal conduct of business. Surely the most natural and simple course is to end the conflict by an appeal to the opinion of the electors, and to make them act as arbiters."

This concession seems at first sight to be unimportant, but appearances are deceptive, and it is, in reality, an innovation which needs careful consideration.

At the present day conflicts between the two Houses rarely occur. If the majority in the two Houses are actuated by different principles, both of them try to come to an agreement, and make attempts to find a common ground on which they can meet. They know that the solution of the difficulty depends upon themselves alone, and upon their mutually conciliatory attitude to each other. When once the dispute can be settled by a third party, the position will be immediately changed, the obstinacy of majorities will increase, and the concessions will be less frequent; each Chamber will wish to show that it knows itself to be in the right, and will have fewer scruples in opposing the other, because it knows that there is an easy method of deciding the matter and ending the struggle.

The dominant thought will no longer be that of mutual conciliation. When once the two Houses are certain that they cannot agree, their one object will be to formulate their opinions in those terms which are most likely to win for them the sympathy and favour of the arbiter, the people.

The referendum is not only open to the grave objection of increasing the temptation to disagree, but it is also liable to determine the dispute in such a manner that the result obtained is either bad or at least more incomplete and inadequate than would have been obtained had other means been adopted.

If the two Chambers continue to keep the same electoral origin—which seems to be the wish of the actual majority of the Senate—then, if the matter in question is important, and its solution too urgent to be postponed, the dispute ought to result in a dissolution. The Crown intervenes in this case without incurring any personal responsibility, takes note of the deadlock, ascertains its gravity and the necessity of ending it by the method laid down in the constitution. If, however, the two Chambers shall be chosen on a different electoral basis—and this seemed to be what the Government desired at first—then, when the revision takes place, some other expedient ought to be devised by which a conflict may be avoided. For instance, mixed commissions might be instituted which should be composed of deputies and senators similar to those which take place in the United States. Were the electoral basis different for each House, a referendum would be an appeal to the electoral body who chose the Chamber, and this would be to subordinate the Senate to the Chamber, and *a priori* to relegate to a second place those authorities who have received the title of senators.

The organisation of the referendum of appeal would moreover be far from simple. Nothing would, in fact, be more complicated. At what precise moment can it be definitely said that there is a conflict? Upon what sort of questions are the people to give judgment? What is to be the result of the popular vote? These are all difficult points.

It might often happen that dispute would not merely arise over the question of maintaining the *status quo* or replacing it by some other definite system. It might not unfrequently be a question of two systems of reform—one desired by the Chamber, the other by the Senate. Can you submit all sorts of projects and counter-projects to the electors? Poor elector! He is to be forced to legislate himself when he has chosen reliable men whose business it is to find the right path in the midst of a labyrinth of controversies.

III. The Corrective Referendum.

In reality all the heat of the discussion in Belgium is concentrated in the third form of referendum. It is proposed that the King should have the right to appeal to the referendum after the two Chambers have voted, in order that it may guide him in exercising his right of consent, and enable him effectually to quash the decision of the parliamentary majority.

Your book is principally concerned with the study of the Swiss institution, its legislative vicissitudes, and its relation to the social and economic conditions of the nation.

But when one reads what you have written, and then thinks of our own country, what vital differences there are between the Swiss and the Royal referendum. The mechanism of the political machinery is apparently identical in both cases. But when the institutions are examined more closely, and due attention is paid to the political surroundings of which they form part, it is obvious that the resemblance is merely superficial, and that the two are quite opposed. The Executive, the Parliament, the Ministry, the organisation of parties, the education of the people—all these primordial elements which constitute the characteristic features of a State are utterly and entirely different in Switzerland and in Belgium.

The King.

In Switzerland the right of appealing to the referendum is not confided to the executive power. It is in the hands of permanently organised groups, such as the cantons, or accidental groups, consisting of a certain number of persons who sign a petition and who are bound by no legal tie. In Belgium the idea is to place the referendum in the hands of the King, who is to be the judge as to whether a solemn appeal to the nation shall or shall not be made.

The justification of this royal referendum is given as follows :—

"The monarch, it is said, does not enjoy in practice the authority which he has in theory and which the texts ascribe to him. By the constitution he has the right to assent to laws, the right of dissolving the Chambers, the right of choosing and dismissing the Ministers. But apart from certain exceptional and unimportant circumstances, it would be morally impossible for the King to avail himself of his prerogative of veto. It would be a power at once too great, too weighty, and too perilous. The King could only refuse his assent, and put himself in opposition to his Parliament, if he felt himself supported by the general will of the country. Every time he refused his assent it would lead to a political upheaval and a dissolution. Every refusal would affect the personal responsibility of the King, and would affect it very seriously should he have wrongly interpreted the state of public opinion, and the same majority be returned after the dissolution. The referendum will solve these difficulties without the necessity of proceeding to extreme measures; it will make the sentiments of the electorate known by national and legal methods. The King will henceforward be able to act with certainty; he will see clearly which side is taken by public opinion, and whether he should or should not refuse his assent."

d

Such is the argument. It seems to me, however, that it contains two errors, one of principle and the other of fact.

In principle the King has the right of sanctioning or refusing laws, not only according to the text of the constitution, but according to the ideas which actuated the national Congress. It is for the King to follow the dictates of his conscience and his reason in the exercise of this right. It is certainly an extremely dangerous and undefined power ; but it is irrational to conclude that because its character is thorny and difficult it is therefore non-existent. The right of sanction, like the veto, when actually exercised, also affects the moral responsibility of the King—there can never be any question of his legal responsibility—but it is impossible to modify this situation by a reform in procedure, and the notion of right cannot be separated from the notion of responsibility.

Two theories are really advanced here. According to the first, which I consider absolutely untenable, the consent of the King must depend solely upon his interpretation of the true feeling of the country. The opinion of the country will be the opinion of half the citizens plus one who enjoy the franchise, and who have answered either yes or no. It is this majority which decides in the last resort as to the justice and utility of the law.

According to a second theory, which seems to me the only one based on law and on reason, the assent of the King must depend on his personal opinion of the justice and utility of the measure under discussion; but in forming that opinion he must give serious consideration to the opinion of the country; and the opinion which he ought to regard is the opinion expressed, according to party rules, by the majority of the deputies who enjoy the confidence of their electors, and who have been chosen by legal methods.

As a matter of fact, it is a great mistake to imagine that the referendum is a kind of present to the Crown. The King will gain nothing by this new right. He will neither be free to consult the people when it pleases him, nor will he be able to retain the power of decision in his own hands after the people have been consulted. If no text regulates the conditions under which the monarch shall exercise his right, he will be at the mercy of mass-meetings and petitions organised by the different parties, or even of disturbances and agitations in the street. The King will be obliged to resort to popular consultations every time that he thinks the Government powerless to cope with a difficulty.

A future Parliament, in order to avoid such a state of things, might draw up an explicit text, which should state the conditions under which the right should be exercised, and should limit it to the case in which a preliminary demand has been made either by a certain number of members of Parliament or by certain provincial and local bodies. These persons or bodies would then become " the ruling powers." On the one hand, the King could not appeal to the people unless those authorities were to agitate for it. On the other hand, if they were unanimous, he could not refuse to grant the referendum if they demanded it. Moreover, the people would be excited by parliamentary discussions, the press would become very noisy, and the party in a minority would move heaven and earth to defeat their opponents.

Various suggestions of a different nature have been put forward by the press. I shall only quote one of them here. It has been proposed that the King should have recourse to the referendum when a law has only passed one of the two Houses by a small majority. Such a provision would be equally disastrous to any freedom of action on the part of the King. Every time that a law is much disputed, and does not obtain a certain specified majority, the monarch must inevitably appeal to the electors, unless he would incur the reproach of being partial.

Laws which bear on matters which are the special province of the King, and which are likely to impose heavy charges on the country, such as military laws and estimates for the construction of fortified works, would in all probability be generally submitted to the electorate, in consequence of the agitation of the opposition.

Let us now turn to another side of the question, and consider the result of the popular consultation. If it is to be regarded as final, then the King has only to submit—he loses all personal freedom in the matter. Supposing, however, that the referendum is only regarded as a solemn piece of advice. Then the monarch is placed in a most embarrassing position. There is no difficulty evidently if there is a large majority; but how is he to decide if the figures are almost equally balanced, or if the number of negative tickets are not equal to half the number of the registered electors? How is he to decide if the total number of electors against the law is less than the total number of suffrages received by the parliamentary majority at the election? How is he to decide if cases of fraud and undue influence come to light which would be sufficient to annul an ordinary election?

Is it not true, then, to say that the Crown will not gain anything by the referendum, neither power or relief?

The referendum will, moreover, imperil the other powers which the monarch actually possesses.

As to the right of veto, it is not necessary to dwell upon it. This right will be entirely lost.

The right of dissolution will be fatally restricted. Those powers appointed by law to make a demand for the referendum will consider themselves bound to point out in how far the parliamentary majority and the people are at variance. How then can the King tell the country that a dissolution is necessary because the Parliament seems to him opposed to the general opinion of the country, when these authorised powers have made no sign or refuse to declare that the Parliament no longer represents the feeling of the nation on some particular point. The right of dissolution ought especially to be preserved from all new complications just now, as its exercise will become a more difficult matter in consequence of the proposed electoral reform by which general, provincial, and communal elections are to be placed on the same electoral footing. Formerly the results of the local elections were made use of to influence the parliamentary majorities, although the composition of the electoral bodies in each case might be very different. In the future it is to be feared that these attempts will be renewed with more semblance of reason, unless public opinion comes at last to realise that local elections are principally concerned with administrative questions.

In short, to introduce the referendum in the interest of the Crown is to pursue an illusion. Instead of being a benefit to the monarch who wishes to preserve a strictly constitutional attitude, it can only bring about many unfortunate complications, and lead eventually to loss of power.

The Parliament.

The Swiss Parliament and the Belgian Parliament have nothing in common. The important points of difference must be specially noticed.

The first is a difference in the fundamental ideas of government. My colleague and friend, M. Dupriez,[1] has recently described it to me as follows:—

"Switzerland is a democratic republic. The principle of popular sovereignty applied in its purest form has produced results in the constitutional organism and on political customs which are quite peculiar to that country. Every man who forms part of the Legislature, Executive, or Judiciary, is appointed for a fixed term. Each person elected is imbued with the idea of the sovereignty of the people, and uses the power delegated to him according to what he believes to be the wish of those who sent him. If he has made a mistake as to their wishes, he hastens to repair his error, and does not think of refusing his

---

[1] Author of that remarkable work, *Les Ministres dans les principaux pays d'Europe et d'Amérique.*

consent. Thus the members of the Federal Assembly whose opinions have been disavowed by their electors do not vacate their seats, the Ministers whose personal wishes are thwarted by the votes of the Assembly or the people nevertheless remain at their posts. In Switzerland the authorities do not resign, they always submit.

The organisation of the Federal Assembly constitutes a second great difference between the two countries. The electoral districts are so mapped out that one of the parties has a great advantage, and the parliamentary majority does not always represent the majority of the electors.

Finally, the third difference consists in the auto nomy of the cantons, and in the fact that the Federal Parliament has only very limited powers. On an average it passes about two or three laws a year. The ordinary session only lasts eight weeks. As to the cantonal assemblies, they scarcely sit longer than our provincial councils.

These three striking features of Swiss political organisation explain why the electors consider themselves authorised to interfere in legislation, either by means of the popular initiative or the referendum. According to their theories they are the great motive power, and ought to command the legislative assemblies to halt, or to advance, or to take a certain direction. Turbulent minorities avail themselves of the initiative as a means of dividing parties, and of the referendum as a means of obstruction.

The country, as a whole, only bestirs itself on certain occasions. It then protests against the parliamentary majority, and either gives the Legislature an imperative mandate to legislate by means of the initiative, or it makes use of the referendum to curb tendencies which are too pronounced. But the electors do not intervene except at long intervals, because they do not live in a unitary country under the direction of a general Parliament whose activity is unceasing. To introduce the referendum into Belgium is to make an attempt to bridge, by means of a badly poised plank, the abyss which separates the system of popular government from the true parliamentary system.

In England and Belgium the deputies are appointed by the electors, but they are not commanded by the electors. They must enjoy the confidence of the country, but they preserve an independence of thought and action. Our political conceptions are opposed to the idea of imperative mandates of any kind whatsoever. The members of the minority as well as the majority represent the nation. They guard between them both private and public interests. The referendum will degrade their position in the eyes of the electorate, who will ask why the choice of representatives is so important when their resolutions are not final. It will weaken their prestige and destroy the principle of their responsibility. Every deputy will realise that his vote is only equivalent to a piece of advice which the electorate may adopt or reject, and that it is the majority of the electors who decide either by tacit ratification or express decision. The position of members and senators will be that of political pioneers, their mission being confined to discovering the land, and to pointing out the advantages and the dangers of the situation.

There are also other drawbacks. If the two Chambers have a different origin, the Senate will be annihilated, and the principle of the duality of the Assembly will only be a hollow mockery.

Again, if the number of electors who are successfully opposed to the Government at the referendum is less than the number of suffrages obtained on the day of the election of the deputies of the parliamentary majority, this majority will be able to say that it is overcome and oppressed by the minority. In this way the dignity and force of Parliament will be irretrievably compromised.

Once a start has been made in the direction of popular concessions, it will not be easy to turn back. Even if the referendum should lead to unfortunate results, it would be difficult to abolish it, because it would be necessary to persuade the people themselves that they have been in the wrong, that they must make a public acknowledgment of the fact, and that they must renounce rights which seem to them to be rights lawfully acquired. No! the step once taken can never be retraced; and when the idea is followed out to its logical consequences by the rival parties, the result will be a series of legislative efforts much more advanced than those proposed to-day.

It will be necessary to revise Article 131 of the Constitution, which relates to constitutional reforms, and Article 85, which deals with the final choice of a new dynasty. These two articles provide a method of popular consultation quite different from the referendum. The country is appealed to for its opinion by means of a dissolution. This system will have then to be discarded as old-fashioned. It will also be necessary later on to introduce the popular initiative, which is an inevitable consequence of the referendum. The people will not only have the right of putting the drag on the legislative coach, they will also insist on giving it a start. Finally, the referendum and the initiative will be introduced with more show of reason for local, provincial, and communal affairs.[1]

The introduction of the referendum into our parliamentary organisation will not be merely a slight modification of the constitution, unnoticeable in its effects: it will be the germ of a new departure, or, to speak more exactly, the commencement of a complete political revolution.

The Ministers.

It is very rare for the chiefs of the administrative departments to resign in Switzerland when they have experienced a rebuff or a check at a referendum.

The attitude of the Belgian Ministers is very different. It is dictated, not by constitutional or legal texts, but by ancient and unchanging traditions.

Let us consider two distinct cases. Suppose, first of all, that an important law is passed by the two Chambers, and is supported by the Ministry, who stake their existence on it either implicitly or in express terms.

As matters stand to-day, should the King refuse

---

[1] The referendum has nothing in common with the inquiry which the local authorities are authorised to institute by Article 75 of the Communal Law, in order to gain information before making a decision.

his assent to such a law, the logical course for him to pursue is to change the Ministry, or even dissolve the Chambers. But if the referendum is introduced into our constitution, it is quite a mistake to suppose that the situation will be simplified. It will instead be extremely complicated, not only before but after the popular consultation.

When the persons or bodies authorised to demand the referendum from royalty exercise their right, or, to speak more generally, when the specified conditions to be determined by a future Parliament shall be fulfilled, the Cabinet will assemble in all haste; they will discuss the point as to whether they are obliged to give their countersign in order that a work which they regard as most important shall be called in question at a popular consultation.

The parliamentary supporters of the party will be convoked in a special meeting. If they are of opinion that the chances are that the consultation will be favourable to them, they will permit the Ministers to countersign without raising any difficulties. If, on the other hand, they consider that an isolated consultation would be a bad piece of policy, and that they would be more likely to succeed in a dissolution, they will decide upon resistance, and begin the struggle from above. The Ministers will be obliged to openly refuse their countersign and to send in their resignation, or allow themselves to be dismissed. If they fear, however, both the consultation and the dissolution, they will then face the referendum with the courage with which we face the lesser of two evils.

Let us then take one step further and consider a

fresh difficulty. Let us suppose that the people have been appealed to, and that they have answered very clearly, and have rejected the law passed by the Parliament and supported by the Ministers. What course is then open to the Ministers and the deputies? According to our present theories the Ministers must retire before a hostile vote of the Chambers on a Cabinet measure. How much more then must they retire before an unfavourable decision of the country itself? How could the majority remain on the front benches as if nothing had happened? How could these Ministers and this majority discuss and pass any other important law? They would be a mere butt for the witticisms of the Opposition, who would declare the Government to be destitute of all moral support. It would be condemned to a policy of in-action until it acquired renewed strength at a general parliamentary election.

The second case is this: Suppose one of the Chambers has adopted an important law in spite of the opposition of the Cabinet. The Ministers have done all in their power to ensure its defeat; they have agitated both by speech and writing, and all to no purpose: they have been beaten. To-day only one course is open to them: they must give in their portfolios. But when once the referendum appears on the horizon, will there not be a great temptation for these Ministers to resist the Chamber, and to threaten it with an appeal to the electorate?

In some countries the unfavourable vote of the Senate is not regarded by the Ministry as having the same significance as an adverse vote of the Chamber. The Senate seems to be somewhat removed from the people, while the Chamber seems to be closely in touch with them. But it would surely be going a step beyond this were the people in Belgium to have the right of personally intervening in legislative decisions.

If the parliamentary majority has no fear of a dissolution, it will show its teeth and resist the Cabinet, and make the latter's existence an impossibility. But in a country where the parties are a periodical check on each other, the majority will generally be in doubt as to the results of a dissolution. In this case it will draw in its horns, and the Ministry will remain in power, in spite of the opposition aroused. This will, in fact, be personal government supported by a latent and extra parliamentary force, the force being a popular one, and only manifesting itself at indeterminate intervals, and on questions which have been cleverly chosen.

When the Cabinet shall make the bold experiment of submitting even the budgets to the people, then the Parliament will cease to be a necessary part of our political organisation; the Ministers and those who support them will be "the sovereigns of the plebiscite."

Parties.

In Switzerland there are numerous dismembered and divided groups, there are passing coalitions and a considerable floating mass of unattached members.

In Belgium, on the contrary, the parties form two armies; they have ancient traditions, and an organisation extending throughout the country. They correspond to the tendencies which manifest themselves in society. The extension of the franchise will perhaps modify their position; it will accentuate the subdivisions. No one, however, expects a radical change to take place in their composition from one day to another. The tendency is for the two existing currents to continue to be the dominant currents for a long time to come without any mingling of the waters.

The advocates of the referendum do not seem to understand the necessity for the existence of parties, and seem also to have no fear of the influence these same parties will exercise upon general opinion. Let us examine the argument advanced with such fre quency that it comes only second to the argument we have just examined in connection with the King. They say "that the referendum must have been invented, even if it did not already exist, in Switzerland, that it is indispensable to a representative organisation, and that it is a happy complement of the right of dissolution." If the nation and the parliamentary majority be out of harmony, it is essential, so they maintain, to find out the points on which the two differ. If these points prove to be numerous, or if there be a general disagreement, the dissolution of Parliament must ensue. If the nation and Parliament be merely at variance on some special question, the referendum is the necessary remedy, the people will be consulted on the one subject, isolated from all others, and the issues will be precisely and openly stated. A dissolution leads to a discussion of persons and programmes; the referendum abolishes personal preferences, and restricts the debates to the examination of a particular law. A referendum and a dissolution are two separate rights, corresponding to two situations which are in reality quite different.

Without raising any doubt as to the competence of the people in legislative questions, this political dilemma is capable of being satisfactorily disposed of in more ways than one. Let us suppose that a party has a large majority, and that the two Chambers pass a bill of the first importance, and that the Crown, before giving its assent, dissolves Parliament. In this case the electoral struggle will surely centre round this particular law. If the Opposition be successful, it is easy to see that the opinion of the country is unfavourable to the politics of the majority. Should the King, instead of dissolving Parliament, have recourse to the referendum, is it not probable that a great many considerations will influence the discussions? Again, if the referendum should result in a negative answer, the real feeling of the people still remains unknown. Did the country only wish to reject the law, or did it wish at the same time to overthrow the majority? One thing is certain, and that is that the electors who supported the majority at the time of the election have now ranged themselves against the law passed by that same majority. The difficulty is to know whether these electors are not discontented with their party as well as with the law. The actual figures obtained at the referendum will always be equivocal in this respect, and the public mind will be full of uncertainty on the point.

The partisans of the referendum shut their eyes to the practical truth. They are ingenuous enough to believe that the electors, when voting, will merely vote on the merits of the question, and that their

judgment will be as unbiassed as that of a stranger
who has only arrived in the country the evening
before. It is a curious mistake, for it is obvious
that the vote of the electors will be a party, and not
a theory vote. The electors are instructed by party
journals; they attend party meetings, they belong to
party associations, they have fought for years on the
the side of a party, and have debated the party programme within their circle. Is it likely that the
elector will be able suddenly to put off "the old
man" when a consultation occurs, and learn to think
in a new manner? Will not even the most thoughtful
and least prejudiced men hesitate before separating
themselves from the flag which they habitually follow?
The idea is to divide political programmes, but will
not these men see a close connection, either logical or
historical, between questions which are supposed to
be separable?

The supporters of the referendum think that it will
be easy to determine whether the discord between
the nation and Parliament exists on a whole series of
questions or on some special one only. They forget,
however, that party programmes are often regarded
by the electors in the light of pieces of cloth which
have still to be made up. They are the expression of
certain tendencies which will be curtailed or developed
at length according to circumstances. They include
also traditional questions, as well as local questions
and questions of organisation. All the articles in the
programme do not possess the same characteristics of
urgency and importance at any one given moment,
but they are all connected by ties of principle or
interest. The political crock is always on the bubble,

and sometimes it is one item and sometimes another that rises to the surface. At certain times the whole programme seems to be summed up in two or three points, sometimes in one only. When the party in power has embodied this special point in a law which appears to it of the greatest importance, is it then possible to distinguish, as the advocates of the referendum seem to wish, between the party and the principle of their law, to separate the father and the child, so to say, declaring all the while that to hit the one is not to strike the other?

Each time that he uses the referendum, the King will be obliged to declare that there is no discord between the parliamentary majority and the country, and that it is not necessary to have recourse to a dissolution. But he will nevertheless be obliged to add that he is uncertain whether all the adherents of the party in power are agreed on such and such a special point, and that he thinks in this respect there may be some difference of opinion between them which may have arisen either before or after the election. Such a proceeding would probably be a great strain on a party, and might lead to general confusion and a possible relaxing of party ties. It seems to amount to an appeal against a compact and well-disciplined group of deputies, addressed to all the forces of the opposition, to all the malcontents within the majority itself, and to all those whose interests are more or less affected by this particular law, and whose hopes in the present or in the future may have received a check. The break up of parties into groups would be a grave danger. A government has as much need of energy as a man has of will-

e

power, and the parliamentary government which does not rest on the solid basis of a faithful majority is a government which is powerless and impotent. Moreover, the horizon is not so clear and cloudless in Belgium to-day that we can afford to weaken our motive powers and content ourselves with representative authorities devoid of force and stability.

Parties are a necessity in a parliamentary system, and in spite of their exaggerations and inconveniences, they are a distinct benefit in our country. They are the intermediaries between the mass of the electors and the leaders. They group and educate the citizens, they register the echoes of general opinion, they subject complaints to a sifting process, they recommend moderation to the turbulent, and tabulate the important matters in the order which seems to them most useful. Once you divide them, break up their ranks, and destroy their programmes, you will have deprived the people of their necessary guides, and you will only have before you a great multitude of errant or indifferent electors.

The People.

The gulf between the Swiss and the Belgians is quite as great as that which separates the Belgians, who have always enjoyed a real independence, from the French, who have been unused to self-government for centuries.

Democracy has had a peaceful existence in Switzerland, for the mountains have afforded it the security of a natural and impregnable fortress. The inhabitants have learnt to regulate their affairs in a patriarchal manner. Cantons with Landsgemeinde still exist there to-day, and the people collect together in the great valleys and decide all civil and political questions as of old. In other places this primitive form of government has had to be abandoned. But the desire to take part in public affairs has become engrained in their natures. They have been accustomed to hear their fathers discuss problems of State, and have received the best of all political educations, that of experience.

The Belgian possesses a great love of liberty. He reasons calmly and with much common-sense, but he is not accustomed to solve administrative and social difficulties by himself. He utilises division of labour, he concentrates his activity on his trade or on his profession, and he confides the task of guiding the politics of the State to the men who seem to share his views. Now all of a sudden, without preparing him in the least for it, it is proposed to consult him directly on the most disputed and difficult questions of legislation.

Two reforms of the first importance are being discussed. On the one hand, the scheme is to extend the suffrage, the result of which will be to summon to the polls considerable numbers of electors who have never taken any part in public affairs, and who have perhaps been rather neglected by the parties and the ruling classes, and who have as yet only vague notions of politics, and aspirations rather than ideas. On the other hand, it is proposed to introduce the referendum, which is an appeal to the people, and which presupposes that their education is already made, and that all classes of society have been in close touch for a long time. There seems to be here a double danger.

But there is yet another striking fact to be noticed, which is this : The Swiss people themselves, whose political wisdom entitles them to rank foremost among the nations of Western Europe, are somewhat cautious and hesitating in the use they make of the referendum. In the Federal Government experience has shown the wisdom of placing certain laws beyond the possibility of popular intervention. Thus budgets, treaties, and all enactments which Parliament may consider to be urgent, are excepted from the referendum.

In your book there is much that is instructive on the question of the vote itself, you dwell on the many reforms that have been attempted or proposed in Switzerland with a view to lessening the dangers of the referendum.

It has been proposed to enlighten the people before the popular consultation by means of the distribution or publication of messages.

If these documents are business-like, the electors find them long and tiresome, and the majority do not take the trouble to read them. If they consist merely of a short abstract, they are ridiculous, and do not teach anything.

Compulsory discussion has also been suggested. But such a discussion presupposes that the speakers will be clear and eloquent, and the audience complaisant, and well up in the course of events. As a matter of fact, no one speaks at the meetings which are held for purposes of debate.

Others again have thought that it would be wise to defer the referendum until the law had come into force, and experience had proved its worth. But this would be too great a check on the impatience of the opposition, and in the end the referendum would fall into disuse.

On the voting day abstentions are numerous. Only 61 per cent. of the electors go to the polls in the case of federal laws. In several places the vote has been made compulsory in the case of cantonal votings. The number of voters has increased; but, on the other hand, the number of blank tickets has increased also. The answer obtained at the referendum has proved to be deceptive and enigmatical. The electors are led to give the same vote by motives which are absolutely opposed. This would be remedied, some reformers think, if the answers were accompanied by a statement of reasons. There are others who claim for the elector the right to separate or amend the proposals submitted. What a dreadful muddle there would be were these plans adopted !

Politicians in Switzerland are not slow to take advantage of the general confusion, and have recourse to all sorts of subtleties of procedure. With a view to carrying measures likely to be unpopular with the majority, they make the strangest combinations of independent groups by tacking on provisions to win their favour. When a law is rejected, they return to the task and modify the form, and present the same law again under new colours. At the third attempt the people become tired of resisting, and allow the law to pass.

There is nothing astonishing in this state of things. The people are competent to choose capable men. They are able to declare their general preferences, and can give judgments on questions which do not require expert knowledge. But to ask them to do more than this is to ask them to do something they cannot perform. They are incapable of making legislative decisions; they have not got the necessary documents, nor the leisure for the necessary study. They are liable to be swayed by special and transitory considerations. Their view is not a trained one, and they naturally cannot see things from the same standpoint as men who have been used to the conduct of affairs.

Moreover, there are certain questions the significance of which would escape them altogether. I will only quote one example which is deserving of special consideration in Belgium, as the Swiss referendum does not reassure us on the point. It is the colonial problem. The founding and development of a colony demand enormous sacrifices of men and money, of activity and devotion, for results which are in the dim future, and which are very difficult to guarantee or even to define. The people, however, are always impressed by present sacrifices, and by reverses which are more or less dramatic. They do not pay any heed to future benefits, and to the development of individual energies. From this point of view it is permissible to think that if the referendum ever became an additional source of power to the King of the Belgians, it would nevertheless be a great weakness for the Sovereign of the Congo.

To sum up what I have been saying at perhaps too great length.

The referendum would be an absolutely new institution in a parliamentary monarchy.

The Crown, whose function it would be to remain neutral between the parties, would not gain in influence, while its authority would be lessened and hampered by many complications.

The Parliament and the Ministry run the risk of being irrevocably transformed. The ancient system of checks and balances would be succeeded by a transitory state of things which might lead either to personal or to popular government.

The unity of parties would be threatened if this sword of Damocles were always hanging over their heads.

Finally, the people, incompetent as they are for the task, would be obliged to come to the polls to give their decision in spite of themselves.

These dangers are not apparent to me alone; they have already been recognised and pointed out by the press and by eloquent party leaders. But the longer one thinks over the question, and the more one reads your book, the more one becomes convinced of the gravity of the situation.

Indeed, in Belgium, it may be said, with a good deal of truth, that if there should ever be a referendum on the referendum, the only voters in its favour would be the authors of the reform.—I remain, yours sincerely,

J. VAN DEN HEUVEL.

LOUVAIN, *March* 10, 1892.

THE REFERENDUM IN SWITZERLAND

CHAPTER I

THE EVOLUTION OF DEMOCRACY IN SWITZERLAND

THE object of this chapter is to give some account of the more important parts of those political institutions which are essentially a product of Swiss democracy, and to examine the various constitutional experiments which have had as their result the direct participation of the people in the work of legislation.

At first sight the task of tracing the evolution of democracy in such a place as Switzerland would seem to be an easy one, on account of the limited field of observation. On closer examination, however, we find that what appeared so simple is really very complicated. More than twenty states have continued to exist side by side in this little corner of the globe, united from time to time, it is true, in defensive alliance, but separated by lofty mountains, differing from the first in language, and later in religion, and enjoying varying degrees of independence from autonomy to partial subjection, with the result that each little state has worked out its own history apart from

A

the rest, and so powerful have been the disintegrating factors that no great current of thought seems to have acted as a stimulus towards unity.[1] It naturally follows that their respective governments were the outcome of very different political ideals. This absolute political separation lasted down to the time of the French invasion at the end of the last century. The Constitution of the 12th of April 1798, which was imposed on the country by France, proclaimed the Helvetic Republic to be "one and indivisible," and it reduced the ancient states to the position of mere administrative departments. Such a complete revolution in the position of century-old institutions, due moreover to foreign intervention, was too sudden and too fundamental a change to be permanent, and Switzerland quickly reverted to the state of a confederation.

Nevertheless, ephemeral though it was, the Helvetic Constitution could not but exercise a considerable influence in the future. It introduced a new principle into the public law of the country, the principle of the sovereignty of the people. From this time forth all the advocates of the "rights of the people" have armed themselves with these magic words, and have made them the basis of a whole series of claims. The Constitution of 1798 was in this way the origin

---

[1] [For a general history of Switzerland the following works are accessible in English :—MacCrackan, *The Rise of the Swiss Republic*, 1892 ; Hug and Stead, *Switzerland*, in the Story of the Nations series, 1890 ; the article on Switzerland in the *Encyclopœdia Britannica*, by the Rev. W. Coolidge ; E. Grenfell Baker, *The Model Republic : A History of the Rise and Progress of the Swiss People*, 1895. An excellent bibliography of works on Switzerland is given by J. M. Vincent, *State and Federal Government of Switzerland*, p. 228.]

of that outburst of enthusiasm for democracy which, a few years later, after the July Revolution of 1830, convulsed the whole of Switzerland. Up to the end of the last century direct legislation by the people had been a fact, though the form which it assumed was accidental. From this time forth legislation by the people was demanded as a right, and publicly advo cated as the only legitimate form of government.

The study of the democratic institutions of our own time becomes much easier if we realise that they, too, have sprung from the very same inspiration, and are the outcome of one and the same idea.

The veto, the referendum, and the popular initiative, all these creations of modern democracy are like organisms, which, in a more or less perfect shape, and with more or less difference in their final form, have all sprung from a single primordial cell. We shall trace their rapid evolution in the second part of this chapter. Let us pause, first of all, to examine the classical and somewhat curious forms of what we might term "historical" democracy.

§ BEFORE 1798.

I. *The Landsgemeinde.*

Direct legislation has been a regular constitutional feature in Switzerland from the very beginning of its history. In the republics of Uri, Schwyz, Unterwalden, Appenzell, Zug, and Glarus the people have never ceased to legislate for themselves and vote their own taxes from the thirteenth century downwards. They met together at least once a year for the purpose in solemn conclave, called the Landsgemeinde.[1]

The Landsgemeinde was an assembly of all the active citizens of the canton, that is to say, of all the "freie Landleute" of the age of fourteen and over,[2] and who were entitled to wear a sword.[3]

[1] The first Landsgemeinde of which we have any precise information was held in the canton of Schwyz in 1294 (Blumer, *Staats und Rechtsgeschichte der schweizerischen Demokratien*, St. Gall, 1850, i. p. 135). The following study of the Landsgemeinde is based throughout on this masterly work of Blumer.

[Before the thirteenth century, however, the inhabitants of the Reuss valley (Uri) met to regulate all the affairs concerning their pasturage, and in Schwyz for purposes of local order from very early times. The records of the Landsgemeinde of 1294 prove that it was then no incipient institution, but a democratic assembly in which the people were sovereign with unlimited powers.

One of the explanations of the origin of the Landsgemeinde is that they were the outgrowth of the feudal manorial court of Hofgericht. The countrymen of the Alpine valleys assembled together at the call of the lord's bailiff or deputy, to witness trials and to act as a popular jury upon disputes arising under the customary law of the district. They did not legislate, they applied the law; they did not elect the magistrate, they received him. In the First Perpetual League they declared that they would only have natives as judges, not foreigners. It would be an easy change, when the feudal power grew weaker, for the people to meet together to elect a man instead of waiting for his appointment, and to assume the general direction of affairs at such meetings. See Rambert, *Les Alpes Suisse*, p. 164. M. Dunant, in *Législation par le peuple en Suisse*, p. 6, says that the word Landsgemeinde dates only from the fifteenth century.]

[2] Towards the middle of the fifteenth century the age of political majority was fixed at sixteen in the cantons of Schwyz, Glarus, and Appenzell, and their example was followed by Zug in the sixteenth century.

[3] Thieves, bankrupts, and malefactors generally, were deprived of their political rights. They were *ehr* and *gewehrlos*, and were forbidden to wear a sword, the distinguishing mark of an active citizen.

[If a man attended without his sword he was not allowed to vote,

It was held in the spring, before the peasants left for the high Alps, on the last Sunday in April or the first Sunday in May [1] The place of meeting was an open space, with the turf for a carpet, and with only the boundless sky above, *unter Gottes freiem Himmel.* What more superb council chamber could be conceived than such a one in these Alpine lands ?

Attendance was compulsory,[2] because on the day

and was, moreover, fined. To the present day men attend the Landsgemeinde wearing swords of very ancient patterns, evidently heirlooms.]

[1] [In Appenzell and Unterwalden the Landsgemeinde is held on the last Sunday in April, in Uri on the first Sunday in May, and in Glarus, if possible, during the month of May. At Glarus and Appenzell (Inner Rhodes) the Landsgemeinden meet in an open space in the town. An excellent historical account, description, and criticism of the Landsgemeinden is given by Rambert in *Les Alpes Suisse* (Lausanne: F. Rouge, 1889). M. Lefèvre Pontalis has described them as they exist at the present day in a pamphlet called *Les Assemblées plénières de la Suisse* (Paris: F. Dentu, 1896), and in the *Figaro* of the 28th of May 1894. Prince Roland Bonaparte contributed two descriptive articles on the subject in the *Figaro* of the 28th May 1890, and in the *Événement* of the 6th of June 1890.

Mr. Irving Richman, in *Pure Democracy and Pastoral Life in Inner Rhodes* (Longmans, 1895), gives a vivid account of a Landsgemeinde held in Appenzell (Inner Rhodes), which, by the way, is the only account I have ever seen of a Landsgemeinde held in the rain. A Landsgemeinde is also described by Adams and Cunningham in *The Swiss Confederation*, pp. 132–33 ; by Vincent, *State and Federal Government of Switzerland*, pp. 106–114; by W. Boyd Winchester, *The Swiss Republic*, pp. 101–107 ; and by MacCrackan, *Teutonic Switzerland*, chap. xi.

The description of Freeman in chapter i. of *The Growth of the English Constitution* is classical (London, 1892).]

[2] A fine was imposed in case of absence. [Mr. Richman, in his book, states that a fine of five francs is still exacted in Inner Rhodes ; and in an article on Compulsory Voting (*Le Vote Obligatoire*), by M. Deploige, in the *Revue Générale* for March 1893

when the Landsgemeinde was held the people had to take an oath to observe the laws and customs of the country. In the early morning, chanting the while their patriotic hymns, these peasant legislators streamed in from all the communes of the canton. The chief magistrate of the state, the landamman, was *ex officio* president of the assembly. A band of musicians conducted him to the platform, erected in the middle of the meadow; the active citizens ranged themselves round him in a circle; farther off outside the circle the women and children [1] and strangers listened and looked on in silence. According to traditional practice, a prayer, recited in unison, and the speech of the landamman, preceded the orders of the day.

Before exercising its principal function, that of legislation, the Landsgemeinde proceeded to nominate the state officials,[2] the governors of bailiwicks, and the deputies for the federal Diet. The elections were made by show of hands. The landamman, with the help of his assistants, declared the result, which no one was allowed to call in question. In case of doubt,

(Brussels), M. Deploige has the following note:—A deputy of the canton of Appenzell writes me that the Landsgemeinde punishes electors who stay away by a fine of ten francs. My correspondent did not, unfortunately, send me the regulation in question.]

[1] [At Glarus the children occupy reserved places in front of the tribune erected for the officials, in order that they may be thus instructed from their youth up in the conduct of public affairs.]

[2] [In Glarus, up to 1857, the candidates had to be entreated to accept office. After many compliments they were elected in spite of their refusals, and the majority accepted the posts offered. Those who declined had to declare upon their honour, or even on oath, that they would not take office before any one even thought of replacing them. See Droz, *Études et portraits politiques*, " Life of Landamman Heer."]

either a second show of hands took place, or the voters separated into two groups and were then counted.[1]

A not uncommon piece of tactics was to call out, " Friends, hands up "—*Hend auf ihr liebe Landlüt*— when any particular name was called out. It was in all probability a ruse employed by the supporters of a candidate to make the doubtful electors take one side or another. There were laws, however, which imposed a fine on this especial manœuvre.

Every free man was eligible for office.[2] The terms were short, with little if any remuneration. The offices were therefore in practice only accessible to persons in easy circumstances, which explains the fact that in the list of landammans the same name occurs again and again.[3]

---

[1] [At Appenzell (Inner Rhodes) the people enter the church by different doors, and are counted as they enter.]

[2] In the cantons of Uri and Glarus those employed as mercenaries in foreign countries were ineligible (Blumer, ii. p. 112). The Swiss were to be found in the Middle Ages in all the armies of Europe, the poverty of their soil and the scarcity of employment having compelled them to enrol themselves in foreign armies. The cantonal governments often used to take advantage of this practice, and would conclude treaties with foreign sovereigns, known as military capitulations, by which they undertook to provide contingents of soldiers. The Federal Constitution of 1848 forbade military capitulations.

[3] [In Uri in the Middle Ages we find one Werner d'Attinghausen in office from 1294–1317. From 1317–30 there is no record. In 1331 we find his son in office, and again in 1333–37, and from 1346–57. Thus father and son were in office at least thirty-seven years. In Schwyz, Conrad ap Yberg and Werner Stauffach alternate from 1291–1314. From 1314–19 there is no record. Then we find a Henri Stauffach in office in 1319. From that time to 1342 there is no record. From 1342–73 we get a Conrad ap Ypberg (thirty-one years), and from 1378 we get a line of Stauffachs. See Rambert, *op.*

After electing the officials the people next proceeded to deal with the internal and external affairs
of the canton.   In such matters the Landsgemeinde
was not only supreme, but a very real and effective
sovereign. The citizens recognised no other laws
than those of their own making ;[1] not a farthing for
taxation left their pockets without their consent.
The state contracted no alliance that was not formally approved by the majority of the nation, and

cit. p. 186. It was the same later on. M. Numa Droz, in his " Life of
the Landamman Heer of Glarus," *Études et portraits politiques*, 1895,
says that from the eighteenth century there had been Landammans out of the family of Heer. Cosme Heer, the grandfather,
had been Landamman from 1828–33 ; Nicolaus, the uncle, from
1803–21 ; and the Heer of the biography eighteen years from
1857–76. The same author gives the following account of the
duties of a landamman in Glarus :—The landamman has to direct
the assembly of the people. He has to preside at the Council of
State of 9, at the Landrath of 40 members, and at the triple
Landrath of 117, which deliberates on the questions to be submitted to the Landsgemeinde. It is the landamman who elaborates the greater part of these proposals. It is he, as a rule, who
draws up the memorial to be sent to each active citizen before
each Landsgemeinde, a memorial which contains all the propositions and arguments in their support. The landamman may be
called upon to take part in many commissions. He is the councillor
of all. Every one goes to him in all the difficulties of life, sometimes for advice on legal matters, sometimes to ask his intervention
in their favour when they apply to the commune for relief. The
landamman has no official secretary to help him in all this. Yet
we find constant rivalry between the different families to obtain
the post, and some curious scenes at election time.

The government of trades unions by general meeting, the earliest
form adopted, presents many analogies with the Landsgemeinde.
See *Industrial Democracy*, by Sidney and Beatrice Webb, vol. i.
chap. 1, " Primitive Democracy."]

[1] In 1733 the Council of Glarus consulted the Landsgemeinde on
the interpretation of an obscure law on bankruptcy. Originally the
Landsgemeinde administered justice and exercised the right of
pardon. (Blumer, i. pp. 270–72.)

no foreigner could become a citizen of the country unless admitted by the Landsgemeinde.[1]

Among the series of laws enacted by the Landsgemeinde, one group ought specially to be noticed, because it throws new light on the political morality of those primitive democracies. I refer to the succession of statutes designed to prevent corruption at elections. The purchase of votes seems, in fact, to have been carried out on a large scale, especially by candidates for the office of bailiff. This was a lucrative post, because the bailiffs were the governors of the subject domains belonging to the little republics, and they did not fail to make the most out of the inhabitants. The existence of these subject domains, it may be mentioned in passing, is one of the curious features of "historical" democracy, and those who theorise about modern democracy will no doubt regard their very existence as a monstrous anomaly, for nothing is more at variance with the principles, if not with the mode of action, of those who claim to rally round the doctrines of the French Revolution.

[1] [It was a very difficult matter to be admitted to citizenship in another canton. For instance, in Appenzell (Outer Rhodes), in 1834, a man had to reside ten years in the canton. An application then had to be made to the Great Council, who minutely investigated the man's antecedents, and submitted the demand to the Landsgemeinde with a favourable report. The candidate then mounted the platform at the Landsgemeinde to be presented to the people, who were the final judges. In Appenzell (Inner Rhodes) he and his family had to take an oath before the people that they were Roman Catholics and went to church regularly. The candidate had to pay a fine for admission. Even if the votes at the Landsgemeinde were in his favour he was ineligible for any public office during his lifetime, but his children were under no disability. At the present day the procedure is very similar, but five years' residence only is necessary, and the candidate is eligible for all offices.]

But in the old-time democracies things bore a different aspect. Their aim was independence, their bias republican, but the rights of man as an abstract idea was still a good deal beyond them. Liberty was much more than an idea, it was an actual fact; not a philosophic theory, but a more or less complicated system of positive rights, based on a series of enactments exactly similar to those by which all other rights had been acquired. Civil or political liberty, once attained, was handed down as an inalienable heritage from those who first acquired it to those who came after them. The freeman, owing neither suit nor service to any feudal superior, no less than the burgess who owned no allegiance to any foreign power, would never dream of quoting in support of their claims to freedom the prehistoric equality of primitive man; still less would they advocate the sovereignty of the people. They produced charters, they appealed to the rights acquired by their fathers, they quoted the concessions and exemptions obtained from former lords.[1] The subject lands, however, had no charters to invoke. They had ceased to exist as seignorial domains, and had become republican property, generally as part of the spoils of conquest. They gained nothing, however, by the change. Their new masters were no more considerate than the old, and the exactions of the republican bailiff fell in no whit behind those of the feudal lords.

A bailiwick was a snug berth for the man who could obtain the appointment by winning the sovereign's favour. In this case, however, the sovereign was an aggregate of some thousands of peasants, all

[1] Cherbuliez, *De la démocratie en Suisse*, Geneva, 1843, vol. i. p. 39.

of them men leading hard and parsimonious lives. The way to the hearts of such men was not to be found by mere flattery: a bribe of money, a good meal, or a flagon of wine were better means to the end, a fact which soon became apparent to any candidate. Already, as far back as the sixteenth century, the Landsgemeinde are found legislating against the abuse. At first such legislation was conceived in merely general terms; then, as the candidates continued to be successful in evading the letter of the law, the statutes took a more detailed form.[1]

Such fits of repentance on the part of a sovereign people, followed by their relapse and by new projects of amendment, seem strange at first, and somewhat difficult of explanation. It would almost seem as if these laws were due to the efforts of defeated candidates, who took this way of revenging themselves on their more fortunate rivals.[2]

[1] [In 1666, 1667, and 1700 the Landsgemeinde of Schwyz fixed a scale of expenses for marriages, baptisms, fairs, and shooting matches, which varied according to the period at which these festivals took place—a higher maximum being allowed in ordinary times, and a lower one in the period just before the Landsgemeinde. This clearly shows that these joyful occasions were utilised for bribery. In Lower Unterwalden, in 1692, "giving, paying, or receiving food or drink" was forbidden during the whole year without distinction of person.—Rambert, p. 223.]

[2] [Rambert, p. 325, says: "The Landsgemeinde have always retained something of the vivacity and impulsiveness of great crowds. It is a nervous government which has fits of exaltation and fits of depression. Glarus, where corruption was so rife, is now a model Landsgemeinde. M. Heer attributes the bribery to the state politics of the time, which were simply concerned with questions of personal interest. Something must be allowed for the spirit of emulation and competition which so quickly infects great crowds when brought together."]

Whatever the reason might be, nothing seems to have put an end to the electoral corruption. Fines, and the exaction of an oath from the successful candidate to the effect that he had not made use of illicit tactics, seem to have been alike unsuccessful. At last the bribery attained the proportions of a public scandal. In 1581 it was said at the Landsgemeinde of Glarus, that if the sale of votes were not put a stop to, it would " demoralise and disgrace the canton."[1] Perhaps if there had been any power superior to the Landsgemeinde, possessing the energy and the will to repress the evil, it might have been eradicated. But the Landsgemeinde was the sole sovereign. The very sinners themselves, with their accomplices, formed part of it. An unusual amount of virtue and will power, therefore, on their part would have been required to put an end to practices the immorality of which did not appear so flagrant to those concerned.

When it became clear that to eradicate the abuse was to attempt the impossible, efforts were made to regulate it and give it an appearance of legality. What had been, up till then, a vice odious to the law, became a duty imposed by the law. Under the new conditions the candidate was obliged to provide a dinner for the electors. In later times a sum of money was substituted, to be distributed in whole or in part among the voters. It goes without saying that in the long run, as far as the successful bailiff was concerned, it was his subjects who provided the funds.[2]

[1] Blumer, ii. p. 116.

[2] [At Glarus, the bailiffs for Thurgau, Baden, and the Rhine valley paid between six and seven hundred florins for the post, and bribed heavily besides.]

Radical as these measures appear, they were nevertheless inadequate. Only one resource was therefore left, namely, to suppress the election itself which gave rise to such fraudulent dealing. This was accordingly done. As formerly in the Athenian democracy, so in the latter years of the old system in Switzerland they had recourse to the ballot.[1] If the lot fell to a man who had not the leisure to devote to the administration of a bailiwick, he put his office up for sale, and parted with it to the highest bidder.

These details may perhaps be resented by enthusiastic admirers of the Landsgemeinde, but that is no good reason for suppressing them. The old democracies will appear in a less poetic but truer light, and truth is our great object.[2]

The rights of the members of the Landsgemeinde,

---

[1] [In Glarus eight citizens were nominated for each post, and a child gave round eight balls wrapped in black, which, when opened, contained seven silver and one golden ball, and the man who had the golden ball was declared to be elected. Schwyz also adopted election by lot in 1692, but it had fallen into disuse by 1706, and it was decided in 1718 that whoever raised the question again should be outlawed. But the law continued in force in Glarus till 1798, and in 1793 they even chose their landamman by lot. Choice by lot was given up when the cantons became part of the Confederation. One writer complains that the method of electing the officers is now very dull by comparison.]

[2] The existing constitutions of these cantons still forbid the purchase of votes in general terms. [In Schwyz in 1830—it ceased to have a Landsgemeinde in 1848—we find that the people after the Landsgemeinde went to salute the magistrates, who gave them little "gratifications." This was no small tax, for there was always a considerable crowd, swelled by all the children of the district. The year 1824 is specially mentioned, for then the people had "cider in casks, and bread and cheese as much as they liked." One might criticise the ancient Landsgemeinden on other points besides those of bribery. See Rambert, pp. 218–22.]

as forming part of a legislative assembly, were not confined merely to sanctioning laws and ratifying treaties. To begin with, each citizen had in theory the right of initiative, and could, therefore, himself bring any proposition before the Landsgemeinde. It was found necessary, however, at a later date, to restrict the unlimited exercise of this privilege. Certain precautionary measures were therefore introduced, and it became the custom, some weeks before the date of the Landsgemeinde, to send in the measures proposed to a council called the *Landrath*, whose members were chosen by the people in the communal assemblies.[1] It was the province of the Landrath to consider all proposals sent to it. Those which it approved, and to which it was ready to give its support, were submitted to the Landsgemeinde before the others.

This preliminary examination undoubtedly had its merits. It acted as a sifting process by which the really useful and suitable measures were separated from the others, and thus recommended to the suffrages of the citizens. As a natural result, the Landrath attempted to claim a new power which

---

[1] The Landrath may be considered as the executive and the Landsgemeinde as the legislative power, though the sphere of each of these bodies was too loosely defined for this to be strictly accurate. The importance of the business affected the size of the assembly. *De minoribus consilium de majoribus omnes.* In course of time the Landsgemeinde came to deal with executive matters, and the Landrath voted the laws; but Blumer especially points out that the ratification of such legislation proceeded from the people. The electors were jealous of their rights, and tolerated no encroachments on the part of the authorities. On several occasions the Landsgemeinde expostulated with the Landrath on account of real or fancied misuse of power.

constituted a grave menace to the rights of the people. It tried to exclude from the deliberation of the Landsgemeinde all the motions to which it had not given its assent. Had this been effected, the popular initiative would have been reduced to the mere right of petition. The people protested, and would not recognise any such power. At Lower Unterwalden and at Appenzell the struggle was exciting and prolonged. Sometimes the people, sometimes the council gained the upper hand.[1]

The way in which the popular initiative was regulated in the canton of Uri is worthy of special notice. Each proposition had to be supported by seven citizens belonging to different families before

[1] Blumer, ii. pp. 132-38; Keller, *Das Volksinitiativrecht nach den schweizerischen Kantonsverfassungen*, Zürich, 1889, pp. 12-27.

[See also Dunant, *Législation par le peuple en Suisse*, pp. 16-23; Deschwanden, *Die Entwicklung der Landsgemeinde in Nidwalden als gesetzgebende Gewalt*, in *Zeitschrift für öffentliches Recht*, vol. vi.; Zellweger, *Geschichte des appenzellischen Volks*, Trogen, 1830-40. The following particulars are taken from Deschwanden :—In Lower Unterwalden, in 1688, we find that no proposition could be submitted to the Landsgemeinde by a citizen unless it had first been discussed by the Landrath. In 1700 it was declared that each citizen had the right to propose anything that was not contrary to the glory of God and the well-being of the country. The government then claimed the right of judging whether the propositions were or were not contrary to the honour of God and the welfare of the country, and under this pretext they eliminated all that displeased them. The Landsgemeinde then abolished these saving clauses. In 1713 a great fire consumed Stanz, and the Landrath attempted to persuade the people that God was angry because they were allowed to make propositions which might be contrary to His glory. The Assembly protested, and the Landrath retired, which prevented the Landsgemeinde from deliberating. Then the people compromised and restricted the right of initiative to those propositions which contained nothing contrary to the glory of God, but they themselves were to be judges of the fact.]

it could be submitted to the vote of the people. This method of procedure was called the *Siebengeschlecht-begehren*—the demand of the seven families.[1]

The preliminary deliberations of the Landrath lessened the importance of the great popular discussions in that it made them less essential; but at the Landsgemeinde perfect freedom of speech was allowed. The landamman consulted the public officials and other dignitaries, as well as the people generally, on each question as it arose. A fine coupled with expulsion from the Assembly were the penalties for interrupting a speaker, but any one who considered himself injured by a speech might demand redress.[2]

The great difficulty was the maintenance of order on such an occasion—a veritable holiday for the hun-

[1] Blumer, ii. p. 131.
. [These seven electors dictated their motion to the Secretary of State at the beginning of the Landsgemeinde, and it was discussed at the Nachgemeinde. It was not till 1823 that the proposition, signed by the seven electors, had to be sent in first of all to the Landrath.

In Glarus the authorities drew up in a memorial a list of measures for discussion. So many interruptions occurred, however, in consequence of the unrestricted right of initiative, that in 1766 the citizens were allowed to unite their propositions in the memorial, which was sent to the communes three weeks beforehand for this purpose. The measures of the Council were discussed first.]
[2] [In Schwyz, in the sixteenth century, we find that the interrupter had to ask pardon of God and the magistrate; and at Stanz he had to kneel in the middle of the ring and say five *pater* and five *ave*. At the present day writers always remark on the freedom from interruption which the speakers enjoy. In Schwyz the injured party who sought redress could demand an explanation of the speaker, and then the Assembly decided if such explanation were sufficient or if the complainant should be allowed to seek legal redress.]

dreds of legislators who attended. Men like these, habitually armed with swords, were only too apt to come to blows when a discussion became heated. As a preventive measure the sale of wine and spirits was forbidden, both directly before the meeting and during its continuance. At Schwyz no one was allowed to carry a stick, and if a disturbance occurred the combatants were imprisoned on the spot. At Glarus the disturber of the peace was deprived of his sword and of all political rights; was declared, in fact, to be *ehr* and *gewehrlos* until he obtained a pardon. It goes without saying that police regulations such as these could only be effectual if the culprits were few in number. When, as sometimes happened, the excitement spread through the whole mass, all attempts at suppressing the tumult were useless, and the debate had to come to an end.[1]

After the different opinions had been expressed, the landamman summed up the amendments and put them to the vote. The citizens voted by raising their right hands, and the landamman counted the numbers and declared the result from the tribune.

The sitting of several hours was not always long enough to exhaust the orders of the day. When night put an end to the meeting, still leaving several matters to be discussed, the legislators arranged for an after-meeting, a *Nachgemeinde*. At this supplementary meeting, which was held a week or fortnight later, attendance was not compulsory. It must have been less well attended than the ordinary Landsgemeinde, because in the canton of Uri on two occasions, in 1705 and again in 1753, attempts were made

---

[1] Blumer, ii. p. 109.

B

to attract people to the meeting by making small payments to those present.

The May meeting of the Landsgemeinde and its possible Nachgemeinde took place in the ordinary course of events, but it remains to be noticed that in case of need the authorities or a certain number of citizens had the right of calling an *Extraordinary Landsgemeinde.*

The Constitution of the Helvetic republic of the 12th of April 1798 respected neither the antiquity of the Landsgemeinden nor the independence of the small republics of Central Switzerland. Their indignation was great indeed when they learned that a foreign power was going to force on them a new constitution. The French spoke to them of liberty, of equality, of the sovereignty of the people, and of political emancipation. What meaning had such language for these mountaineers, already sovereign legislators, and free as the eagle that soared over their own Alpine snow heights, ignorant of the meaning of feudal privileges, and emancipated for centuries from the rule of monarchs and aristocrats? They perceived merely the emptiness of all these promises, and felt the hollowness of the revolutionary phraseology. Their fathers had founded a genuine democracy; the democracy the invader would establish was only a theory on paper.

A touching letter addressed to the French Directorate on the 5th April 1798, expresses their sentiments on the matter. It is, unfortunately, too long to give in full. The following is an extract:—

"Nothing can in our eyes equal the misfortune of

losing the Constitution which was founded by our ancestors, which is adapted to our customs and needs, and which has for centuries enabled us to reach the highest attainable point of comfort and happiness. Citizen directors, if you should have really come to the determination to change the form of our popular governments, allow us to address you on the subject with frankness and freedom. We would ask you if you have discovered anything in our constitutions which is opposed to your own principles. Could any other conceivable form of government put the sovereign power so exclusively in the hands of the people, or establish among all classes of citizens a more perfect equality? Under what other constitution could each member of the state enjoy a greater amount of liberty? We wear no other chains than the easy fetters of religion and morality, no other yoke than that of the laws which we have made for ourselves. In other countries, perhaps, the people have still something to wish for in these respects. But we, descendants of William Tell, whose deeds you laud to-day; we, whose peaceful enjoyment of these constitutional privileges has never been interrupted up to the present time, and for the maintenance of which we plead with a fervour inspired by the justice of our cause,—we have but one wish, and in that we are unanimous: it is to remain under those forms of government which the prudence and courage of our ancestors have bequeathed as a heritage; and what government, citizen directors, could more accord with your own?

"We who address you are inhabitants of those countries whose independence you have so often

promised to respect. We are ourselves the sovereigns of our little states. We appoint and dismiss
our magistrates at will. The several districts of our
cantons elect the councils which are our representatives, the representatives of the people. These are, in
short, the very foundations of our constitution. Are
not your own identical ? "

The *Act of Mediation* of 1803 gave back a certain
degree of their former independence to the cantons.
Then the little peasant republics returned to their
old traditional policy, and the people once again
assembled every year to debate on public matters,
to make their laws and appoint their magistrates.[1]

The Landsgemeinde meets to-day just as it did
in the Middle Ages. The same ceremonial is still
observed. There is the prayer in which all join
before the proceedings, the procession, and the speech
of the landamman, the voting by show of hands, and
the oath of fidelity taken by the people to observe
their laws and customs. Except for certain encroachments of the central government in the domain of
cantonal sovereignty, the power of the Landsgemeinde
has remained essentially the same as in the olden
days. It still legislates and votes the taxes, approves
the estimates and the budget, appoints the officials
and the magistrates. In the constitutions of the
cantons the Landsgemeinde is declared to be the

---

[1] [Napoleon nevertheless introduced certain habits of order which
were not without their influence on the Landsgemeinden held
after his fall. Under the *Act of Mediation* the discussions at the
Landsgemeinde had been restricted to the subjects which had been
sent in to the Great Council and published one month beforehand.
This is the practice now universally followed, with slight variations
in the date fixed.]

sovereign legislative power, and attendance at its
meetings is enforced as a civic duty.[1] The citizens
have still in principle the right of initiating laws, and
of freely discussing, "under the free heaven of God,"
the propositions brought for their consideration.[2]

The demand of the seven families — *Siebenge-
schlechtbegehren* — that peculiar feature which has
existed from time immemorial in the Constitution of
Uri, did not disappear until 1888. Any elector since
that date may bring forward a proposal in the Landsgemeinde, provided it is in writing, is clearly expressed, contains an epitome of the arguments in
its favour, bears the signature of the proposer, and is

[1] [Each Landsgemeinde canton has a "Landbuch," which is an
official record of the Landsgemeinde. Some of these Landbücher
are very ancient, and date from the fifteenth century. They were
the only thing in the nature of a written constitution which the
cantons possessed ; they were merely a collection of laws, decrees,
and traditional practice which were altered from time to time.
The fact that the cantons are now obliged to have a written constitution which is guaranteed by an outside power, which they
are bound to observe, and which they cannot alter without the
same sanction, forms no slight limitation of their power. These
cantons found the greatest difficulty in drawing up a written constitution, and it was not until after 1850 that all the Landsgemeinde
cantons succeeded in drafting constitutions. The document drawn
up by the government of Uri in 1820 is very characteristic :—"We,
Landamman, Council, &c., hereby declare that we have never had a
written constitution contained in one document, but our constitution rests on the following principles, consecrated by the usages of
centuries and by legal enactments, which, with the protection of the
Almighty, we hope to transmit to our descendants." Then follows
a meagre list of six articles.]

[2] [It is interesting to compare the Town Meeting in the New
England States with the Swiss Landsgemeinde. See Professor
Bryce's description in the *American Commonwealth*, vol. i. p. 590,
&c., 1893. For a detailed account of the power of each Landsgemeinde, see Dunant, *op. cit.* pp. 14–23 ; also Signorel, *Le Réfe-
rendum législatif*, pp. 120–24, 1895.]

forwarded before the end of March to the Landrath,
which makes a report on the subject at the Landsgemeinde.   The mover either makes a speech in
support of his own bill, or gets somebody else to
defend it for him.[1]   The other states have constitutional provisions of much the same character.

In the half canton of Lower Unterwalden proposals
must be sent in to the Landrath before the 1st of
March.   The official *Gazette* publishes them within
ten days.   Within three weeks of publication, any
elector has the right of submitting counter-proposals
and amendments to the Landrath.   The Landrath
examines these new motions, and can in its turn
supply others.   But no proposals may be modified at
the Landsgemeinde.   They are there put to the vote
as originally drafted.[2]

The canton of Glarus is an exception, for its constitution states expressly that the Landsgemeinde
has the right of accepting, modifying, or rejecting
the propositions which are presented to it, as well as
the power to send any measures back to the Triple
Council for reconsideration or ratification.[3]

---

[1] *Verfassung des Kantons Uri*, Arts. 26 and 28. [An amendment of
the constitution cannot proceed from a single person.   It must be
supported by fifty signatures at least.]

[2] *Verfassung des Kantons Unterwalden nid dem Wald*, Art. 41.

[3] [In Glarus, according to the Constitution of 1887, citizens send
propositions to the Landrath to be inscribed in the memorial which
contains the orders of the day for the Landsgemeinde.   These
motions, if supported by ten votes in the Council, are incorporated
with an explanatory clause one month before the Landsgemeinde
assembles.   The rejected motions are also included in the memorial, but without any recommendation.   If the Landsgemeinde
accepts one of these latter motions, the Landrath is bound to include
it in the next memorial with an explanatory clause.   A law cannot

The stranger who witnesses a Landsgemeinde never forgets the experience, and is always profoundly impressed. The grandeur of such a scene has affected even such eminent contemporaries as Cherbuliez,

be amended until three years after its promulgation unless it is prejudicial to the country.

In Appenzell (Inner Rhodes) the Constitution of 1892 stipulates that the right of making propositions belongs to all citizens, but the motions must previously be sent in to the Great Council. If the Council will not undertake to present a particular motion, any citizen may do so, provided it contains nothing contrary to the federal or cantonal constitution. The regulations in Upper Unterwalden are the same.

In Appenzell (Outer Rhodes), where they only vote and do not discuss matters at the Landsgemeinde, the Great Council, or a group of electors equal in number to the Great Council, may propose any law to the Landsgemeinde, but in the latter case the Council has to report on it first.

Thus at the present day everything passes, first of all, through the hands of the Council. They cannot, however, suppress or throw out motions. They can only comment adversely.

Mr. Irving Richman gives the following account of the popular initiative in Inner Rhodes:

"It has long been a constitutional rule of the state that no measure can be presented at the Landsgemeinde unless it has been passed upon by the Great Council. An inference from this might be that the Landsgemeinde merely goes through the form of accepting and rejecting what the Great Council has accepted and rejected beforehand. And in matters of slight importance this is usually the practice. But that it is not the practice in matters of more than slight importance is shown by the following incident: To the year 1891 it had been the prerogative of the Great Council to choose the cantonal member of the Ständerat or Senate. In the Landsgemeinde of that year a citizen brought forward a measure (previously passed upon adversely by the Great Council) to annul this prerogative and place the election of Senator in the hands of the Landsgemeinde. The vote was taken and the measure passed."

It would also seem that several measures proposed by the Council have been rejected by the Landsgemeinde, the people being more conservative than their councillors. See *Pure Democracy and Pastoral Life in Inner Rhodes*, J. Irving Richman, 1895.]

Dubs, and Welti, all of them confirmed opponents of the popular veto and the referendum.

"The people in a pure democracy," wrote Cherbuliez, "is a being morally complete in itself, a unique personality with an actual existence quite distinct from that of the individuals who compose it. The people in a representative democracy is only an abstract quantity without any corporate life, a mere numerical result whose component units feel and act for themselves as if there were no common tie between them."[1]

"The Landsgemeinde," said M. Welti in his great speech against the referendum in the Federal Assembly of 1892, "has nothing in common with the referendum. It is a real and living thing, while the other is nothing but a dead form of democracy on paper. In the Landsgemeinde each man feels that he is also a citizen. In the Referendum the ballot-paper is his substitute."[2]

"A Landsgemeinde," wrote Dubs, "held on a spring day, under God's free sky, with the very women and children taking part in it outside the circle, with the mountains as a background, those bulwarks of our freedom—this is the finest and most ideal personification of democracy. Anything and everything that might be offered in exchange would only seem a feeble reflection of this living union of the people."[3]

[1] Cherbuliez, ii. p. 134.

[2] Protocol of the deliberations of the National Swiss Council concerning the revision of the Federal Constitution, 1871-72.

[3] Dubs, *Le droit public de la Confédération suisse*, Geneva, 1878, i. p. 210.

[M. Curti, in his article on the Referendum in Switzerland in the *Revue Politique et Parlementaire* for August 1897, p. 245, says

The admiration of these men, though sincere, is by no means blind. They realise thoroughly that Landsgemeinden are like rare plants. They can only live in special surroundings. Their admiration, moreover, is shared by nearly all their fellow-countrymen. The Swiss, taking them as a whole, have a weakness for the Landsgemeinden of their little cantons. They are historic curiosities, relics of the past, which the lofty mountains seem to have preserved from the adverse influences of feudalism and monarchy. No one imagines, however, that they could be transplanted to a new soil.[1] Nowhere else could we find the conditions universally regarded as essential to the proper working of direct legislation. Such countries must necessarily be small,[2] and contain a compara-

that "the success of the Landsgemeinden depends on the favour of the heavens. They are magnificent to behold in fine weather, but if a shower comes the business is treated with rather undignified haste, while whole groups leave the meeting."]

[1] Orelli, *Das Staatsrecht der schweizerischen Eidgenossenschaft*, p. 107; Ernst, *Die Volksrechte im Eidgenössischen Bunde* in the *Monat Rosen*, 1883-84, p. 245; E. Naville, *La démocratie représentative*, p. 2; Brunialti, *La legge e la libertà*, i. p. 259; Dubs, *Die schweizerische Demokratie in ihrer Fortentwicklung*, pp. 30-32.

[2] [The longest dimensions of any one of the Landsgemeinde cantons does not exceed thirty miles. Appenzell (Inner Rhodes) has the configuration of a circle, the diameter of which is only ten miles across, and the seat of government is almost central. The population of these Landsgemeinde cantons when we first know anything of them cannot have exceeded 1500 men. The number of registered electors in October 1896 was 4495 in Uri, 3824 in Obwald, 2877 in Nidwald, 8323 in Glarus; in Appenzell (Outer Rhodes) 12,214, and in Inner Rhodes 3005. In addition to a small territory and small population, the political unity of a canton must be beyond discussion. The natural effect of Landsgemeinde is to bring out geographical divisions, to which also correspond divergencies of interest and moral differences. After the Reformation there was a Protestant and a Catholic Landsgemeinde in Glarus, and a Protestant and a Catholic Landsgemeinde in Uri.]

tively limited number of inhabitants.[1] Nor can there
be found in the world at large such simplicity of life
and social relations, which come upon an observer of
these primitive democracies almost as a revelation.[2]

The inhabitants of these cantons are occupied with
agricultural and pastoral pursuits. They do not, therefore, come in contact with all the complicated and
difficult problems which press so urgently for solution
outside their frontiers. They rarely find it necessary to
make new laws. Their relations with each other are
regulated by custom, and this is all-sufficient. Their
magistrates, who are upright and experienced men,
have an exceptional position. They are universally

[1] Both Zug and Schwyz have been obliged to give up their
Landsgemeinde since 1848 owing to the growth of population.
[The outlying districts were jealous of Schwyz, and broke away
and formed a canton of Schwyz-Exterior in 1832. There were
struggles between the two, the Confederation intervened, and
the matter was compromised by the Landsgemeinde being held
at Roththurm in between the rival places. The parties, however,
fought over the elections, and maligned the men to be elected,
until at last the meeting became a free fight. Another Landsgemeinde was held, at which five Federal Commissioners were
present to keep order. The result was that the Landsgemeinde
was given up, and Schwyz now has practically six Landsgemeinden.
It is divided into six districts, and each has a *Bezirksgemeinde*, consisting of all the male citizens who have attained their majority.
They assemble once a year, on the first Sunday in May, or they
may be summoned at other times by the district council, or when
one-fifth of the voters demand it. They elect the judges of the
district and the other officials. They levy taxes, approve expenditure, and make binding agreements (Arts. 78-90, Cons. of Schwyz).
There were after the Reformation no less than eleven Landsgemeinden in Switzerland—two in Appenzell, two in Unterwalden
two in Glarus (a Catholic and a Protestant one, which united in
1836), two in Uri, two in Schwyz, and one in Zug. There are now
six.]
[2] See a very interesting monograph by M. Béchaux, *Une démocratie modèle l'Unterwald*, Paris, 1888.

respected, and, thanks to the authority with which they are endowed, they find no difficulty in directing the great assemblies of the people. Then, too, democracy can never degenerate in these countries into demagogy. It can never become the oppression of the minority by the majority. The two principal causes which rouse the great mass of people to act as despots are differences in religion and social inequalities. These do not exist in the cantons with Landsgemeinden. The inhabitants are religious, and join in the same form of worship. They are neither very rich nor very poor, but possess a modest competence. The enmities of religions and of class and class do not find anything to thrive on, and the country is preserved from those unfortunate laws which in other countries make democracy sometimes so dangerous to true liberty.[1]

II. *The Referendum in the Grisons and in Valais—The Rittinghausen System.*

The Landsgemeinde was composed of all the citizens of the country, and all the local assemblies habitually held in the several communes were merged on this occasion in one great central gathering. This general assembly was due to the need of ascertaining public opinion on matters of common interest, and of having a concerted plan for the defence of the country. Such a meeting was only possible, however, where

[1] [It will be remembered that the word Landsgemeinde simply means "National Commune," and that the principle of the mass meeting obtains in almost every local division of Switzerland. See Preface.]

the territory was small. Hence, when this condition failed, as in the Grisons and in Valais, it was out of the question to collect all the people in one day at the same spot. Thus, while the more ancient cantons summoned their inhabitants together in one large assembly, the Grisons and Valais had to leave the business of debating on matters of general interest to their little communal assemblies. In the one case, legislation was the work of the entire nation solemnly convoked for the purpose in a Landsgemeinde; in the other, it was none the less the work of the nation, but of the nation acting in sections, and subdivided into a number of local assemblies or *Gemeinden*. In the former, the limited area of the country made it possible to give a central organisation to popular legislation; in the latter, the people had to be content with a strictly federal system.

The canton known as the Grisons was essentially a federation of separate communes which during the thirteenth century had succeeded in wresting their independence bit by bit from their feudal superiors, so that by the fourteenth and fifteenth centuries they were in a position to contract alliances between themselves. They first formed three leagues—the Grey League, the League of the House of God, and the League of the Ten Jurisdictions. Finally, towards the end of the fifteenth century these three leagues coalesced and formed the Rhœtian republic, and became an allied canton (*zugewandte Ort*) of the Swiss Con federation.[1]

---

[1] Hilty, *Das Referendum im schweizerischen Staatsrecht*, in the *Archiv für öffentliches Recht*, Zweiter Band, pp. 171 and 176.
[See also Hilty, *Die Bundesverfassungen der schweizerischen Eid-*

A Federal Assembly, consisting of delegates of the communes of the three leagues, sixty-three members in all, was held every summer. The meeting-place was alternately Ilanz in the Grey League, Coire in the League of the House of God, and Davos in the League of the Ten Jurisdictions.[1] This Diet was a deliberative and consultative assembly. Its members came to it furnished with definite instructions, which it was the custom to read out at the beginning of the session. Their function was to discuss and consider questions before them, but any decision they might arrive at was only of a provisional nature, and was adopted with the saving clause *ad referendum*,[2] that

---

genossenschaft, an historical treatise written by request of the Federal Council on the occasion of the six hundredth centenary of the First Perpetual Alliance of August 1, 1891; *Revue de Droit International*, xxiv., 1892, pp. 384-405, 476-89, *Le Referendum et l'Initiative en Suisse*. Also Benoist, *Une démocratie historique* in the *Revue des deux Mondes* for August 1891; Vulliemin, *Geschichte der schweizerischen Eidgenossenschaft*, i. p. 130. Also *Rechtsquellen des Canton Graubünden*, with an introduction by Wagner and Von Salis, in the *Zeitschrift für schweizerisches Recht*, vol. iii. part 2, vol. iv. part 1, and vol. v. part 3; "The Early History of the Referendum" in the *Historical Review*, vol. vi. p. 674, by W. A. A. Coolidge. The referendum system is fully described by Simler in his *De Helvetiorum Republica* (1577), and by Sprecher in his *Pallas Rhœtica* (1617). Ganzoni, in *Beiträge zur Kenntniss des bündnerischen Referendums*, p. 15, points out that though the Rhœtian and Swiss historians describe the referendum very fully, yet there is very little trace of it in the Rhœtian law, merely a few enactments on the subjects. It was not until 1794 that the whole system was elaborately set forth on paper, reformed and regulated.]

[1] Curti, *Geschichte der schweizerischen Volksgesetzgebung*, Zweite Auflage, Zurich, 1885, p. 11. This remarkable work is the best history of the democratic ideas and institutions of Switzerland.

[2] [The words occur apparently for the first time in Vulpius' narrative, *Historia Rhœtica*. He died in 1706. See "Early History of the Referendum," *Historical Review*, vol. vi. p. 681.]

is, to be referred back to the constituent bodies, the communes, with whom the final adoption or rejection really rested.[1] Thus the communes themselves were the real sovereigns of the country. In order to enable these bodies to exercise their legislative power, a committee of the Diet prepared at the end of each session a report of the debates, together with a list of questions. In this list were set forth the different subjects upon which the communes were required to exercise their sovereign power of sanction or veto. It had to be printed, to be expressed in a clear manner without unusual words, and to be in the language spoken by the people to whom it was addressed.[2] The communes received the papers from the hands of messengers, who had to obtain an acknowledgment of their safe delivery. This was called *das Ausschreiben auf die Gemeinden*.[3]

[1] [Mr. Coolidge, in his article on "The Early History of the Referendum," *Historical Review*, vol. vi., p. 681, says that there was also another assembly, a sort of standing committee, called the Beitag, which also had to refer matters back to the communes. He quotes the following passage from Simler, *De Helvetiorum Republica* : " Quoties causæ publicæ agendæ sunt quarum tamen causa non placet indici senatum totius Rœtiæ, tum hi tres præcipue et præterea aliquot alii ex singulis fœderibus convocantur; sed non habent plenam statuendi potestatem verum acta ad communitates fœderum separatim referuntur, et quod major horum pars statuerit, ratum est."]

[2] According to a decree of 1794. Before that, by a decree of 1587, the questions had been drawn up exclusively in German. Three languages are spoken in the Grisons — German, Romance, and Italian. The members of the Great Council, as a rule, speak in German, but they can also use Italian or Romance. There are three Romance dialects—the Oberland, the Oberalp, and the Engadine. There are three or four newspapers in the Romance language.

[3] Another mode of ascertaining the opinions of the communes

When once a commune was duly informed of some question, the citizens collected together to agree upon their answer.[1] These communal assemblies, which were distributed throughout the whole territory of the Grisons, each reproduced the chief features of the Landsgemeinde in miniature. There was this difference, however: the Landsgemeinden were really sovereign, whereas the answer of one commune was not decisive for the whole country unless it happened that this was the opinion of the majority of the communes.

As a rule, the questions submitted to the Referendum were not of a legislative nature. Decentralisation was carried so far in the Grisons that each league dealt separately with all matters touching civil or criminal law, and in the League of the House of God these subjects were even within the competence of each commune.[2]

was known by the name of *das Reiten und Fahren auf die Gemeinden,* in which messengers were sent to the sovereign communes instead of circulars.

[1] The electoral qualifications were not fixed by any general regulation for the whole country. Each commune settled the matter as it liked.

[2] The questions which were the special province of each league were also referred back to the communes of the league, and decided by the vote so obtained. Finally, everything within the special sphere of the communes was decided by an appeal to the citizens in their local assemblies or gemeinden. (Ganzoni *Beiträge zur Kenntniss des bündnerischen Referendums,* Zürich, pp. 12 and 45.)

[Herr Ganzoni remarks that "the Referendum has been the corner-stone of every constitution in Rhœtia up to the present day." It existed in three distinct strata. There was, first of all, the referendum from the Hochgerichte to the villages. The Hochgerichte, or jurisdictions, which are described above as communes, were primarily the units for judicial purposes. They were also the centres of political organisation. Below them were the villages

The referendum was therefore applied more especially to administrative matters of general interest and
to questions of foreign politics. The majority of the
communes decided, for instance, such a matter as the
creation or suppression of the judiciary; they approved
the Federal budget, and gave their consent to the
public expenditure; they passed police laws like those
against vagabonds or those for the suppression of
epidemics;[1] they acted as sovereigns in all the rela-

possessing land in common, and these were known as Dorfschaften.
In 1839 we get the system further elaborated, though this is probably only a codification of customary usages. The envoys from each
village met in the chief assembly of the Hochgericht. When they
had agreed on any matter, the "little council," or executive authority
of the Hochgericht, had to issue a circular to the various villages
inquiring the opinion of each on matters specified therein. A discussion then took place, the result was reported by the envoys, and
the council announced which side was supported by the majority of
villages. Secondly, there was a referendum from the Diet of each
league to the component Hochgerichte of the league. The Diet of
each league was composed of envoys from the Hochgerichte of the
league, but in the Grey League, or Graue Bund (graue = grafen,
counts), the feudal lords were also members of the Diet, which had
therefore not such popular tendencies as the other leagues. The
referendum was chiefly used as a means of ascertaining the views
of the Hochgerichte, although when ascertained they were not
necessarily final. In the League of the Ten Jurisdictions the
referendum was much more important; and in the League of the
House of God, which had been consecrated by the Bishop of Chur,
the referendum was of extreme importance, as everything was laid
before the Hochgerichte. Thirdly, there was the referendum from
the Diet of the Three Leagues to the Hochgerichte, described above.
See Coolidge, "Early History of the Referendum."]

[1] [Hilty (*Le Referendum et l'Initiative en Suisse*, in the *Revue de
Droit International*, 1892, No. 4, p. 317) does not seem to agree
with this. "The right of voting possessed by the citizens of these
republics (in the Grisons and Valais), the necessary majority, and
even the matters to be submitted to the vote, were not settled by
any precise rules in either country. Questions of general police
and financial matters were considered as outside the sphere of the

tions of their state with other states; they nominated and recalled the ambassadors; they ratified treaties; they declared war in the last resort, and concluded peace. With them rested the responsibility of planning the defence of the country, for it was their province to sanction the construction of fortresses. In addition to these powers the communes were a sort of Court of Appeal, the resort of any person who considered himself injured by the decision of any inferior authority.[1] Towards the end of the month of January, a Congress, composed of the president and three deputies from each league, twelve in all, met at Coire, for the purpose of examining the answers of the communes, and of ascertaining the decision of the majority.[2]

A more delicate and difficult mission than that of their Congress can scarcely be conceived. The difficulty lay in the fact that the questions to be answered by the communal assemblies were not drawn up in such a manner that their replies could be only either Yes or No. A very great latitude was left these bodies in the exercise of their vote. The idea was that, since they had the power of wholly accepting or entirely rejecting the proposals of the Diet, it was possible to accept or reject conditionally. After all,

referendum, and a good deal could be included under these heads. For instance, in the Grisons a forest law, which was necessary but unpopular, was enforced for a long time under the title of 'General police regulation concerning forests.'"]

[1] Ganzoni, pp. 27–69.

[2] The majority which decided a question was not the majority of the electors of the whole country, but that of the communes. The communes were the political units, and each possessed one or more votes according to the ratio in which it contributed to the taxes. (Curti, p. 11.)

the communes were the actual sovereigns of the country, and hence it logically follows that they had the right to modify the projects of law submitted for their consideration, and were justified in making amendments. As a matter of fact they did make considerable use of these prerogatives. Sometimes they took the course of refusing to entertain the propositions submitted them, and consequently declined to give any answer except one to the effect that the time was not ripe for the solution of such matters. If the question were so thorny that silence on their part would have been inexcusable, they escaped responsibility by sending an answer with a double meaning. Heaven only knows how the members of the Congress were able to evolve any sort of order out of this chaos, or how they discovered the leading idea among the many and varying answers. They must often have had to content themselves with evolving a majority out of a mere preponderance of opinion in one direction or another, or even sometimes have been obliged to issue their questions afresh. We find them more than once giving vent to their extreme irritation, and upbraiding the communes either for sending an answer in terms much too general to be intelligible, or for not sending any answer at all. In 1712 the members of the Congress almost threatened to strike. They decided, in fact, not to reassemble unless the majority, at least, of the communes provided them with answers. The communes, on the other hand, re-echoed the complaints and protests of the Congress. They declared that it had acted arbitrarily in estimating the majority, and that it credited them with intentions they never conceived. They ultimately demanded that a detailed report of the result of the examination of the votes should be communicated to them, in order that they might be able to check the proceedings of the Congress.[1]

Such were the general features of the referendum in the Grisons. It is interesting to compare this old institution with the system proposed at the time of the Revolution of 1848 by Rittinghausen, who, with Victor Considérant and Ledru Rollin, defended the practice of direct legislation by the people against Louis Blanc, Émile de Girardin, and Proudhon.[2] This

[1] Ganzoni, pp. 29-75.

[2] [Rittinghausen went to Paris in 1848 in order to propagate an idea which he had propounded in his journal, the *Westdeutsche Zeitung*, and at the Parliament of Frankfort. In his works he violently attacks the representative system, and calls the legislative assemblies "the incarnation of incapacity and evil intentions." He then goes on to consider what other form ought to replace the representative system, and arrives at the conclusion that direct legislation by the whole people "is the only government worthy of an enlightened nation, the only one by which the theory of the sovereignty of the people becomes a reality." His principal works are *La législation directe par le peuple ou la véritable démocratie*, Paris, 1850; *La législation directe et ses adversaires*, Brussels, 1852; *De l'organisation de la législation directe*, Cologne, 1870; *Réfutation des arguments produits contre la législation directe*, Cologne, 1872; *Die direkte Gesetzgebung durch das Volk* (Zürich: Schw. Grütliverein, 1893). Some of Rittinghausen's work has been translated into English. See Three Letters on "Direct Legislation by the People; or, True Democracy" (London: James Watson, 1851). "The Difficulty Solved; or, The Government of the People by Themselves," by Victor Considérant (J. Watson, 1851), is a translation of one of the pamphlets of Rittinghausen's chief supporter.

The introduction of the referendum into, at least, one Trade Union in England is ascribed to the influence of these pamphlets. John Melson, a Liverpool printer and a Trades Unionist, urged the

system is all the more interesting as a Belgian politician has recently characterised it as the ideal towards which all democrats ought to strive.[1] "The time has now come to explain," wrote Rittinghausen, "how direct legislation can be organised."

The people are to be divided into sections, each containing a thousand citizens.[2]

Each section is to assemble in a place suitable for the purpose—a school, town hall, or public building —and then will proceed to elect a president, who will direct the debates in the mode hereinafter mentioned.

Every citizen shall be allowed to take part in the discussions.[3]

The voting will take place at the end of the discussion.

After the examination of the result the president of the section forwards the number of the votes, for and against, to the mayor of the commune. The mayor makes a return of the votes in all the sections of the commune, and communicates the result to his official superior, who goes through the same process for his district. He then forwards the tale of votes,

adoption of direct legislation by his Union instead of legislating by what was known as a delegate meeting. He was unsuccessful at first, but, as a result of his efforts, the delegate meeting was superseded in 1861 by the Referendum (*Typographical Circular* for March 1889). See "Industrial Democracy," by Sidney and Beatrice Webb, 1898, vol. i. p. 21, note.]

[1] Lorand, *Le Referendum*, 1890, p. 23.

[2] "It is not essential that there should be a thousand citizens in each section. This number will obviously have to vary according to the density and distribution of the population in the different countries."—Rittinghausen, *La législation directe*, p. 39.

[3] ["Consequently every mind is at the service of the country."— Rittinghausen, Three Letters, &c., Letter II., p. 13.]

for and against, to the head of the department, who in his turn transmits the result of the vote in his department to the minister, who collects the total results for the whole country. By this process it can be known accurately how many citizens have approved and how many would reject any particular measure. Its fate is decided by the will of the majority. The following are the general rules for the debates: The president shall direct the discussion. No bills shall be presented to the people. The only initiative possessed by the ministry, elected by the whole people for a certain time, consists in determining that on such and such a day, in all the sections throughout the country, meetings will be held for the purpose of deliberating on such and such a subject. When a certain number of citizens demand a new law on any matter whatsoever, or a change in some law already in existence, the ministry must, within a certain prescribed interval, summon the people to act in their sovereign capacity as legislators; and it is only in matters of external policy that the ministry will be able to submit propositions, to be deliberated on by the people, which have not previously been indicated to them by the number of citizens fixed by law.[1]

The law will emanate organically out of the discussions themselves.[2] In order to attain this result, the

---

[1] "I am of opinion that every Power is a tyranny in the bud, and that democracy will never be able to neutralise it sufficiently unless by taking from it all initiative in legislation."—Rittinghausen, p. 39.

[2] "Laws prepared by commissions will happily become impossible under this system, for their admission would also necessitate the admission of every proposition involving alterations. Now, with the privilege of making amendments, it would be easy to see that

president will first of all bring the *principle* of the law up for debate. He will then lead up quite naturally to the subordinate questions in their turn.[1] When all the results shall have reached the ministry, a drafting commission will draw up the text of a clear and simple law, which will have the advantage of not giving rise to several interpretations.[2]

Louis Blanc, without knowing anything of the working of the Rhætian referendum, noticed immediately among the defects of the Rittinghausen system the drawback which we criticised when considering the history of the referendum in the Grisons.[3]

all direct legislation would be only a brilliant dream, a utopia." Rittinghausen, p. 34.

" The right of amendment is a compromise, and the law does not tolerate compromises.—*Id.* p. 216.

[Every project of law produced by any commission whatever is of no value, inasmuch as it is not the work of the general mind, and is tainted by the self-interest of those who have prepared it."]

[1] [Rittinghausen gives an example. He takes the subject of prescription in criminal matters. First of all the president would start the discussion on the question, "Shall there be prescription in criminal matters or not?" Then he will pass to the question, "Shall prescriptions be the same for felonies, misdemeanours, and police contraventions?" Then, "After what period shall there be prescription for felonies?" The voter marks the figure he wishes to prevail upon the ticket. The president puts the same question relative to misdemeanours, and afterwards as to police contraventions.] It will perhaps be feared that the presidents of many of the sections will not know how to put the questions in the order required by direct legislation; but have we not the press, which will make it its business to discuss all the matters before the time fixed for the debates, which will thrash out the subject in all its bearings, and, in a word, will guide those who have not the good sense requisite to put a few questions of principle? But such cases will be rare."—Rittinghausen, Three Letters, &c., p. 14.

[2] Rittinghausen, *La législation directe par le peuple et ses adversaires,* Brussels, 1852, pp. 24-26.

[3] [Rittinghausen himself foresees that three objections will be

"Frankly speaking," said Louis Blanc, "nobody will have any confidence in the system. Moreover, M. Rittinghausen does not seem to realise that eight figures, and only eight, combined in every possible way, two and two, three and three, four and four, can form as many as 40,000 combinations. A law containing eight principal clauses could therefore give 10,000 assemblies for 10,000 different bills. How would he propose out of these 10,000 opinions, all differently expressed, to extract the will of the people, who are thus directly governing themselves? And what is it that he proposes the ministry should add up? 'When all the data are in the hands of the ministry,' says Rittinghausen, 'a commission shall draft the text of a clear and simple law.' The task before your commission is to frame a *clear and simple law*

brought against his scheme, and, as he considers, answers them satisfactorily.

1. That the people are too ignorant. He combats this by urging that in legislative assemblies real talent is swamped by the mediocrities, but in the popular reunions opportunity will be given for all lights to shine. There will, moreover, he says, be no tumult or disorder in these popular assemblies; for when the people deliberate, it is quieter and more dignified than the great legislative assemblies. Free masses, he says, "listen generally to every opinion, and I have often remarked that they do not scruple to sacrifice a favourite orator to the first-comer with better arguments." Personal animosity will give place to an enthusiasm for principles. Direct legislation will elevate and improve the press, whose columns will no longer be soiled by the efforts of parties to mutually annihilate each other.

2. That the people will not have time for law-making. The matters for legislation will not be numerous. At the end of three years, after deliberating twice a week in the sections, the people will hardly have anything to legislate about.

3. That direct legislation is not the ideal of democracy. Rittinghausen admits this, but says it is the decisive step to be taken towards the brilliant future which humanity has before it. See Three Letters, &c., pp. 17–28.]

out of five, six, even ten thousand bills, and to do it, moreover, in such a way that it shall be the expression of the direct *united* will of five, six, or ten thousand sections, who will each have given a *different* reason for their vote. I defy any commission to do it. It is absurd even to suppose that *this clear and simple law*, when finally drafted, would be regarded by the various sections as the exact expression of their wishes, and as the result of the *direct self-government of the people*, when such a law is not the exact reproduction of their work. It is just as far-fetched to imagine that this commission could possibly compose, out of so many *data*, the text of *a clear and precise law*, without exercising a power a hundred times more irritating than that of a legislative assembly elected by universal suffrage. For it might happen, indeed it would almost always happen, that, from the very fact of the multiplicity and diversity of the data, the text of the clear and precise law would not harmonise exactly with any of the proposals drawn up by the majority of the sections. They would then say to the drafting commission: You not only make a law quite different to what we desired, but you have done so in the face of our formally expressed wish to the contrary. You are arrogant usurpers." [1]

Rittinghausen was deeply wounded by this biting criticism.[2] Although he believed thoroughly in his

---

[1] Louis Blanc, *Plus de Girondins*, quoted by Rittinghausen, pp. 140-42.

[2] "You, Louis Blanc, the renowned writer, are the only one who needs an explanation of my system. The proletariat has always understood me without the slightest effort; to them my scheme has always appeared clear, and devoid of all superfluous or incom-

system, which he considered as his own invention,[1] he was so much disturbed by the attack of Louis Blanc that, without seeming to be in the least aware of it, he threw over an essential part of the mechanism of his institution.

"Let the drafting commission," he wrote, "just try to follow that constitutional tradition which has shown itself to be representative, and the people will soon make up their minds. For, after all, a drafting commission is not indispensable. WHAT IS THE GOOD of insisting on FORMULATING THE TEXT OF A LAW when the answers to the questions, once in the hands of the central authority, will serve the same purpose? If only the counting of the votes be honestly carried out by that central authority, the people can, if they please, dispense with the services of the drafting commission."[2]

And after having written that, Rittinghausen enters the lists against the Anarchists. Has he, however, any right to attack them? He upholds against

prehensible phrases with double meanings."—Rittinghausen, p. 143.

[1] Rittinghausen wrote in answer to Proudhon: "The direct legislation of the Greeks, Romans, and Germans has never been organised as I propose. My method will infallibly be adopted, for it is the only organisation that is reasonable. I can claim it as my own invention, and it is neither more nor less than the art, hitherto unknown, of producing laws spontaneously and organically from the free deliberations of the whole people. I can claim to have made the science of legislation enter upon a new phase."—*Id.* p. 184.

[2] Rittinghausen, p. 146. [For a scathing criticism of Rittinghausen, see *Idée générale de la Révolution au XIX Siècle*, by Proudhon, in vol. ix. of his complete works. See also an article by M. Agathon de Potter, called *Rittinghausen et son système*, in the *Philosophie de l'Avenir*, 19th year, No. 176.]

Proudhon "*the necessity of a social interpretation of natural right.*"   But where could one find in his mutilated system, without its drafting committee, any "social interpretation of right" stated, as he demands, *in the text of a clear and simple law which will not admit of several interpretations?*   Rittinghausen has condemned his own work.   He has himself proved that his invention belongs to the domain of dreams and utopias.

It is therefore very gratifying to see M. Lorand bringing up the subject again to-day, and trying to put it in the place of honour.   What a curious turn of fortune's wheel.[1]

A referendum much like that of the Grisons formed part of the constitution of Upper Valais.   This canton was allied to the Confederation, and was divided into seven districts called *Dixains.*   The Upper Valais was governed by a "Great Council," in which sat the Bishop of Sion, the president of the canton, and twenty-eight deputies nominated by the councils of the *Dixains.*[2]   All affairs of importance which occupied the attention of the Council were

[1] [Direct legislation has also its advocates in France to-day.   It is advocated in the *Petite république française* of the 2nd of February 1895, and in an article in the *Almanach de la question sociale* of 1895.   There is in Paris a league, founded in May 1895, called the "Socialist and revolutionary league for republican, socialistic, and direct revision by the people, deliberating and voting in its assemblies."   On the 11th November 1895 a memorial on the subject was presented to the Chamber of Deputies in Paris, signed by the leaders of the socialistic party.   See Signorel, *Le Referendum législatif,* pp. 147–53.]

[This meeting is first mentioned in 1339 under the name of *concilium generale.*   Later it was called the Landrath, and took

communicated to the people, who discussed them in the communal assemblies. The results of their deliberations, and of the popular votings, were transmitted to the president of the canton and to the Chancellor, who laid them before the Great Council. No law could come into force unless it had been accepted by the majority of the *Dixains*—that is to say, by four out of the seven.[1]

place regularly twice a year. The object was not to unite the districts to each other, but to control the action of the Bishop. See "Early History of the Referendum," Coolidge, and *Rechtsquellen des Cantons Wallis*, Heusler, 1890 (Basle, Detloff).]

[1] Hilty, *op. cit.* 172. [From instances given by Professor Heusler in his introduction to *Rechtsquellen des Cantons Wallis, Zeitschrift für schweizerisches Recht*, vol. vii. and ix. (or published separately in 1890, Basle, Detloff), it would seem that some measures at least required the assent of every Dixain. These instances are quoted by Coolidge, "Early History of the Referendum," *Historical Review*, vol. vi. p. 678, who says that no measure was valid unless it obtained the whole of the votes. This system lasted in Valais down to 1802, when Napoleon then incorporated the canton with France, and the referendum disappeared. In 1815 it was restored, and we get the first constitutional statement of this popular right : "The Diet exercises the legislative power. Laws are drafted by the Council of State, and cannot be enforced until they have been referred to the councils of the Dixains and sanctioned by the majority of these councils. When there is a question of financial laws, of military capitulations, and of naturalisation, these are referred not only to the councils of the Dixains, but to those of the communes. The referendum is not applicable to the affairs which concern the Valais as a Swiss canton." In 1839 the referendum gave place to the veto (see p. 75), and it was no longer the majority of the Dixains, but the majority of the people, that decided the matter. The right of legislation by the people is now restricted to financial matters only.]

III.—*Popular Institutions in the Canton of Berne.*

Communal assemblies were also held in the canton of Berne from the fifteenth to the seventeenth century, for the purpose of deliberating and voting on questions of general interest. In external character they resemble the local gemeinden of the Grisons, but from the point of view of public law they approximate to a very different type. The communes of the Grisons were independent of each other, and on an equality among themselves. Their assemblies each formed a part of a sovereign nation ; when united, they constituted the supreme power in the state. The communes of the canton of Berne, on the contrary, had not been able to preserve their freedom. They had fallen into a state of dependence on the town, and were governed by the patrician families of Berne. There was no question of their participating in any way whatever, either directly or indirectly, in the sovereign functions of government. They neither elected the deputies nor gave their assent to the laws. Politically they were non-existent. They were, in fact, possessions of the city of Berne, and had to provide her with the sinews of war—soldiers and money. If the inhabitants of the country sometimes met in con sultation about affairs of state, it was not in virtue of any right to do so. It was the result of a manifestation of good-will on the part of the government, who, when in a critical position, wished to assure themselves of the support of the country, or even to shift the responsibility of an important decision on to the shoulders of the people.[1]

To put it shortly : The referendum in the Grisons was *compulsory ;* in the canton of Berne it was only *optional,* the option resting with the government. The communal assemblies in the Bernese territory were presided over by a member of the council of the town, or by the president of the commune. Attendance does not seem to have been compulsory. Only now and again, when some very important question came up for discussion, was the delegate of the council who presided over the gathering obliged to ask if everybody were present.[2] The age of political majority was fixed at fourteen years. In 1503 children of twelve could take part in the voting. From 1535 to 1546 eighteen was the statutory age, and then it was reduced again to fourteen.[3]

The first popular meeting took place in 1449. The city of Berne applied to the people for authority to exact a special tax to meet the debts contracted during a war. From this year up to the end of the fifteenth century there were eight similar meetings. In the sixteenth century we hear of sixty-eight, and in the seventeenth only one, in the year 1610. Most

---

[1] [M. Hilty says that the object of these popular consultations was twofold. In the first place, to get at the voice of the people, which was by no means the voice of God in the eyes of the aristocratic council, but which was nevertheless instructive. In the second place, the object was so to direct public opinion that the government would not meet with an obstinate resistance on the part of the people should it wish to embark on a more or less uncertain enterprise.—*Le Referendum et l'Initiative en Suisse, Revue de droit international,* 1892, p. 389.]

[2] Von Stürler, *Die Volksanfragen im alten Bern,* Berne, 1869, p. 14.

[3] Von Stürler, *op. cit.* pp. 14–15.

of the questions submitted to the people were of a military character—such as the undertaking of an expedition, the conclusion of peace, the making of treaties and alliances, the expediency of prohibiting the enlistment of citizens as mercenaries, the imposition of a war tax, and, at a later date, religious matters. At the time of the Reformation the people were called upon to decide in the communal assemblies whether they would adopt or reject the new form of worship. Finally, very occasionally they discussed economic questions.[1]

The city of Berne, as sovereign, decided on the subject to be discussed, and fixed the time for its discussion, and also settled the form in which the appeal to the people should be made. These appeals were carried out in three different ways.[2] Sometimes the city of Berne summoned deputies from the country districts to a council. In this case, circulars were addressed to the communes stating the question that was pending. It requested the inhabitants to meet together to deliberate on the matter, and to entrust their resolutions to two deputies who were to appear on a certain day at Berne. On the appointed day each deputation announced to the council the view taken by its commune, and these opinions were embodied in the formal report. At a later date the government

---

[1] [In January 1590 a very interesting consultation took place. The Bernese Council had signed a peace with the Duke of Savoy, by which treaty Berne kept Vaud and abandoned its ally Geneva to the Duke. The people of Berne would not accept the treaty, the peace was not adhered to, and Geneva was saved for the Confederation.]

[2] Von Stürler, *op. cit.* pp. 16–18.

communicated its own decision to the communes. It would be difficult to say, considering the optional nature of the referendum, how far the government took the will of the country into consideration. Von Stürler, the historian of the ancient Bernese referendum, has estimated that fifty consultations resulted in favourable replies to the previously expressed opinion of the government. The people gave a negative answer on fourteen questions only. In the remaining cases we are either ignorant of the result, or the people merely stated beforehand that they would be content to leave the matter in the hands of the government.

This method of getting to know the feeling in the country was frequently employed in early times, but Berne ceased to have recourse to it later on, and, instead, sent her own delegates from the city to the country districts.[1] The presidents of the communes were ordered on such an occasion to call the inhabitants together. The delegate from Berne first of all greeted his audience in the name of the government, and stated the reason for the summons and the subject to be discussed. If he were asked to do so, he explained the matter more in detail; then, finally, he took the vote of the meeting by

[1] [The reason for this is given by the chronicler Anselm, who says that the government in 1509 "preferred to send their own messengers rather than make their subjects quasi-councillors, for such a proceeding rarely happened without being harmful to those in authority; for these country-folk were apt to encroach on the rights of the government, to discuss other matters, and to support and create intrigues and misunderstandings." As a matter of fact, we find that these peasants, when they were once consulted, profited by the occasion to give utterance to many grievances. See Hilty, *Revue de droit*, &c., 1892, p. 389.]

saying: "Will those who agree with our lords and masters of Berne remain in their places? Will those who are of a contrary opinion go to the side?" The result of the vote was communicated to the government by the delegate, or by a letter from the president of the commune. When Berne did not think it advisable to send out members of her government as delegates, she issued a circular letter to the presidents of the communes, in which the object of the referendum was indicated. The communes were allowed a specified time in which to consider their answers. Each president then assembled the electors and directed the discussion on the matter. After the debates he drew up a report of the meeting, signed it and sealed it, and sent it to the Council at Berne.

Then these reports were sorted according to their contents into two groups, those for and those against the project of the government. Each commune, whatever its population, possessed one vote, and an absolute majority of the communes decided the question.

The practice of thus consulting the people fell into disuse in the seventeenth century. The Bernese patrician families, who had organised themselves into a powerful and exclusive oligarchy, would not, from that time onwards, allow the inhabitants of the country districts to have any controlling voice. However, on two occasions the rural inhabitants succeeded in treating on equal terms with their lords of the city. In 1513 the government was obliged to promise not to contract any alliance without the consent of the people, and in 1531 it undertook not to go to war unless the people had previously given their assent.

These conventions, by which the referendum became a popular right, and, therefore, part of the constitution, continued to be observed for some time. Unfortunately, the peasants lacked cohesion and guidance. They had the advantage of numbers, and could, in times of excitement, force the government to yield to their demands. To maintain their position, however, they required leaders endowed with energy and perseverance, they needed an understanding between themselves, and a certain amount of discipline; but they had none of these. Their isolation and impotence resulted in the triumph of the patrician families, who were the sole and uncontrolled legislators down to 1798.[1]

---

[1] [1. In discussing the history of the referendum before 1798, one might also notice the traces we find in Zürich, in Geneva, in Lucerne, and also a curious form of military referendum known as the *Kriegsgemeinde.*

In Zürich we find the city council consulting the communes by a very similar method to that employed by Berne. Delegates were sent to the communes to explain the matter, and brought back the opinions of the people in each locality. They only seem to have been consulted on matters of foreign politics or administrative affairs of great importance, and the answers sent back were long, and contained a full account of their reasons for voting as they did. They voted on such questions as the alliance with France, on religious questions arising out of the Reformation, and on foreign enlistments. The first official mention we get of the referendum in Zürich is in the *Waldmannischer Spruchbrief* of 1489, and in the *Kappeler Brief* of 1531, which are almost our only authorities.

This letter contains a promise on the part of the government not to commence any war against the wish of the country, and to ascertain the views of the good people of the country upon all important affairs. The referendum disappeared in the seventeenth century, and those who attempted to revive it were punished as traitors. Bluntschli attributes its disappearance to the exhaustion after the struggles of the Reformation, combined with unlucky foreign wars and the visitations of the plague, when the

D

§ AFTER 1798.

I. *Public Law in the Federation and in the Cantons from 1798 to 1830.*

Under the old system Switzerland was a confederation of states, having no federal constitution properly
speaking, nor any central organised authority. The
confederate cantons were independent states, sove-

bare necessity of existence dwarfed all political aspirations of a
popular nature. A very amusing extract is given by M. Dunant in
Législation par le peuple en Suisse, p. 34, which shows, as he says, that
democratic notions were not very advanced in Zürich at that time.

2. The history of popular rights at Geneva is interesting because
of their connection with the writings of Rousseau. Geneva did not,
however, become part of the Swiss Confederation until 1815. We
find the government in the fifteenth century in the hands of a
council of fifty, which was afterwards increased to sixty, and then
to two hundred. These councils took over all the rights which had
belonged up to that time to the general council of all the citizens;
but in order that the laws and decrees passed by them should come
into force, they had to be approved by the assembly of the citizens.
The aristocratic government established under the influence of
Calvin reduced the powers of the popular assembly. They no
longer had the right of deliberating on the laws and on the constitution ; they had only the right of voting, not of discussing. In the
eighteenth century (1707) a democratic reaction took place, and
under the popular pressure certain reforms were granted. The
elections were to take place by secret ballot, and no new law could
come into force without having been approved by the assembly of
the citizens, which was to meet every five years.

Further disturbances took place, however, and France, Berne,
and Zürich intervened in 1738, and a new constitution was drawn
up. Under this constitution the assembly of citizens had full rights
of legislating, but the right of initiating laws was reserved to the
authorities. All citizens had, however, the right of petition. At the
time of the French Revolution, 1794, the assembly of citizens declared
that they alone had the right of approving, rejecting, modifying,
interpreting, or abrogating laws or edicts ; and by a revision of the
constitution in 1796, the right of initiative also was given to the

reign within the limits of their respective frontiers. They established, according to their inclinations, in the one place a democratic government,[1] in another an exclusive aristocracy,[2] and in others a federal republic.[3]

A common danger, and the need of combining their separate forces against powerful enemies, had given birth to the Swiss Confederation. This alliance was strengthened by the desire to settle by arbitration the disputes which arose between the states. The bond was still further cemented by common financial interests in the administration of the domains or

assembly, or to 700 citizens in the case of an ordinary law, of 1000 in the case of an amendment of the constitution. When Geneva was incorporated with the French republic, these rights were curtailed, and it was not until 1830 that the people regained their position. See Fazy, *Les Constitutions de la République de Genève*, 1870.

3. A system of appeal to the people by the authorities was in operation in Lucerne in 1513, but it only lasted until 1525.

4. We find in the military history of Switzerland a sort of military referendum. In the case of the more important campaigns the districts used to send certain councillors with their captains, so that a parliament could be practically held on the field. This parliament often concerned itself with the most important matters, such as armistices and terms of peace, and their conclusions were announced to the districts by means of the councillors. In many cases, too, we find a sort of military Landsgemeinde of the whole army, which decided any great military question. The battle of Marignano and the battle of Bicocca were both resolved on after this fashion.—Hilty, *Das Referendum im schweizerischen Staatsrecht*, in the *Archiv für öffentliches Recht*, vol. ii. p. 203.]

[1] [As in the Landsgemeinde cantons.]

[2] [*Cf.* Berne, Zürich, and Lucerne.]

[3] [*Cf.* the Grisons, which belonged to the class of friendly allies, who were more or less under the protection of the cantons. There were also feudal seigniories, ecclesiastical principalities, such as Bâle, republics of various kinds, and even one monarchy, Neuchâtel, besides the bailiwicks of the subject territories.]

subject territories which the states had acquired, and which were held in common.

The adjustment of these different interests led to the annual meeting of a Federal Diet, in which each state was equally represented. The members of the Diet were merely delegates bound by instructions given by their states. If a new question were raised they had to return to refer it (*ad referendum*) to the government of their canton, which alone had the right of coming to a decision. As a rule no decision obtained the force of law unless it were unanimously adopted by the Diet.[1]

[1] [In the earliest times the Diets met at uncertain intervals ; later it became the custom for them to meet regularly in July. The Diet was held in any canton, and even on foreign territory ; but from the fifteenth to the eighteenth century they usually assembled at Baden, and after that at Frauenfeld. Each deputation in later times reported itself to Zürich on its arrival, for Zürich was practically the presiding canton. They were then informed of the hour of the opening. The first part of the session was public, when the premier deputy of each state publicly greeted the Federation in the name of his canton. The deliberations which followed were held in private. These were afterwards drawn up into a report, of which each deputation received a copy, with the necessary particulars attached. As a rule each canton was represented by two deputies, the allies by one only. The premier deputy was generally the first magistrate of the canton, with the exception of Berne, and the second deputy an important member of the council. Sometimes the younger members of the aristocratic families were sent as "Councillors of the Legation," in order that they might get to know the important members of the Confederation. [See Hilty, *Die Bundesverfassungen der schweizerishen Eidgenossenschaft*, pp. 320–21.

There were, in fact, two kinds of Diets : the general Diets, or *allgemeine Tage*, which were chiefly concerned with ratifying treaties of peace (see Hilty, *Eidgenössische Abschiede*, ii. 518, 525 ; iii. 638, 646), and the Federal Diets of the twelve cantons, which the allies did not necessarily attend. After the Reformation we get Diets of those of the same faith, *Konfessionelle Sonder-*

The wars carried on by the combined cantons to defend the independence of their country created at first a strong feeling of unity between them. After the lapse of years, however, the memory of the glorious struggles of the past became dim, the federal tie relaxed, and at the time of the Reformation, when the country became divided into Catholic states and Protestant states, a complete rupture seemed imminent. The religious schism caused Swiss to arm against Swiss, and separate private alliances were formed, based upon a common faith and religion; so that when the day came for them again to defend

tage, held at Lucerne and Aarau, and those of the cantons who were over lords of bailiwicks, *Syndikatstage*, which met at Frauenfeld and Lugano. The Diets were more or less of the nature of diplomatic conferences. We find them settling the differences between cantons (1348); drawing up a military code, and legislating about fairs and the protection of churches and convents (1393); drawing up a new constitution (1481); coming to an agreement about coinage for ten years (1389), and then later for fifty years (1425). There were various police regulations agreed on at these Diets, concerning the pursuit of murderers, the prohibition of the *Vehmgericht*, laws against vagabonds and idle people who would not work, against Jews and sorcerers, also regulations for the protection of the trade routes, and on navigation and fisheries. It was at one of these Diets in 1477 that Burgundy was sold to Louis XI. for 150,000 florins (see Hilty, *Eidgenössische Abschiede*). Although a state might have two deputies, it was only considered to have a single vote. *Cf.* Bluntschli, *Geschichte des schweizerischen Bundesrechtes*, i. p. 419;] Blumer, *Handbuch des schweizerischen Bundesstaatsrechtes*, i. pp. 3–18; Id., *Staats und Rechtsgeschichte der schweizerischen Demokratien*, i. pp. 328, 360, ii. pp. 74–85; Curti, *Geschichte der schweizerischen Volksgesetzgebung*, Berne, 1882, pp. 13, 38.

[The "Referendum" was often made use of to drag out the embarrassing or difficult questions, for by constantly referring things back it was easy to prevent anything definite being settled. *Cf.* Benoist, *"Une démocratie historique"* in *La Revue des deux Mond* , January 1895, p. 285.]

their native country against an enemy, the weakened sentiment for a common Fatherland was no longer powerful enough to rouse all Swiss people to gather under the same flag. Thus, when the armies of the Directory invaded the country at the end of the last century, though the French troops were here and there heroically opposed, yet the resistance offered was partial, isolated, disconnected, and consequently ineffectual. The invader, moreover, found willing supporters among the people themselves. The ideas of the Revolution had preceded its armies, and in certain social circles they had aroused an ardent sympathy for France. This was natural enough, for at the time of the French Revolution three-fourths of the citizens of Switzerland were nothing more or less than political nonentities. In the aristocratic cantons the peasants of the country districts were excluded by the burghers or the patrician families of the principal towns from all share in the government. In the subject territories the whole of the inhabitants were in a state of complete dependence on the sovereign states. How could men thus robbed of their heritage resist the seductions of the new ideas of liberty, equality, and the sovereignty of the people? They joyfully hailed the arrival of the French, whom they regarded as saviours. The feeling of patriotism, the love of independence, and the sentiment of nationality had been extinguished by the grievances of a state of political helotism.[1]

The French, once masters of the country, swept away all the institutions peculiar to the people, and the historic forms handed down from the past. They

[1] Curti, *Geschichte*, &c., pp. 91–92.

endowed Switzerland with her first constitution, *the Constitution of the Helvetic Republic* of the 12th of April 1798. The old Swiss Confederation, the frontiers of the several cantons, the separate sovereign states, the subject countries, and class privileges were all abolished. By a sudden transition, forcibly effected, without any previous preparation for such a change, a military republic was set up in the place of the old Confederation, divided, moreover, into prefectures, and furnished with a representative government, in which the sovereignty was vested in the general body of citizens, and which established political equality, freedom of opinion, and liberty of the press.[1]

This complete revolution of the old order of things was a piece of ill-considered Radicalism. The fragile constitutional structure of the Helvetic republic was scarcely erected before it cracked on every side. Its authors had not only violently broken away from tradition, but the constitution was not a national production, and it had not been consecrated by the people.[2]

[1] [Switzerland was divided into eighteen prefectures, consisting of the cantons, the allies, and the bailiwicks, parcelled out, not according to the historic past of any of them, but according to physical geography. The obligation of military service was imposed, their religious festivals were diminished, and, as a set off, they had freedom of commerce and industry, both of which were unknown to them.]

[2] [Provision was made in this constitution for amendments of the constitution by popular consent. Title XI. was as follows:—
"Art. 106. The Senate shall propose these changes, but propositions of this character shall become resolutions only after having been twice decreed, a space of five years intervening between the decrees. These resolutions shall then be rejected or ratified by the Great Council, and, in case of ratification only, shall be laid before

Some attempts to modify or otherwise revise this constitution were made by Bonaparte, who, acting as "mediator," summoned the Swiss delegates to Malmaison towards the end of the month of April 1801, in order to submit the scheme of a new constitution for their consideration. This draft made some important concessions to the Federalist party, whose aim was to preserve the cantonal sovereignty from the would-be centralisers. It was provisionally adopted on the 29th of May 1801 by the Legislative Council of the Helvetic republic, but was altered by the Centralist party on the 24th October 1801, and remodelled again by the Federalist party on the 27th of February 1802.

Finally, after a great deal of political agitation, we get the Constitution of the 20th of May 1802. This last is the only one of all the ephemeral constitutions of the epoch which is of interest to us, and then not so much by reason of its contents as from the manner in which it came into operation.

All the citizens who had reached twenty years of age were called upon to ratify this constitution in their respective communes. For this purpose registers were placed for four days in the various communal chanceries, in order that each citizen might enter his name as either accepting or rejecting the constitution. The result was that 72,453 citizens voted for it and 92,423 voted against, while 167,172 refrained from voting altogether. Although

the primary assemblies for adoption or rejection." "Art. 107. If the primary assemblies accept them, they shall become a fundamental part of the constitution." This provision never came into practice. See Borgeaud, p. 260.]

the majority of those who actually voted had pronounced against the constitution, those who had not voted at all either way were considered as having tacitly expressed approval, and therefore it was declared to be adopted.[1]

Such was the first appearance in federal law of the popular veto on a matter directly affecting the constitution.[2]

[1] [The words were : "The project has received the assent of the great majority of the citizens in Helvetia who are qualified to vote." It was therefore declared to be "the fundamental law of the republic."]

[2] [There were many precedents in France for submitting the constitution to the popular vote. The Constitution of 1793 was submitted to the people in their primary assemblies, and the result announced on the 1st of August was that 1,801,918 were in favour of accepting it and 11,610 were against it. It has been proved by M. Taine and others that the vote was not free. This constitution, however, never came into force. The next constitution, that of the year III., was also submitted to the people and accepted by them by 1,057,390 votes against 49,977, and this time the vote seems to have been an honest one. The Constitution of the year VIII. was also submitted to the acceptance of the French people. It received 3,000,000 votes in its favour, and only 1500 were registered in opposition. This voting did not take place in the primary assemblies, but in the capitals of the communes, by signatures publicly inscribed in registers specially set apart for the purpose. This system, which had been proposed in France by Bourdon at the time of the Revolutionary commune, was practically a register of those who disapproved of the government. It is not strange, then, that there should have been a certain reluctance to sign in opposition. Bonaparte was appointed Consul for life in 1802 by one of these plebiscitary votings, and from that time they ceased to be of importance as a method of legislation, though plebiscites were taken in 1804 and 1815.

Nothing is more natural, therefore, than that the Swiss Constitution, framed under the influence of France, should have been submitted to the people. It is interesting to compare the contemporary systems of constitutional votings in vogue in Massachusetts and New Hampshire with the French and Swiss system, especially as

The Federalists nevertheless objected to the new constitution, on the ground that it made too many concessions to the Centralist party. They attempted to bring about a fresh revision in September of the same year. Napoleon therefore intervened, and forced on all parties his *Act of Mediation*, which was intended to put an end to the political strife, the result

Condorcet, the author of the *Lettres d'un bourgeois de New Haven* (Paris, 1788), was the soul of the committee appointed in 1793 to draw up the French Constitution. ¹ The "projet Girondin" of 1793 has been described as "the result of a systematic union of the principles of New England and those of the eighteenth-century French philosophy. . . . In it the primary assemblies take the place of the town meetings." (Borgeaud, *Adoption and Amendment of Constitutions*, pp. 206-7.)

In Massachusetts, as early as 1778, the new constitution was submitted to the town meetings for ratification and rejected by them. In 1779 the people were asked whether there should be a convention to draw up a constitution. This was decided in the affirmative. A constitution was framed and presented to the town meetings, and finally, in 1780, it was found that |a majority of more than two-thirds had pronounced for its ratification. In New Hampshire the first Constitution of 1779 was rejected by the town meetings. A second plan was accepted in 1781 on the condition that certain alterations be made, and in 1783 the Constitution was finally adopted. In 1791 the town meetings were asked to declare whether they wished any amendments, and an affirmative answer being obtained, a convention was elected to prepare them. The reformed constitution was then divided up into a number of subjects, which were submitted separately to the approval of the citizens. Some were accepted and some rejected, and the convention took up the work again, and the Constitution, as finally drawn up, obtained a two-thirds majority. The example of these states was followed by Mississippi in 1817, and Missouri in 1820. In 1821 the practice was adopted by New York, and since that time it has become almost universal (Oberholtzer, *The Referendum in America*, ch. 2). In Switzerland no federal constitutional question was brought before the people until 1848, and the cantons, with the exception of those with Landsgemeinde, did not begin to submit their constitutions to the people until 1830, and it was not until 1848 that

of which had been no less than half a dozen constitutional experiments in the space of five years.[1]

The *Act of Mediation* of the 19th of February 1803 drew up a constitution for the Swiss Confederation, but it also contained separate constitutions for the different cantons.[2] It is, as Cherbuliez expressed it, a cross between the historic law of Switzerland and the philosophic law of the French Revolution, a compromise between old facts and new ideas. It lays down as a principle "that there no longer exist in Switzerland either subject lands, or privileges of place, birth, persons, or families." This is the advance. It maintains, however, the cantonal sovereignty. "The cantons shall exercise all the powers which have not been expressly delegated to the federal authority," and in this the new constitution adheres to tradition.

The constitutions accorded to the cantons varied in the different states. The Landsgemeinden were re-established in the democratic cantons, but certain modifications were introduced with reference to the age of political majority, and the popular initiative

the Federal Constitution made voting on constitutions compulsory. The point I wish to bring out is, that although Switzerland may be said to have invented the referendum in matters of ordinary legislation, yet the principle that a sanction by popular vote is necessary for the adoption of a constitution was known and acted upon in America for more than fifty years before it was nationalised in Switzerland. Where there had been popular votings in Switzerland, the vote of individuals was not considered; it was always the vote of the commune that counted except in the Landsgemeinde cantons, and even there voting on a written constitution was a novelty. See Borgeaud, *op. cit.* bk. i. ch. 2 ; bk. ii. ch. 2, 3, 4; also Lowell, *Governments and Parties in Continental Europe*, pp. 244–45.]

[1] Blumer, *Handbuch*, &c., vi. pp. 21–33 ; Curti, *Geschichte*, &c., pp. 105–11.

[2] Blumer, i. pp. 33–45 ; Curti, 111–17.

in legislative matters.[1]   The referendum reappears
in the Grisons with a more systematic organisation.[2]
In the other cantons—that is to say, in the states
already sovereign before 1798 and not included in
the preceding category [3]—as well as in the new cantons
created out of the territories which used to be subject
to the original cantons,[4] the Act of Mediation established representative government based on equal
electoral districts.   In the old sovereign cantons the
balance of political equality between the citizens was
considerably altered in favour of the towns, who were
allowed a share in the representation of the canton
quite out of proportion to the number of their active
citizens.[5]

The constitutions imposed by the Act of Mediation did not survive the decline in the fortunes of
their author.   Before the fall of Napoleon, when his

[1] Keller, *Das Volksinitiativrecht*, &c., pp. 7, 10, 18, 25.

[2] Ganzoni, *Beiträge*, &c., pp. 78–85.

[3] Basle, Berne, Fribourg, Lucerne, Schaffhausen, Solothurn, and
Zürich.

[4] Aargau, St. Gall, Ticino, Thurgau, and Vaud.

[5] At Basle and at Schaffhausen the towns sent one-third of the
representatives; in Berne, Zürich, Lucerne, Fribourg, and Solothurn
the proportion was a fifth.

[A few other points may be noticed about this constitution.
The Diet was not held two years following in the same place,
but met in turn at Fribourg, Berne, Solothurn, Basle, Zürich, and
Lucerne.   The canton in which the Diet was held was the "presiding canton."   The deputy of this canton was called "the
Landamman of Switzerland."   He was the president of the Diet
and the head of the republic, and he had the right of convoking
extraordinary Diets.   The presiding canton was obliged to provide
a guard of honour for the deputies of the other cantons, and to
lodge them suitably and pay the current expenses of the Diet.   (See
Hilty, *Die Bundesverfassungen*, &c., pp. 423, 427).   This has given rise
to the tradition that certain cantons have an especial right to be
represented in the Federal Council.]

star began to pale, the aristocratic spirit revived in the states that had formerly been sovereign, and particularly in Berne. These cantons had undergone a considerable reduction in territory by the conversion of the subject countries into independent states, and they now manifested a decided intention of re-entering into their possessions and of extending their domains to the limits of their original frontiers. The intervention of the Allied Powers, however, happily averted this, and the Congress of Vienna insisted on the independence of the existing states. They also created three new cantons—Geneva, Neuchâtel, and Valais.[1]

These twenty-two cantons took an oath, on the 7th of August 1815, to observe the "Federal Agreement."[2] By this agreement "the XXII sovereign cantons of Switzerland—to wit, Zürich, Berne, Lucerne, Uri, Schwyz, Unterwalden, Glarus, Zug, Fribourg, Solothurn, Bâle, Schaffhausen, Appenzell (the two Rhodes), St. Gall, the Grisons, Aargau, Thurgau, Ticino, Vaud, Valais, Neuchâtel, and Geneva—unite for their common safety and for the preservation of their liberty and their independence against all foreign aggression, as well as to preserve internal peace and order. They mutually guarantee their constitutions, which shall be established by the supreme authority of each canton, in conformity with the principles of the Federal Agreement.[3] They also mutually guarantee their re-

---

[1] Blumer, i. pp. 45–49.

[2] Blumer, i. pp. 49–57 ; Curti, pp. 119–23.

[3] ["It regarded the point as already won that the public law of the different cantons was or should be codified. A copy of the constitutions was to be deposited in the archives of the Diet " (Borgeaud, *Adoption and Amendment of Constitutions*, p. 27).]

spective territories" (Art. 1). "The Diet to which the
sovereign cantons have entrusted the general affairs
of the Confederation shall deal with them according
to the rules laid down in the Federal Agreement. It
is composed of the deputies of the XXII cantons,
who vote according to the instructions given by their
governments. Each canton has one vote.[1] . . . For
important decisions (war, peace, or alliances) three-
fourths of the votes are necessary. In all other
matters that have been declared to be within the
province of the Diet by this present Federal Agreement an absolute majority is sufficient" (Art. 8).

The Act of Mediation being superseded, the cantons
were left free to change their respective constitutions
as they liked. The Federal Agreement laid down one
principle only to which all the cantons were obliged
to conform   "The Confederation declares this principle to be inviolable: that since the XXII cantons
have been generally recognised as such, there are no
longer in Switzerland any subject countries, and, in
the same way, the enjoyment of political rights can
never in any canton be made the exclusive privilege
of any one class of citizens" (Art. 7).

The cantons with Landsgemeinden profited by the
freedom of choice thus restored them to organise the
right of the popular initiative on a more democratic
basis.[2] On the other hand, a retrograde movement

---

[1] [In refusing the cantons a representation proportional to the
number of their inhabitants it made it possible for the small cantons to combine to oppress the large ones, with the result that
the great cantons were sure to revolt sooner or later against the
majority of the Diet. See Duvergier de Hauranne, *La Suisse et
la révision de sa Constitution, Revue des deux Mondes*, 1873, p. 762.]

[2] Keller, *Das Volksinitiavrecht*, pp. 10 and 18.

took place in Zug. The Landsgemeinde was deprived of the right of sanctioning legislation, and only retained the popular election of the magistrates.[1]

The Grisons remained faithful to the referendum,[2] and the Valais, which had been separated from Switzerland from 1802 to 1813, reintroduced it in a new form into the new Constitution of May 12, 1815. The clause runs as follows: "The Diet shall exercise the legislative power. Bills are to be prepared by the Council of State, but cannot come into force until they have been referred to the *councils* of the Dixains and sanctioned by the majority of the councils. Financial laws, military capitulations, and the naturalisation of aliens shall be referred not only to the *councils* of the Dixains, but also to those of the communes." Thus it was the councils of the Dixains, together with the councils of the communes, and no longer the electors, who from henceforth accepted or rejected the laws.

In the other cantons, and particularly in those in which the aristocracy had formerly been the ruling power, the principle laid down in Article 7 of the Federal Agreement remained a dead letter. The ancient aristocracy was already only too apt to manipulate the constitutional revisions to their own advantage. They were favoured in their designs by the general course of foreign politics, which always exercised a great influence in Switzerland, and which at this time tended towards reaction and to a return of the old state of things. The qualifications necessary to be an elector and for eligibility to office were retained. That was the first attack on the principle

[1] Curti, *Geschichte*, &c., p. 127.　　[2] Ganzoni, pp. 86–90.

of political equality proclaimed by the Federal Compact.   Later on the system of indirect election was adopted, by which the legislators practically recruited themselves.   The burghers of the dominant towns maintained their influence in the direct elections, and managed, moreover, to secure the larger number of the seats conferred by indirect election.   None of these reactionary constitutions were submitted to the people for their ratification.[1]

"The Act of Mediation," says Cherbuliez, "had created an aristocracy of ability; the Restoration re-established an aristocracy of birth and the predominance of certain localities, the time-honoured forms of which were quite out of harmony with any principle adopted by the new generation.   The control exercised by the nation over its government was not active enough to be efficient.   There existed no means by which the majority of the representatives could be influenced according to the

[1] Blumer, *Schweizerischer Bundesstaatsrecht*, i. p. 57.   It is therefore not quite correct to say with M. Laveleye (*Le gouvernement dans la démocratie*, ii. p. 149) that "from 1802 it became the rule that every constitution, whether it were that of a canton or of the Federation itself, had to be accepted by the majority of the active citizens or electors."

[M. Borgeaud, *op. cit.* p. 264, says of these constitutions: "They were generally the work of councils more or less restored from the old régime, or of new assemblies chosen by the privileged classes; the only exceptions to this were the little Landsgemeinde cantons and the cantons of the Grisons and Geneva.   In the two Unterwalden the constitution was adopted by popular assemblies. Glarus, Uri, and Schwyz simply made a digest of their traditional institutions, depositing copies of them in the archives of the Diet. In the Grisons the constitution was a real Federal compact; the sovereign communes were called upon to ratify in the manner usual among the old leagues.   At Geneva . . . the constitution was submitted to the people 'by reason of their natural right.'"]

wishes of the people, and in the interests of the country as a whole. All the positions of honour in the state were monopolised by certain families, and thus an oligarchy of nobles was formed very much like that condemned by the Revolution of 1798. They were soon confronted in every state by an opposition party, whose aim was to put an end to the political disabilities created by the Constitutions of 1815. Freedom of the press, the extension of electoral rights, the separation of powers, and the power of removing public officials, were the important points in their programme. This progressive party was not without its supporters in the legislative bodies, but it was nearly everywhere defeated by a hostile majority of the legislators, who obstinately declined to grant any concessions.[1]

Such was the position of affairs when the French Revolution of 1830 occurred with the suddenness and force of an explosive, and by its example pro-

[1] [Only four states revised their constitutions before the French Revolution of July 1830, and only in one state was the revision submitted to the people. The canton of Vaud revised its constitution in May 1830, and granted the exercise of political rights to all citizens who could show a certain moderate property in real estate or mortgages, and the electoral assemblies chosen by them received the right to approve *in the future* all constitutional amendments. The actual constitution, as then drawn up, was not submitted to the people. It revised its constitution again in 1831.

In Ticino, the proposal to revise the constitution was made in 1829, and carried out in 1830. Sovereignty was declared to reside in the whole body of citizens, and the exercise of political rights was dependent merely on a small property qualification. The constitution was laid before the people in their district assemblies, and on July 4 it was accepted in all the districts but one. It was the vote of the districts, and not of the individuals, that was counted in the general result. Lucerne and Appenzell (Inner Rhodes) revised their constitutions in 1829. See Borgeaud, *Adoption*, &c., pp. 265-76.]

E

duced a general break-up of the existing state of things in Switzerland.[1]

In the space of one single year, during the year 1831, no less than eleven cantons[2] set up new constitutions, modelled on the programme of the Liberal party.[3] Between 1830 and 1834 there were altogether twenty revisions of cantonal constitutions, and,

[1] ["Then during the hot July days," says Henne am Rhyn, "we waited in vain for messengers from Paris, until one fine morning we saw the French mail-post enter Basle flying the tricolour. The Bourbons had fallen, the king had fled, and the Revolution was master of Paris. The news produced an extraordinary commotion in Switzerland. We knew that the storm was about to break over us too, and we waited."

Almost everywhere great popular meetings were held. The leaders harangued the people. Resolutions were adopted and carried to the capital by delegates. Then when it was necessary— for ordinarily a mere threat sufficed—arrangements were made to move *en masse* upon the seat of government, and the authorities were called upon to recognise the sovereignty of the people, and to convoke a constitutional convention as quickly as possible to revise the charter. In general, the rulers, not having permanent troops at their disposal, yielded without serious resistance. The Federal Diet having met in extraordinary session in December 1830, adopted the following decree :—

"The Federal Diet unanimously approves the principle that each state in the Confederation, by virtue of its sovereignty, has the right to make whatever amendments to its constitution it may judge necessary, provided they be not contrary to the Federal Agreement. The Diet will therefore not interfere in any way in such constitutional reforms as have already been effected or are about to be." See Borgeaud, *op. cit.* pp. 269–70.]

[2] Chatelanat, *Die schweizerische Demokratie in ihrer Fortentwicklung*, Berne, 1879, p. 14.

[3] [In the cantons of Valais and Schwyz the contest was more prolonged and more serious, and also in Basle, when the city refused to admit the citizens of the rural communes to an equality. In Neuchâtel, the King of Prussia, who was its sovereign, suppressed the insurrection by force. Ticino and Geneva did not make any change, nor did the purely democratic cantons of Uri, Unterwalden, Zug, Glarus, Appenzell, and the Grisons.]

except at Fribourg, the new constitutions were everywhere submitted to the people for their ratification.[1]

The cantons proclaimed the sovereignty of the people, and gave it visible expression in the form of universal suffrage and the constitutional veto granted to the electors. Proportional representation—that is to say, equality before the law of both the towns and the country districts—was in the main realised. The right of petition, the liberty of the press, the freedom of trade, and a more liberal law of settlement were also guaranteed.

The legislative power was vested in the Great Council, an assembly consisting of one chamber directly elected by universal suffrage. The executive power was placed in the hands of the Small Council, or Council of State, whose members were nominated by the Great Council, and who collectively controlled the administration.[2]

If at this point we pause and take a survey of the cantonal constitutions of Switzerland, we see that the character of the government in by far the larger number of them is that of a *representative democracy*. It is, in fact, the prevailing form, except in the cantons with Landsgemeinden, in the Grisons, and in Valais. We shall trace in the following pages how this representative democracy was superseded by a system of *direct democracy*, how the Great Councils gradually ceased to monopolise the attributes of sovereignty, and especially how they came to share their legislative attributes with the people.

---

[1] Vogt, *Referendum, Veto, und Initiativ*, in the *Zeitschrift für die gesammte Staatswissenschaft*, Tübingen, 1873, p. 360.

[2] Curti, pp. 124–25; Blumer, pp. 59–61.

II. *The Growth of the "Rights of the People" in the Cantons.*

The representative system underwent its first modification in 1831 in the canton of St. Gall, one of the new states formed in 1803.

Some time before the meeting of the constituent assembly which was to draw up a new constitution for the canton, there appeared in St. Gall an anonymous pamphlet, entitled *Volkstümliche Ansichten* (Popular Prospects). Its author insisted on the necessity of allowing the people to intervene directly in the work of legislation. "The constitutional rôle of the electors," he urged, "should not be limited to the mere approval of laws. It ought also to be possible for them to make their own laws on any subject they may desire, and therefore they need far greater powers than the mere right of addressing petitions to the Great Council."

The difficulty was to find any feasible plan by which it should be possible for the people themselves to act as legislators—a difficulty especially felt at this time, when no other form of direct legislation could probably be conceived except that which obtained in the small cantons. The author of the pamphlet, recognising the impossibility of a Landsgemeinde at which all the electors of the canton of St. Gall should be present, proposed to hold instead a number of small Landsgemeinden, allotting one to each district of the canton, which should be attended by the electors within that district. Every measure should be adopted by two-thirds of these Landsgemeinden before it could become law, and each Landsgemeinde, whether large or small, had one vote. "For a first attempt," as M. Curti observes, "this was not a bad scheme."

It is not difficult to imagine the excitement such novel proposals would cause, and the opposition they would be sure to encounter. For the democrats, the main thing was to secure the triumph of their prin ciple—in other words, to obtain public recognition of the justice of direct legislation by the people.[1]

The philosopher and parliamentary orator of the party, Felix Diog de Rapperswyl, undertook to champion the cause in the constituent assembly. "The people are sovereign," said Diog. "The people, and the people alone, should exercise the supreme power. Their will should be law. Sovereignty cannot be delegated. A sovereign who acts only through deputies may be said to have abdicated. The people have been declared to be of age. It is therefore out of the question that the Great Council should be constituted its guardian." According to Diog, republicans could not take too many precautions against the despotism of a parental government. He even went so far as to claim for the citizens the right of accepting or rejecting simple adminis trative orders. "If he were logical," his opponents said, "he ought to demand not only that the people should make their own laws, but that they should possess the executive and judicial powers as well."

---

[1] [Those who advocated popular rights always did so on theoretical grounds, and based their claims on principles of abstract right. They never seem to have urged the utility of the measure. It was on practical grounds they were always opposed.]

His answer to this was: "When I can prescribe how a thing shall be done, and according to what principles justice shall be administered—in a word, when I am legislator, what does it matter to me who executes my laws or who applies them? It is not a question of who shall be administrator, but rather, what he shall administer" Diog did not confine himself to demanding a referendum on all legislative measures; he also claimed the initiative for the people—that is to say, the power of the electors to bring forward their own bills. "Sovereignty does not consist merely in the negative right of refusing or vetoing a law, but in the positive right of commanding what one wishes. The people cannot rest contented with sanctioning laws; the very laws themselves ought to be the actual expression of their will." The Parliamentarians, in reply to Diog, said: "The mass of the electors are not as yet enlightened enough to act as legislators, nor have they the requisite leisure. They will fall into the hands of a few leaders, who will deceive them as to the true value of the laws. They will be the victims of the propaganda of demagogues and anarchists" It seemed probable that the question would be solved by brute force, for the Parliamentarians would not give in, and disorderly mobs began to besiege the place where the constituent assembly held its sittings. But, on the 14th of January 1831, Dr. Henne made a proposal which he thought would reconcile all parties. He suggested that, three weeks before the opening of the parliamentary session, the orders of the day of the Great Council should be published, so that the people might have an opportunity of expressing their wishes. Moreover, the laws, when discussed and finally adopted by the Great Council, should be examined by a committee of citizens appointed by the people, and this committee, like the Roman Tribunes in the days of the Republic, should be empowered to veto any new law of which they disapproved. The majority of the Parliamentarians were willing to support the compromise of Henne, but the democrats would not abandon their proposed system of direct legislation. When the matter came to the vote, it was the democrats who were defeated, by 66 votes to 75.[1]

As the *veto* is quite an obsolete institution at the present day, it is not without interest to notice the way in which it was organised in St. Gall. The following are the articles of the Constitution of the 1st of March 1831 which relate to the subject:—

Art. 2.—The people of the canton are sovereign. Sovereignty, which is the sum of all the political powers, resides in the whole body of the citizens.

Art. 3.—It results from this that the people themselves exercise the legislative power, and every law is submitted to their sanction. This sanction is the right of the people to refuse to recognise any law submitted to them, and to prevent its execution in virtue of their sovereign power.

Art. 135.—The approval of laws reserved to the people by Article 3 of the Constitution applies, namely—

(a) To all branches of legislation, civil and criminal, and to the treaties which relate to these subjects.

(b) To all fiscal laws of general import.

(c) To the laws relating to the administration of the communes.

(d) To all laws on military matters.

Art. 136.—The laws mentioned above come into force forty-

---

[1] Curti, *Zur Geschichte der Volksrechte*, Zürich, 1881.

five days after their publication, if the people have not refused to sanction them before the expiration of this delay.

Art. 137.—As soon as fifty citizens of a political commune demand it, a communal assembly must be held to decide whether the law submitted to them shall be opposed or not.

Art. 138.—If the majority of the communal assembly resolve to raise no opposition, the law is considered to be approved by the commune. In the contrary case, the Amman of the commune shall communicate the result at once to the Amman of the district, and he in his turn shall advise the "Small Council" by sending them a copy of the report of the meeting.

Art. 139.—This document should indicate the number of active citizens in the commune who have respectively voted for or against the proposed law. Non-voters are classed as voting in the affirmative.

Art. 141.—If the number of those who have rejected a law exceed the total number of citizens by one, the law falls through.

Out of the total number of registered electors, 9190 accepted the Constitution, and 11,091 rejected it; but there were 12,692 who did not vote, and these were counted as having accepted it. It was therefore declared to be adopted "by a large majority."

The example of the canton of St. Gall was followed in 1832 by the newly formed half canton of Rural-Basle,[1] and, after a lapse of some years, by Lucerne in 1841, by a Conservative government which had just come into power.[2]

A section of the Conservative party in Zürich, who had overthrown the Radical authorities in 1839, attempted in the same way in 1842 to introduce the

[1] Blumer, *Handbuch*, pp. 61-62. [The period of delay was only fifteen days in Basle.]

[2] Ernst, *Die Volksrechte im eidgenössischen Bunde*, in the *Monat Rosen*, 1883–84, pp. 248–50. [The period of delay was fifty days.]

veto into the Constitution of Zürich.[1] The petitions
addressed to the Great Council in support of the plan
urged that laws which had been sanctioned by the
people would be better observed, would have more
authority, and would last longer than laws made
without their approval; while the collaboration of
the people and the Council would ensure that perfect understanding so desirable between electors and
elected. In the Great Council stress was laid on the
fact that the veto would be a check, and that in the
absence of anything like a royal veto in a republic
of this kind, it would act as a set-off to the omnipotence of the Great Council. At Zürich, as everywhere
else, doubt was thrown on the legislative capacity of
the people, who, it was said, would probably prove
both selfish and shortsighted. "But," objected one
speaker, "if the people are capable of pronouncing on
constitutional laws, why should they suddenly become
incompetent when it is a question of ordinary laws?
Why should they be unable to judge of one particular
law when, by electing their representatives, they are
obliged to form an estimate of the legislative work of
those representatives for several years?"

The veto, although advocated with much ingenuity,
obtained but few supporters. In the Great Council
only 54 votes were given for it, whilst there were
115 against. The reason was, that since it had been
adopted by the Conservative Government of Lucerne,
the Liberals distrusted the scheme, and regarded it
as a reactionary institution.

"It is scarcely possible," Cherbuliez wrote in 1843,

---

[1] Stüssi, *Referendum u. Initiativ im Kanton Zürich*, pp. 9-12; Curti,
Geschichte, pp. 142-48.

"to regard the veto as a harmless innovation, especially when one recalls that in St. Gall it was used to reject a liberal law on the relations of Church and State, and that the same influence which has recently effected changes in the Constitution of Lucerne in obedience to ultramontane prejudices, has also been the very one to introduce the legislative veto."[1] And further on, when criticising both the referendum in the Grisons and the veto, the same author wrote: "The legislative veto in its two forms, and particularly in the first, constitutes the worst kind of democracy, for the people are never so incapable of considering the general interests of all as when they are broken up in local assemblies. There is only one opinion in Switzerland on the referendum, and that is, that it is an obstacle to the rational development of political and civil institutions, it frustrates the most urgent improvements, and negatives those justifiable reforms in the system of organic laws on which the intellectual and moral condition of the nation depends."[2] Nevertheless the veto was but a timid step on the road along which the Swiss were destined to proceed much farther.

In comparison with later institutions it was the least disturbing of reforms, inasmuch as it had been arranged in such a manner as to render any real popular intervention as difficult as possible. In St. Gall, for instance, before a commune could meet to exercise the veto, fifty electors. had to transmit a written demand to the president·of the commune, and then the negative votes given in the commune

[1] Cherbuliez, *De la démocratie en Suisse*, Geneva, 1843, i. pp. 94–95.
[2] Idem, ii. p. 43.

were not counted in the total unless these votes had constituted the actual majority in the commune itself. In Rural-Basle the law could only be rejected by two-thirds of the total number of active citizens.

In 1839 the Valais revised its constitution and substituted a new institution for the referendum of 1815, which might be called the "compulsory veto."

"All laws, military capitulations, financial decrees, or acts of naturalisation resolved on by the Great Council cannot be enforced until thirty days after their publication. Within this interval the majority of the citizens of the Valais may reject any such law if they think fit. For this purpose the president of the commune is required to convoke the primary assembly on the third Sunday after the publication of a law. He will make a report of the voting and forward the same to the president of the *Dixain*."

As in the cantons with the veto, no law could be rejected save by an absolute majority of the registered electors. But in the Valais the meeting of the communal assemblies was made compulsory by the constitution; while in St. Gall, Lucerne, and Rural-Basle these assemblies were only held upon the express demand of a certain number of electors. There was a fresh revision in Valais in 1844, when all trace of the veto disappeared, and the compulsory referendum appears in its place.

"All laws, military capitulations, financial decrees, and acts of naturalisation shall be referred to the primary assemblies, and shall not come into force until they have been adopted by a majority of the citizens who have taken part in the voting."

If we compare the texts of the two laws, it is easy to grasp the difference between the veto and the referendum. The veto is in reality the right of the body of electors to *reject* within a given time a law passed by the Great Council. The requisite majority, however, is that of the electors *actually registered.* The referendum is the right of the electoral body to sanction new laws—that is to say, to either *accept* or *reject* them within a specified interval. This right belongs, not to the majority of the *registered* electors, but to the majority of those who have *voted.*[1]

In 1846 the Constitution of Berne conferred upon the Great Council the right of submitting laws or decrees to the electors at their discretion.

"The political assemblies (that is to say, all the active citizens living within the jurisdiction of a parish) are to be called together to vote on matters which shall be referred to their decision by law. Such issues will be decided by the majority of the aggregate number of citizens actually voting in the whole canton."

This is the *referendum at the option of the Great Council.*[2] A similar provision was subsequently inserted in most of the cantonal constitutions, but it was expressed in greater detail, and was more carefully defined.

The canton of Vaud about this time adopted an institution which had hitherto been unknown outside the little cantons with Landsgemeinden. According

---

[1] ["In other words, the men who do not vote at the referendum are neglected, while in the veto they are treated as if they had voted affirmatively."—Lowell, *Governments and Parties in Continental Europe,* 1896, p. 249.]

[2] Whenever the term *optional referendum* is used in the course of this work, it means the referendum *at the option of the electors* —that is to say, the popular voting which a certain number of electors have the right to demand in the case of a law passed by the Chamber. M. de Laveleye is wrong in speaking of the Bernese referendum of 1846 as a referendum at the option of the people. —*Le gouvernement dans la démocratie,* ii. p. 150.

to the Constitution of 1845 (Art. 21), if 8000 citizens demanded a popular vote on any question whatever, whether it were the making of a new law or the repeal of one already in existence, the legislative assembly was obliged to comply with this demand. This was the *popular initiative*, unlimited as to its scope.

The veto was not introduced into the Constitution of Vaud, because of its essentially negative character. "Laws submitted to the referendum," said a speaker, "are, no doubt, sometimes accepted; but when they are rejected, the positive wishes of the country still find no expression. How can you reasonably expect the people to pronounce immediately on a new and complicated law? By means of the initiative they will be able to obtain the laws they wish, and can demand the repeal of those they do not care for, after having had experience of their working."[1]

From 1830 onwards the cantons began to introduce modifications into their constitutions, all conceived in a more or less democratic spirit. In some cases the form of a representative democracy was still retained, but in others there was a distinct trend towards a system of pure democracy. The result was that one canton after another repealed the reactionary clauses in their constitutions which had been inserted at the time of the Restoration. Of all the legislative work of 1815 the Federal Agreement was soon the only thing left intact, the only surviving relic of an epoch that had passed away.

The Federal Agreement was merely a contract made between sovereign states acting through their

[1] Curti, *Geschichte*, pp. 148-58.

respective governments, and not a constitution drawn up by the representatives of the people and adopted by the electorate.   The Federal Diet which it had created was not composed of representatives of the Swiss nation, but of the ambassadors of the sovereign states, bound by definite instructions.   It expressed the wishes of a majority of the states, not of the majority of the Swiss people.   It was not so much a legislative assembly as an international congress.   In all these respects the Federal Agreement was directly opposed to the principles which were embodied in the cantonal constitutions.   It therefore became necessary to revise it, in order to make the public federal law harmonise with the public law of the cantons. The aim of the Radical party was to effect a complete rupture with the past, and to let nothing remain which should recall the sovereignty of the several states.   For the Federal Diet they wished to establish a national assembly which, like the Great Councils of the cantons, should consist of one Chamber, whose members should be elected directly by the people.

They were only partly successful, however.   They effected a compromise with the Federalists, the result of which was to introduce the system of two Chambers into the Confederation.[1]

[1] [One of the immediate causes of the new constitution was the war which followed the attempt of the seven Catholic cantons to secede.   These cantons—Lucerne, Uri, Schwyz, Unterwalden, Zug, Fribourg, and the Valais—formed themselves into a confederation called the "Sonderbund," for purposes of mutual defence of territory and powers.   A war followed, in which these cantons were defeated and forced to rejoin the Confederation.   But it was felt that some change in the constitution should be undertaken.   The direction of that change was due to the influence of the French Revolution of 1830 and the democratic ideas prevailing in the

By the terms of the Federal Constitution of 1848 " the supreme authority of the Confederation is vested in the Federal Assembly, which is composed of two sections or councils, to wit: (*a*) the National Council; (*b*) the Council of States " (Art. 60).

The National Council is composed of representatives of the Swiss people, chosen in the ratio of one member for each 20,000 persons of the total population. Fractions of upwards of 10,000 persons are reckoned as 20,000. Every canton, and in the divided cantons every half canton, chooses at least one representative (Art. 61).

The elections for the National Council are direct. They are held in federal electoral districts, which in no case shall be formed out of parts of different cantons (Art. 62).

Every Swiss citizen who has reached twenty years of age, and who in addition is not excluded from the rights of an active citizen by the legislation of the canton in which he is domiciled, has the right to vote at elections (Art. 63).

Every Swiss citizen who is a layman, and who has the right to vote, is eligible for membership in the National Council (Art. 64).

The National Council is chosen for three years, and is entirely renewed at each general election (Art. 65).

The Council of States consists of forty-four representatives from the cantons. Each canton appoints two representatives; in the divided cantons each half canton chooses one (Art. 69).

Members of either council vote without instructions (Art. 79).

At the same time the Constitution of 1848 created a *federal executive authority*, which, under the Federal Agreement of 1815, had existed only in name.

cantons. This constitution was first of all discussed by a commission of twenty-five members. It was accepted in the Diet by 13½ votes against 6½, and on the 1st September 1848 by 15½ cantons and 169,743 electors against 17,899.—Hilty, *Die Bundesferfassungen*, &c., p. 402.]

The supreme direction and executive authority of the Confederation is exercised by a Federal Council composed of seven members (Art. 83).

The members of the Federal Council are chosen for three years, by the councils in joint session, from among all the Swiss citizens eligible to the National Council. But not more than one member of the Federal Council shall be chosen from the same canton. The Federal Council is chosen anew after each election of the National Council (Art. 84).

The *rights of the people* were recognised by the Constitution of 1848 in two ways. The electors could, firstly, demand the revision of the constitution then in force; and, secondly, they could accept or reject a new constitution—rights which applied equally to cantonal and federal constitutions.

The *cantons* are bound to ask of the Confederation the guarantee of their constitutions. This guarantee is accorded, provided (c) that the constitutions have been ratified by the people, and may.be amended whenever the majority of all the citizens demand it (Art. 6).

The *Federal Constitution* may be amended at any time (Art. 111).

Amendment is secured through the forms required for passing federal laws (Art. 112).

When either council of the Federal Assembly passes a resolution for the amendment of the Federal Constitution and the other council does not agree, or when fifty thousand Swiss voters demand a revision, the question whether the Federal Constitution ought to be revised is, in either case, submitted to a vote of the Swiss people, voting Yes or No. If, in either case, the majority of the Swiss citizens who vote pronounce in the affirmative, there shall be a new election of both councils for the purpose of preparing a draft of the revised constitution (Art. 113).

The revised Federal Constitution shall come into force when it has been adopted by the majority of Swiss citizens who take part in the vote thereon and by a majority of the states (Art. 114).

The Federal Constitution of 1848 had the effect of making the representative system temporarily popular, and seemed likely to arrest the tendency of public cantonal law to become purely democratic. Schwyz and Zug gave up their Landsgemeinden, and the referendum disappeared from the constitution of the Valais. This proved, however, to be only a passing check. Thurgau in 1849, and Schaffhausen in 1853, adopted the system of the veto, whilst in 1852 the referendum again made its appearance in the Valais in the following form :—
"Every change in the financial system, and every proposed increase in taxation, must be submitted to the people for ratification" (Constitution of the 23rd December 1852, Art. 72).

In the same year the initiative gained a foothold in Aargau, but its scope was much narrower than in the canton of Vaud. "Any law in force shall be wholly or partially changed or modified when a demand to that effect is made by 5000 citizens, giving their reasons for desiring such a change, and provided also that when the proposed change is brought before the electors in the communal assemblies, the majority of those voting shall be in favour of such a change."

The following year the referendum in the Grisons was modernised, and from henceforth the adoption or rejection of laws depended on the majority of the electors who voted, and not, as heretofore, on the majority of the communes.

In 1856 Solothurn adopted the *optional referendum, i.e.* the referendum at the option of the electors, though, as a matter of fact, it was called the veto "Laws shall be submitted to the people

F

for their acceptance or rejection when 3000 electors demand the veto, giving their reasons within thirty days after the publication of a law. The fate of the law is decided by the majority of the electors taking part in the vote."

In 1858 the constituent assembly of Neuchâtel decided that for the future every loan or financial undertaking exceeding the sum of 500,000 francs should be submitted to the people for their ratification. This was the *financial referendum*, and it was adopted in 1861 by the canton of Vaud, and later by several others. The people of Neuchâtel had introduced this form of referendum in consequence of a vote of the Great Council by which a very high subsidy had been given to a railway of merely local importance.

The progress of democracy up to this date had been somewhat uncertain. Fears were entertained of the results of the direct interference of the people, owing to their inexperience, their shortsightedness, their caprices and passions. It seemed as if the mind of the masses had not yet reached that stage of political maturity when it would be safe to dispense with the tutelage of the ruling classes. The Great Councils, after drawing back several times, at length regretfully relinquished their prerogatives, and shared their powers with their electors.

The time came at last, however, when all counsels of prudence and moderation were thrown to the winds. Soon after 1860 a perfect wave of democracy seemed suddenly to sweep over the country, carrying all before it, and in a very short space of time the representative system was ousted from the position which up to that time it had succeeded in maintaining. Rural-Basle was the first to break through the barriers which the authorities had succeeded in raising, with the result that the people became really and effectively sovereign.

The veto of 1832 was suppressed, as being an institution that was out of date. Its place was taken by the *compulsory referendum* and the *popular initiative*. "No law or important decree can come into force without having been approved by the referendum; and, furthermore, any 1500 electors have the right of provoking a vote of the people at any time on the question of the repeal or amendment of a law in force" (Constitution of the 6th of May 1863). This was the greatest advance that had as yet been made by any canton towards direct legislation by the people.

A few years after, Zürich, Berne, Solothurn, Thurgau, and Aargau, within a few months of each other, followed the example of Rural-Basle, and adopted the compulsory referendum; while all except Berne adopted the popular initiative. At Berne the Radical majority had voted subsidies to new railways which had exceeded the ordinary revenue of the state. The Conservative minority thereupon urged the adoption of the financial referendum, thinking that it might put a stop to any increase of the deficit. The radical Democrats cleverly managed to excite both parties in such a manner that a race for popular favour took place between them, and neither Radicals nor Conservatives would let themselves be outdone by the other in proving the

confidence they felt in the people.[1] Large sections
of both parties, therefore, agreed in supporting a
compulsory referendum (1) on all laws; (2) on the
orders of the Great Council, involving an outlay of
more than 500,000 francs for the same object; (3)
on the state budget when drawn up for a period of
four years.[2]

At Zürich the debates were concerned with the
practical rather than the theoretical aspect of reform,
and the discussions centred round the questions of
compulsory voting, and of open as opposed to secret
voting. The advanced democrats proposed to divide
the people into sections, which should assemble on
the same day in the principal place of each district
to debate and vote on the laws. The advantages of
this scheme, they maintained, were as follows:—In
the first place, it will provide for a preliminary public
discussion, which is essential if the referendum is to
contribute to the political education of the people.
Secondly, at these sectional assemblies the deputies
will get to know the needs of the people, they will
be made acquainted with the objections of those
in opposition, and will discover the omissions and
weak points of the law in question. The meetings
will thus differ from the meetings got up in the
ordinary way by the different parties, where laws are
never discussed except from one point of view, and
the explanatory messages of the government, so far

[1] Bandelier, *Du Referendum au point de vue jurassien Porrentruy,*
1869, p. 15 ; Gengel, *Die Erweiterung der Volksrechte*, Berne, 1868,
p. 11.

[2] Law of the 19th of May 1869 to carry out Article 6, section 4,
of the Constitution.

from being impartial commentaries, are themselves only expressions of personal opinions. It has been said that the press will inform the electors of the advantages and disadvantages of a law. This may be true for the electors who read journals of all shades of opinion, but the great majority of men only take in one newspaper.

The other side dwelt successfully on the inconveniences of the popular vote, on the difficulty of introducing what was termed compulsory political instruction, and on the impossibility of discussing one or more laws seriously in a popular assembly which could only meet for a few hours.

After the revisions of 1869 there were only three and a half cantons in which the representative system still held its ground. They were Geneva, Ticino, Fribourg, and Basle-City. To-day Fribourg is the only one. Everywhere else the Great Councils have ceased to be the sole legislative powers, and the electors themselves may now propose or ratify laws.

When we examine the causes of this general transformation of representative democracy into pure democracy, and the reasons for the displacement of the centre of political gravity; when we search among the contemporary pamphlets and interrogate the politicians of those times, we find a general agreement that all the cantonal constitutions which resulted from the revolutionary movement of 1830 were fundamentally defective. They were hastily framed by men beside themselves with enthusiasm for democracy. They were incongruous from the very first, and were constructed with a complete disregard of the laws of political equilibrium. The dominant

idea of the framers of these constitutions was to ensure political equality, and to establish the sovereignty
of the people as an unassailable principle. They
believed that this problem was solved when they
had given every citizen a right to vote, and had
vested all the powers in the direct representatives
of the nation. The whole authority of government
was accordingly concentrated in a single assembly,
the Great Council. The logical application of their
principles implied that there could be no independent
authority. The Great Council was itself sovereign
by delegation; and it would have been a contradic-
tion to admit any independent power side by side
with it. The Great Council was not only the legislative assembly of the canton, but it was itself the
source of all the powers not expressly attributed to
it by the constitution. It elected the judicial authorities, and it appointed and dismissed the members of
the government. There was no separation of powers
in a constitution of this kind. The other parts of
the body politic, dependent as they were on the legislative assembly, were absolutely incapable of acting
as checks on it. By the very fact of their origin
they were reduced to the position of subordinate
authorities, either administrative or judicial. Unfortunately the councils themselves did not provide
any safeguards against too hasty legislation on their
part. In the absence of any external controlling
power, it was especially important that measures
should not be rushed into laws, but that their progress should be slow and deliberate, and that there
should be certain delays fixed by law. The regulations for debate in the majority of the Great Councils

did not, however, contain any such provision. It is true that in some cantons measures had to undergo a second and even a third reading, but administrative orders were generally free from this restriction. Moreover, there was nothing beyond the power of the Great Council, no executive measure which it could not enforce by an order or resolution as soon as it believed itself secure from an immediate reaction of popular opinion. The Great Council was everything, and did everything. The men who imagined that they had put an end to despotism in 1830 were mistaken. They had only substituted the omnipotence of the elected council for the omnipotence of the aristocratic families. Democracy had not really been established. The work was yet to do. Although all were agreed as to the necessity for a revision, politicians could not come to an understanding as to the nature of the revision itself. Some proposed to reform the existing system, others to abolish it. The former party did not like the idea of taking a leap in the dark. They were willing to take measures against the omnipotence of the Great Council, in whose hands all the powers were now collected, but they were also desirous of retaining the representative system.

The other party, however, would be satisfied with nothing less than a complete reform. "That the people are sovereign is a point on which we are all agreed," they said; "but under the representative system, as soon as the people have once delegated their authority to their representatives, that sovereignty becomes a mere farce, and they are cheated out of their rights. Hence checks of doubtful efficacy are not sufficient to provide against the abuse of power by the representative assembly. The evil must be cut off at the root by abolishing representation." The parliamentarians, for their part, proposed to limit the duration of each assembly to one or two years, and to put both the right of dissolving the Great Council and the election of the executive in the hands of the people.[1]

These were measures of which the "democrats" approved, only they did not wish to stop here. "As long as the Great Council can legislate at will for the people," they said, "and as long as the people submit to their rule, we shall not be a true democracy. The people are sovereign, the sovereign is he who commands, he cannot be commanded, and, therefore, the people being sovereign, must make the law. The function of the members of the Great Council should be to act as councillors of the people, to make complicated and difficult questions clear, and to generally instruct the people. But the people themselves must

---

[1] The right of dissolution is recognised by the Constitution of Aargau (Art. 29), of Solothurn (Art. 25), of Rural-Basle (Arts. 2 and 53), of Thurgau (Art. 5), of Berne (Art. 22), of Schaffhausen (Art. 44), of Lucerne (Art. 44). In all these cantons the government is obliged to bring the question of the dissolution of the Great Council before the electors as soon as the requisite number have made a demand to that effect.

[It will be noticed that these cantons are all German cantons. "The German cantons," says Mr. Lowell, p. 230, "though more socialistic, are less ready to be guided and controlled by the government, while the French are inclined to respect public authorities, and regard them as commissioned to rule the people as their superior wisdom may direct. Hence it is in German Switzerland that we find most highly developed those institutions which are intended to limit the powers of the Great Council and enable the people to protect themselves against any possible oppression on its part; that we find, in short, the greatest desire to substitute a pure for a representative democracy."]

have the right of initiating, discussing, and sanctioning their own laws." Such were the views of the democrats, and the abuses of power by the parliamentary majorities at once justified and ensured the success of the " democratic " claims, which enlisted to a certain extent the sympathies of the mass of the people. Public opinion at length became sufficiently aroused for both parties to exploit it in their own interests. Sometimes those in opposition headed their programme with "Extension of the rights of the people," hoping by this means to attract all malcontents to their standard and thus get into power. Sometimes the party in power made use of the cry, fearing a possible defeat, and wishing to arm themselves against the time when they too should be in a minority. The parliamentarians, who had treated the democrats as " demagogues " and "anarchists," began to see that they must advance with the times, and adopt some of the new ideas. But their concessions were niggardly in the extreme. They included, for instance, the veto, but they hedged it round with so many checks that it was almost impossible for it to be used. They also added the referendum at the option of the Great Council, and then, after a good deal of hesitation, the referendum at the option of the people. The parliamentarians considered that the Great Council was the sum of the intelligence of the canton, and ought therefore to be the principal legislator, the intervention of the ignorant mass of the people being advisable only very occasionally, and under exceptional circumstances. The democrats regarded the matter from quite a different standpoint, and never ceased

clamouring and agitating until the triumph of the
compulsory referendum and the popular initiative
was assured—until, in fact, they had established the
modern forms of legislation by the people. Direct
legislation proved infectious, and spread from canton
to canton, its introduction being mainly due to its
inclusion in the programmes of political parties.

It still remains an interesting question whether
the representative system would have been so easily
dethroned if the constitutions of 1830 had been
differently framed,; if, for instance, a second Chamber
had been set up side by side with the Great Council,
or if, at least, the government of the canton had
not so frequently fallen into the hands of fictitious
majorities obtained by gerrymandering the constituencies. My own opinion is, that even had these
things been differently organised, yet the result would
have been the same. The one idea of the constitution makers of 1830 was to introduce an all-powerful
authority into the machine of government. No
system of checks was devised, and, as a result, they
were obliged to seek for some controlling force outside the constitution, and found it in the people, who,
unintelligent and wayward though they might be,
could alone exercise a real control over the Great
Council. The sovereign people were the only limit
which could possibly be placed on the encroach
ments of this sovereign assembly and on the omni
potence of the Great Council, and in this fact lies
the explanation of the evolution of democracy in the
Swiss cantons.[1]

[1] [Mr. Lowell also comes to the same conclusion, "that the
ultimate basis of the demand for the referendum, the real founda-

III.—*The " Rights of the People" in the Confederation.*

The question of revising the Federal Constitution of 1848 arose for the first time in 1864, and was the result of a commercial treaty made with France on

tion of the belief in the right of the people to take a direct part in legislation, lay in the defective condition of the representative system." He points out that the Swiss had no experience of representative government. "Except for the Grisons and the Valais, with their peculiar federal structure, the cantons either made their laws by means of Landsgemeinden, or else the country districts were ruled by the dominant city, and the city by a few patrician families; while the Confederation itself was so loosely organised, that the Diet was not a true legislative body, but rather a congress of ambassadors.

"It is curious that in Switzerland alone, among the countries north of the Alps, representative government did not arise spontaneously. The fact is, that owing to the absence of royal power, which was the great unifying force in the Middle Ages, the country did not become sufficiently consolidated to have a central legislature, and no one of the separate communities that made up the Confederation was large enough by itself to need a representative system. . . . The result was, that when representative institutions were copied from other countries, the Swiss were not accustomed to them. In the first place, they did not know how to provide the necessary checks and balances; and in the second, they had not learned to make their Chambers reflect public opinion. The people had not acquired the art of limiting or controlling the representative bodies. They continued to be jealous of the men they elected, and the legislatures were—or, what for political purposes is the same thing, were believed to be—out of sympathy with the majority of the people.

"The struggle for political equality was, therefore, no sooner at an end, and representative bodies based on universal suffrage were no sooner established, than the demand for direct popular legislation began. Its introduction has acted like oil upon troubled waters. The referendum, by putting an end to doubts about the real opinion of the majority upon disputed questions, has removed at once a means of agitation and a source of discontent." See *Governments*, &c., pp. 238, 246.]

the 30th of June in that year. This treaty granted
the right of settlement in Switzerland to all French-
men, without distinction of creed. The Constitution
of 1848, however, only granted the right of free
settlement to those Swiss citizens who belonged to
the Christian faith. The Swiss Jews immediately
availed themselves of the treaty to demand a revision of the Federal Constitution in order that they
might be placed on the same footing as their French
co-religionists. On the 30th of September 1864 the
Federal Assembly ratified the treaty with France,
although the rights of settlement accorded were contrary to the provisions of the Constitution of 1848.
On the same day, however, it invited the Federal
Council to report on the question as soon as possible,
and to present a scheme in which the right of settlement should not be affected by the religious belief of
the citizen. The Federal Council replied to this
request by a message of the 1st of July 1865. In
their report, however, they did not confine themselves
to the one subject, but enumerated several points
which, in their opinion, might be profitably added or
amended. Most of these suggestions were concerned
with the right of settlement; the others proposed that
the federal government should have its legislative
domain extended, and should be empowered to take
measures to protect literary and artistic copyright, to
regulate commerce and transport, and to establish a
uniform system of weights and measures.

On the 14th of January 1866 the electors were
summoned to vote on the new articles proposed by
the Federal Assembly. Of the nine amendments
which were submitted to the referendum, two only

found favour with the people, and these only obtained a small majority. They were the amendments which conferred the right of civil equality on the Jews, and which established a uniform system of weights and measures.[1]

Many Radicals, while approving these new clauses, had nevertheless voted No, because they were not satisfied with a mere partial revision, and they hoped by bringing about the rejection of these amendments to lead up to a total revision. Their tactics were successful, and it became patent after the popular voting of the 14th of January that the Constitution of 1848 would have ere long to be very considerably altered.

The Radicals of German Switzerland were at the head of the party of revision. They wished to limit the autonomy of the cantons, and to strengthen the central government, partly in order to give the great German cantons a preponderating influence, and partly also to be able more easily to restrict the liberty of the Church in the Catholic cantons. Their programme may be summed up in three phrases—one army, one system of law, and no ultramontanism.[2] The citizens of the larger cantons, notably Berne and Zürich, were not only engaged on a campaign to bring about a federal revision; they were also striving to obtain

[1] [The first amendment obtained 170,032 votes, while 149,401 were recorded against it. The second, on weights and measures, obtained 159,202 for and 156,396 against, but it was rejected by a majority of the cantons, and so fell through. It is the only instance in which a law that has been sanctioned by a numerical majority has failed to obtain the necessary cantonal majority. The net result is that only one law came into force.]

[2] Von Segesser, *Sammlung kleiner Schriften*, iii. p. 347.

an extension of popular rights in the cantons—the two agitations going on at the same time. We have already seen that the compulsory referendum was the result of their efforts in Berne and Zürich, and that Thurgau, Solothurn, and Aargau followed their example.

From this time onwards it became certain that the federal revision so ardently desired by the Radicals would have to be undertaken in a democratic spirit, and that any addition to the powers of the central government must be accompanied by an extension of the rights of the people. To transfer the right of legislating on civil, criminal, and commercial matters from the Great Councils to the Federal Assembly, without at the same time giving the Swiss electors an opportunity to pronounce on these same subjects when embodied in federal laws, would have deprived the people in the democratic cantons of the fruit of their recent victories, and would have been a retrograde step.

The democrats, who were in reality struggling for the rights of the people, recognised this so clearly that they made centralisation their aim, as the surest way of obtaining the referendum in federal matters.

Long before the question came up in the Federal Assembly, the contest between the parliamentarians and democrats began in the press and in pamphlets. The following is but a summary of the arguments used by each side.

The parliamentarians possessed a champion of the first order in M. Dubs, a distinguished lawyer and member of the Federal Council. M. Dubs expressed his ideas on the subject in a pamphlet which made a great sensation.[1]

"We ought," he wrote, "to try to reconcile the liberty of action necessary to the representatives with the rights that are inherent in the sovereign people. The people delegate power to their deputies, who are responsible for its proper use, and ought therefore to be accorded a certain latitude; but, at the same time, the people ought to possess some guarantee against the independence of their deputies. Without some such safeguard their sovereignty is imperilled, and there is a risk of its becoming a mere empty phrase. Now, how is it possible to reconcile these two essentials?

"(1) The people must ratify the constitution of the state. They should have the right to accept or reject it, not as a whole, but article by article. They ought besides to be able to revise it at any time, in whole or in part.

"(2) The electors ought to have the power of demanding new laws, but the Chamber should remain free to deal with their petition. As to the laws already voted by parliament, a certain number of the electors, to be fixed hereafter, ought to have at all times the right of demanding the repeal of a law by presenting a petition to that effect, which should also contain the reasons for desiring such a change. If the adversaries of a law can collect the requisite number of signatures, the electoral body will be consulted, and will decide whether the law in question shall remain in force or not.

"(3) There should be no longer general elections at

---

[1] Dubs, *Die schweizerische Demokratie in ihrer Fortentwicklung*, 1868.

fixed intervals, but the electors should be able at any time to bring about the dissolution of the Chamber, or, in other words, to dismiss their representatives.

"(4) The people ought to appoint and dismiss the members of the government. They ought also to settle disputes between the government and the Chambers."

The system of M. Dubs was the result of a train of argument in which the conclusions were rigorously and correctly reasoned out. When, however, his opponents began to reckon up the democratic reforms included, they regarded them as quite insufficient. There was no referendum, either compulsory or optional; nothing but the right of initiative, limited to the repeal of existing laws. They could never be content with such trifling concessions.

The views of the democratic party were defended by M. Gengel, the editor of the *Bund*.[1]

"Under the system to which the name representative democracy has been given, the sovereignty of the people is only a fiction; the people are, in fact, subordinate, and the supreme power is in the hands of the Chamber. To say that popular sovereignty and universal suffrage are one and the same thing is ridiculous. Once the elections are past the electors have no possible influence over the Chamber. They do not take part in the sittings; they do not read the parliamentary reports, even if they exist; and in the newspapers they only get mutilated and abbreviated accounts of what has taken place. In order that popular sovereignty should not be an empty phrase, and democracy a lie, the people ought themselves to

---

[1] Gengel, *Aphorismen über demokratisches Staatsrecht*, Berne, 1864.

approve their laws, appoint the executive, and elect the judges." [1]

Gengel was also a zealous advocate of the compulsory referendum. "Under a democratic system," he said, "all the laws passed by the Chamber ought to be submitted *ipso jure* to the sanction of the people. When the representatives know that the laws will finally go to the people, they will make it their business to frame them in harmony with popular ideas and needs, and will try to supply the omissions. Having the final decision in their hands, the people, too, will make a careful study of the laws. With the compulsory referendum the people will give their votes as a matter of course, whereas in the case of the optional referendum they will only do so after a certain amount of agitation. The optional referendum is a weapon of opposition. It can only reject. The compulsory referendum, on the contrary, is the means of expressing the popular will and ratifying the acts of those in power. The optional referendum does not occur, like the compulsory referendum, at certain stated intervals. It is the outburst of a discontent which has been smouldering and increasing, until at last it breaks out when opportunity offers. It is, in fact, a safety-valve. But the compulsory referendum is the normal and peaceable exercise of an established right, by a people that has attained its political majority. Those who advocate the optional referendum attempt to restrict the exercise of this popular right to the smallest possible number of cases. The compulsory referendum, on the contrary, is the solemn recognition and practical affirmation of the sovereign power of the people."

[1] Gengel, *Die Erweiterung der Volksrechte*, Berne, 1868.

Another publicist, M. Bernet, entered upon the task of demolishing the veto with great vigour.

"The statesmen of 1830 invented the veto as a sort of lightning-conductor for democratic claims. It was necessary to give the people something, but their object was to give as little as possible. The veto was a *pis aller*. The legislation on the veto was, generally speaking, a sad piece of bungling—*eine traurige stümperei*. The legislators have tried to stifle the expression of the popular will by all kinds of devices. They either fixed the necessary number of signatures at a very high percentage of the total, or they counted those who were absent as having accepted; or the period during which the operation of the law was suspended, in order to allow the demand for the referendum to take place, was made as short as possible. The result has been, therefore, that for the greater part of the time the veto has only been a counterfeit of a popular right."[1]

The referendum itself was severely criticised by M. Dubs.

"The people are asked," he said, "to give a deliberate judgment, either affirmative or negative, directly after the publication of a law. But, as a rule, the people will not be disposed to give their decision under these conditions. They will prefer to wait and see how the new law works. And what is the objection to their doing so? The mistake which is made by those who theorise about democracy is in imagining that the people think as easily and as rapidly as they do themselves. It is not abstract theory, but

[1] Bernet, *Nach zwanzig Jahren*, 1868.

practical experience, that instructs the great mass of
men. Their judgment is as sound as that of Parliament as long as they have been allowed to form it in
their own way.[1] If you introduce the referendum
Parliament becomes merely a consultative committee.
Its responsibility disappears, because it no longer decides anything definitely when the people pronounce
in the last instance. You would do better to suppress
the Parliament and replace it by special committees
composed of competent men, whose duty it should be
to draft bills. Under the present system the majority
of the deputies exercise the functions of a jury; they
listen to the debates carried on by specialists, and
vote in the best interests of the people. If, however,
the people are to be the judges of their own interests,
there is no need for such a jury.

" Does any reasonable man think that the sum of the
votes given in the communes is the exact expression of
the national will? This may be true as regards quantity, but not as regards quality; for such small local
assemblies always judge everything from an egotistical
and utilitarian standpoint. It has been said that the
referendum is an excellent means of politically edu-

[1] Dubs, *Die schweizerische Demokratie in ihrer Fortentwicklung*,
pp. 16-19. M. Buzberger, a deputy, expressed the same idea at a
later date in the National Council. "The people," he declared, "can
scarcely be expected to pronounce upon a law unless it has been in
force a certain time." And M. Taine also says : " A people, when
consulted, would probably be able to say what form of government
pleases them, but not what form of government they need. They
will only find that out by experience. You must give them time to
see if the political structure is adequate, solid, and capable of resisting gusts of fanaticism ; whether it be suited to their customs,
to their occupations, their character, peculiarities, and eccentrici-
ties " (*L'Ancien Régime*, Preface, p. 11).

cating the people. This would be true enough if the people were united in one large assembly, and heard the laws discussed first in principle and then in detail, and could listen to the arguments advanced by competent men on both sides. The referendum is not, however, of much use if each individual elector has to study the law by himself. Where are the great mass of men to find the time to do this, even if they possess the will ? The great majority will always vote on party lines, or else in accordance with the oracles of the village inn, or the advice of any man in whom they have confidence."

M. Hilty answered the criticisms of M. Dubs by setting forth the advantages of the referendum. According to him, "the majority of votes, whether for or against a law, will be recorded in such a calm and decisive manner as to leave no room for dispute ; the people will no longer be subordinate ; the referendum will be the best means of interesting the mass of electors in public affairs ; popular voting is a natural and necessary factor in law-making, and laws so made will have a truly national character." [1]

The Federal Assembly met in November 1871 for the purpose of discussing the question of revision.[2] The President of the National Council, M. Brunner,

---

[1] Hilty, *Theoretiker und Idealisten der Demokratie*, Berne, 1868. [M. Hilty concluded by referring to the referendum "as the stone which the builders rejected, and which nevertheless became the head stone of the corner."]

[2] [An appeal had already appeared in the official Gazette of August and September 1870, inviting all Swiss citizens, communes, or corporations to transmit to the Federal Chancery their desires with reference to the constitution. See *Feuille fédérale*, October 22, 1870, for the result ; or Borgeaud, p. 298.]

in his opening speech, touched upon each of the important points in the programme of revision. " The question to be decided," he said, " is to know whether the direct intervention of the people in legislation is admissible, and what should be the limits assigned it. These are the points upon which opinions clash. Since the majority of the cantons have accepted the referendum, it has in my opinion become impossible, politically speaking, to effect any revision of the Federal Constitution which shall involve increased centralisation without at the same time bestowing upon the Swiss people as a whole the right of which the majority of them have been deprived as members of a canton." [1]

The Assembly was unanimous as to the necessity for a new constitution which should entail a greater amount of centralisation.[2] Differences of opinion arose only on questions of detail. The referendum therefore seemed to be inevitable.

It encountered, however, a good deal of opposition among the more eminent members of the Chamber. A speech of M. Welti, in particular, made a great impression. The following are some extracts from it:—

[1] This quotation and those that follow are taken from the " *Report of the debates of the Swiss National Council on the revision of the Federal Constitution*," 1871-72.

[2] [In 1870 the war between France and Germany had broken out, and the success of the Germans pointed very significantly to the results attained by centralisation. Moreover, there was the danger that Switzerland could be invaded by one or other of the hostile armies, and the necessity of giving the central government greater power in military matters became apparent. In 1869 the National Council had proposed to revise the constitution by means of nine amendments. They now decided to examine each of the articles of the constitution in turn, to see if they required modification.]

" It has been asserted several times that the representative form of government is inadequate, and that it ought to be looked upon as dead and buried. Yet the freest and greatest nations are, nevertheless, those living under this form of government. It is no invention of politicians, but the outcome of natural causes, and cannot therefore be quietly put on one side.

" The representative system will always reappear in some shape or another. Many reproaches have been levelled against this present age, especially since 1830. It has been said that it is a period of political over-production, that the wants of the people have not been comprehended, and that we have gone too fast. The reproach is an honourable one, for, at any rate, the power has not been used by any one section representing property, money, or the church, as is so generally the rule nowadays. But once introduce the referendum, and all the elements which we believed we had succeeded in repressing will again rise up to confront us; and twenty years hence, perhaps, the sovereign people will have fallen under the yoke of social autocrats, the great manufacturers and the clergy.

" Up to the present time the people, in spite of the absence of the referendum, have not lacked the means of getting rid of an institution they disliked. We have universal suffrage, the freedom of the press, the right of public meeting, and in each house a *Vetterli*.[1] These are the real guarantees of liberty. If we do not make use of them, the fault lies, not with our institutions, but in ourselves. For

_____
[1] A rifle.

my part, I am convinced that the people will be found incapable of fulfilling the functions of a legislator."

M. Gonzenbach also made a speech much to the same effect, and said: "When there is an assembly consisting of one house, as in the cantons, the referendum may perhaps be looked on as a necessity · but in the Confederation, when we have two councils, the fact that laws have to run the gauntlet of two houses is a better guarantee than the popular vote. If you wish to cite an example of a state that is really free and well organised, and which has attained a high intellectual level, you do not think of quoting the cantons with Landsgemeinden or the Grisons or Valais. Progressive ideas are not the privilege of the masses, but of isolated individuals. It is a mistake to suppose that the referendum will make it easier to execute the laws. A law which has been accepted by only a small majority will be very difficult to enforce."

M. Ziegler replied to these criticisms in words which have since been often quoted.

"You call the people incapable," he said, "yet they · are eminently capable of electing representatives, which is quite as difficult a task as voting on laws. How can it be said that the people are incompetent to vote on laws when it is an established principle that ignorance of law is no excuse for breaking it, and in the ordinary affairs of life every one is required to know the law he lives under?"

M. Carteret, of Geneva, of whose pronounced

Radicalism there can be no doubt, repudiated alike the referendum, the veto, and the initiative. He was, however, a supporter of the popular right of dissolving the Assembly, by which the electors would be able to change their delegates when they no longer represented their wishes and their ideas. He proposed that the National Council should adopt an article framed as follows:—"The question of the renewal of the Federal Assembly shall be brought before the electors when 30,000 citizens who have the right to vote shall make a demand to that effect."

"Such a method of dissolving the Federal Assembly," said M. Scherer, "is a violent measure, and one that it would be hardly ever advisable to adopt, especially as the public officials are now elected for such short terms as to make it unnecessary. The people can at present always weed out those they may dislike by refusing to re-elect them."

When put to the vote, this motion of M. Carteret was rejected by 61 votes to 38.

The referendum at the option of the Federal Legislature was suggested by M. Borel, and met with even less encouragement. "A referendum which is dependent on the good-will of the councils," M. Brunner remarked, "will not help us much. A similar institution was introduced into the Constitution of Berne in 1846, giving the Great Council the option of submitting a law or a decree to the people when they thought it advisable. The minority made several attempts to induce them to use this power, but the majority always refused to accede to their request." "This form of the referendum," M. Scherer said, "would only be used when the councils are afraid to take the responsibility of a law on themselves, and wish to shift the burden of it on the people." The referendum at the option of the Legislature was rejected by 64 votes to 34.

M. Anderwert was willing to go further in the matter of making concessions to the people, and proposed the veto. "It is admitted," he said, "that the people ought to have some direct influence over legislation secured to them. Experience has proved that the actual voters are not usually a large proportion of the total number. In the cantons this is partly due to lack of interest and deficient education, but in a greater measure also to the geographical peculiarities of the country. We cannot expect, therefore, to be much more fortunate in the votings on federal laws. It is quite conceivable that the most important laws may fail owing to the indifference of the majority and the opposition of a weak minority. We ought, therefore, to consider carefully whether a well-arranged veto would not be preferable to a referendum."

The organisation of the veto as proposed by M. Anderwert was very simple. A certain interval was to be fixed during which the operation of every new law should be suspended, in order to enable its opponents to place their negative votes in the urns provided in the chancery of each commune. If, at the end of the suspensory period, the votes, when counted, proved that a majority of the registered electors were opposed to the law, it should remain a dead-letter. The veto, which had become merely an historical institution at the date of the federal revision, only obtained 19 votes against 69.

The compulsory referendum found an ardent supporter in M. Scherer. "The veto," he said, "merely confers the power of refusal. Failure to say No is regarded as tantamount to acquiescence in everything. This system, therefore, counts the indolent on the one hand, while on the other it has the effect of rousing the passions of the rest of the population, who possess more energy and activity. The referendum is a most effective method of politically educating the citizen. In order to give his vote he must necessarily study the questions at issue, and make up his mind whether any particular law is framed in the best interests of the country, and whether the time is ripe for introducing a law of this kind. The political societies, the press, and the government messages which will be attached to the bills, will provide excellent opportunities for the citizen to get information and instruction. Finally, it is quite in harmony with the spirit of republicanism that the representatives of the people should explain to their constituents the motives which induced them to support any particular proposal, and should, moreover, be able to do so without incurring any loss of prestige."

"The referendum should be preferred to the veto, then, because it makes the citizen think, because it contributes to his self-respect, and because it combats that indolence which is the great danger of republicanism. It will have this further advantage, that we shall make fewer laws, but that they will

be clearer and shorter, and we shall get rid of legis
lation framed to suit the exigencies of the moment."

The majority of the Federal Assembly were in
favour of the referendum, but they thought it sufficient to grant any five cantons or 50,000 active
citizens the right of claiming a direct appeal to the
people. In technical terms, they rejected the compulsory referendum, but supported the optional referendum. They were actuated by a fear that the
electors would get weary if they were obliged to vote
on all federal laws when their time was already so
much taken up with the questions that arose in their
own canton or commune. The optional referendum
seemed to offer the electors every facility for getting
rid of unpopular laws. It was, moreover, a compromise between the adherents of the representative
system and the partisans of the compulsory referendum. It then became necessary to settle the
scope of the referendum, and to determine the
subjects on which a demand could be made.
M. Brunner proposed, but without success, that
only the essential principles underlying a law should
be submitted to the people. M. Buzberger replied
that if a vote is to be a really popular one, a law
must be submitted to the people in its entirety, in
order that the people should not afterwards say that
if they had known the details they would not have
accepted the principle of the law.

M. Scherer made a distinction between laws and
resolutions. " Laws are concerned more especially
with the internal organisation, with the political
life and domestic politics, of the state. Our policy

with regard to matters outside this sphere finds its expression in resolutions, and financial matters are generally settled by means of resolutions. It would not be suitable to confine the referendum to certain subjects. Such a limitation would, in fact, be impossible, because the different kinds of laws cannot be classified without infringing the rights of the people. But the right of issuing decrees ought to belong exclusively to the Federal Council. Were such resolutions submitted to the referendum, it would be impossible to have a good administration, for, as a rule, and especially in the case of finance, peace and war, resolutions require to be carried out promptly." The Federal Assembly finally decided that the referendum might be demanded (1) on all laws, (2) on all resolutions which were not of special urgency.

There still remained a difficult question, and one which, in the eyes of many of the deputies, appeared the most important of all. It was this: Should a majority of the Swiss people alone decide the fate of a law, or should a majority of the cantons be required as well?

The Radicals of German Switzerland were anxious that if a majority of Swiss electors had pronounced for or against a law, that law should be declared to be accepted or rejected as the case might be. They feared their plans for centralisation would receive a check if laws had to be referred for approval to the cantons as electoral units.

The Catholic deputies and the deputies of Romance Switzerland, however, made the cantonal vote a condition of their adherence to the referendum.

The President, M. Brunner, attempted to allay their apprehensions in his opening speech. ' " The fear that a referendum of the Swiss people without the addition of the restraining vote of the states will lead to our becoming a unitary state seems to me," he said, " to be based only on theory. It is true that, in a confederation of states, all centralising steps lead towards the establishment of a unitary state, and it follows from this that the present Federal Constitution is a great step in that direction. Nevertheless, the cantons up to the present time have found an ample guarantee of their constitutional sovereignty in the strongly federal feeling which prevails in the Assembly itself. A further guarantee is the existence of the same feeling among the Swiss people, where it is even more strongly marked, and it will make itself felt when they have to pronounce on the work of the Legislature. The history of our country, the diversity of our political life, the natural repugnance of our people to anything approaching bureaucratic government, will be for a long time an insurmountable obstacle to our becoming a unitary state."

M. Dubs and M. Segesser, the leader of the Right, brilliantly defended the rights of the cantons, but they did not succeed in winning their case. The National Council, by 54 votes to 52, and the Council of States, by 20 to 19, decided that laws, when submitted to the popular vote, needed but a majority of " the people " to decide their adoption or rejection.[1]

To the optional referendum thus organised, the

[1] [It will be remembered that a constitutional law has to be accepted or rejected by a majority of the people and the cantons.]

popular initiative was added. This gave any 50,000 citizens, or five cantons, the right of demanding, firstly, that the Federal Assembly should draft a law or a decree on any subject desired; and secondly, that they should repeal or modify any law then in force. The initiative found supporters even amongst the opponents of the referendum. Thus M. Feer Herzog, who opposed the referendum, supported the initiative, because "it establishes a right which is the natural inheritance of the people, because it is already foreshadowed in the right of petition guaranteed by the existing constitution, because it is not merely a piece of state mechanism, but depends on a long experience of the laws by the people and on agreement as to their defects, because it merely wants good sense to enable it to work, because it respects and even strengthens the representative system, because it is of the essence of the sovereignty of the people, because it is the spontaneous manifestation of the real will of the people."

"By means of the initiative," M. Scherer said, "the sovereignty of the people finds real expression, and acquires its natural influence over the legislators. Moreover, it will afford the authorities a valuable indication of the popular will, and it ought therefore to be welcomed by them." "It would be better," he added, "not to submit to the people actual bills prepared by a group of citizens, but to leave the drafting of the measures to the councils."

On the 12th of May 1872, the constitution, as drawn up by the Federal Councils, was submitted as it stood to the popular vote. In thirteen cantons out of the twenty-two the majority of the electors voted No. The total number of votes was 255,609 for and 261,072 against the constitution. It was therefore rejected by a majority of the people and by a majority of the cantons.

The opposition which proved so successful came principally from the Catholic and the Romance speaking cantons. The former feared the consequences on religious politics, and the latter were actuated by a dislike of centralisation.[1]

The constitution as then drawn up proposed to transfer from the cantons to the Federal Government — (1) the organisation and administration of the army; (2) the right of superintendence over dike and forest police; (3) the right to make legislative enactments for the regulation of fishing and hunting; (4) the right of legislating upon the construction and management of railroads; (5) the customs revenue without the obligation of indemnifying the cantons; (6) the power to legislate on the protection of workmen engaged in unhealthy and dangerous employments, and on the labour of children in factories; (7) the supervision and power to legislate on the transactions of emigration agents, and on organisations for

[1] [For the first time in Swiss history party lines were determined by race, and it may therefore be regarded as fortunate that this constitution was rejected. The feelings on the question of revision were so strong that it affected even the Federal Council. M. Dubs resigned as a protest against the new constitution, and M. Challet-Venel was refused re-election by a majority of the Assembly because he had opposed revision. Only one other Federal councillor has ever been refused re-election if he desired it, Herr Ochsenbein in 1854, and no other Federal councillor has resigned because he disapproved of the policy of the Chambers. See Droz, *Études et portraits politiques*, p. 359.]

insurance not instituted by the state; (8) the power to make, by law, general provisions for the issue and redemption of bank notes; (9) the civil law; (10) civil procedure; (11) criminal law; (12) criminal procedure; and (13) electoral legislation.

This draft provided not only a highly centralised constitution, as can be seen from the provisions mentioned above, but it was, in addition, an act of religious persecution.

(1) Priests were rendered liable to military service. "No person shall on account of a religious belief release himself from the performance of a civil duty."

(2) The churches were forced to submit to decisions of the civil authority. "The free exercise of religious worship is guaranteed within the limits compatible with public order and good morals. The cantons and the Confederation may take suitable measures for the preservation of public order and peace between the members of different religious bodies, and also against encroachments of ecclesiastical authorities upon the rights of citizens and of the state. The order of the Jesuits and the societies affiliated with them shall not be admitted into any part of Switzerland, and their members are forbidden to teach in the church or in the schools."

(3) It deprived the Church of all its marriage jurisdiction. "No limitation upon marriage shall be based upon sectarian grounds, and no one shall be forced to submit to any ecclesiastical jurisdiction in the matter of marriage."

(4) Finally, though it left elementary education to the cantons, it opened a door to the interference of the central authority. "The Confederation may

fix by legislative enactment a minimum standard to be exacted from elementary schools."

Some months later, in October 1872, the general elections for the renewal of the Federal Assembly took place. Fifty-six of the seventy-eight members who had voted for the constitution rejected on the 12th of May were re-elected, and twenty-seven of the thirty-six members who had opposed it. This result was not what one would have anticipated from the electors after the referendum of the 12th of May; but, as a matter of fact, it was not that the electors had changed their minds, but that the constituencies had been skilfully gerrymandered. Although the party of revision had gained only a show of success, they did not fail to declare in speech and writing that the electors had given them a vote of confidence.

When the Chambers reassembled in December, seventy-four deputies of the National Council supported a motion by which the Federal Council was invited to report and make proposals on the way in which a revision of the Federal Constitution could again be undertaken. The motion was adopted unanimously. The Federalists and Catholics themselves desired revision, though only on condition that cantonal sovereignty was not seriously affected thereby. The efforts of the Radicals were directed to breaking up what they termed "the unnatural coalition of the French Protestants and German Catholics." With a view to bringing the former round to their anti-clerical programme, they threw over certain provisions and certain articles relating to the unification of the law. For instance, there was an article (No. 55) in the

H

scheme of 1872 which declared that ".civil law and civil procedure are within the province of the Confederation. The Confederation shall also have the right to legislate on criminal law and criminal procedure." This article now disappeared, and was replaced by the following article :—" The Confederation has power to make laws on matters of civil rights, on all legal questions relating to commerce, and to transactions affecting chattels (law of commercial obligations including commercial law and the law of exchange), on literary and artistic copyright, on the collection of debts, and on bankruptcy. The administration of justice remains with the cantons save as affected by the powers of the Federal Court." But, on the other hand, fresh provisions inimical to the Catholics were added.

(1) Primary instruction shall be placed exclusively under the direction of the secular authorities (Art. 27).

(2) No one shall incur penalties *of any kind whatever* on account of religious opinion (Art. 49). This was a prohibition of excommunication.

(3) Contests in public or private law which arise out of the formation or the division of religious bodies may be brought by appeal before the competent Federal authorities (Art. 50). The object of this article was to enable the Old Catholics to rob the Roman Catholics.[1]

(4) No bishopric shall be created upon Swiss

[1] [The Roman Catholic Church of Switzerland is governed by the same forms and authorities that are usually found in other countries. The Old Catholics are a body of seceders who separated from the Roman Church during the agitation caused by the proclamation of the doctrine of Papal infallibility.]

territory without the consent of the Confederation (Art. 50).

(5) The prohibition of the Jesuits, which was part of the programme of 1872, "may be extended also by Federal ordinance to other religious orders whose action is considered dangerous to the state or disturbs the peace between the sects" (Art. 51).

(6) The foundation of new convents or religious orders and the re-establishment of those which have been suppressed are forbidden (Art. 52).

(7) The control of places of burial is placed in the hands of the civil authority (Art. 53).

The tactics of the German Radicals were completely successful. The spectre of ultramontanism was so persistently dangled before the eyes of the French Protestants that their hatred of the Church overcame their objection to centralisation. Those who had been enemies yesterday now became good friends. There were no longer Centralists or Federalists; they were all anti-clericals. *Wir haben auf dem Rücken der Ultramontanen mit den Waadt-Ländern Frieden geschlossen*—"We have concluded peace with the Vaudois by trampling the ultramontanes under foot"—is what I was told last year by a Radical deputy whom I was questioning about the Federal revision, and the compromises, and the political jobbery of this time; and he chuckled still with pleasure to think of his youthful achievements.[1]

Whilst the Radical fanatics were then rejoicing over their fallen adversaries, the ultramontanes, the articles in the abortive scheme of 1872 which were concerned

1 [In the National Council the new constitution was adopted by 103 votes to 20, and in the Council of States by 25 to 14.]

with the rights of the people underwent certain modifications. The first thing to be dropped was the popular initiative, which had conferred upon any 50,000 electors the right to demand that the Federal Assembly should draft a new law'or repeal an existing one. The optional referendum, too, underwent certain alterations. It was now settled that a demand for the referendum must come from eight cantons, while the proposal of 1872 had required only five. As a matter of fact, it would have made it too easy for the Catholic cantons to oppose the Federal Assembly if five cantons had been the minimum. To avoid the reproach of being anti-democratic in the suppression of the initiative, the number of signatures necessary for demanding the referendum was lowered from 50,000 to 30,000. After these modifications the article introducing the referendum read as follows :—

Art. 89.—"Federal laws shall be submitted for the acceptance or rejection of the people if the demand is made by 30,000 active citizens or by eight cantons. The same principle applies to Federal decrees which have a general application, and which are not of an urgent nature."[1]

The new constitution was accepted on the 19th of April 1874 by 340,199 votes against 198,013, and by 13½ cantons (Zürich, Berne, Glarus, Solothurn, Basle-City, Rural-Basle, Schaffhausen, Appenzell (Outer Rhodes), St. Gall, the Grisons, Aargau, Thurgau, Vaud, Neuchâtel, Geneva). It was rejected by 8½

---

[1] [A new article was also added, experience having proved the need of it. "In counting up the votes of the states, the vote of a demi-canton is counted as half a vote. The result of the popular vote in each canton is considered to be the vote of the state" (Art. 121.) Thus everything is made to rest finally on the people.]

cantons (Lucerne, Uri, Schwyz, Unterwalden, Zug, Fribourg, Appenzell (Inner Rhodes), Ticino, Valais), all of them Catholic.[1] The *Bund* of Berne summed up the result in these words. "The vote of Sunday," it said, "has been a defeat for the Ultramontane party only. Ultramontanism has received a fatal blow."

Attempts have been made since the constitution has come into force to revise Article 89. We shall have occasion to notice them later, but up to this time nothing has resulted from them.

[1] [The number of cantons by which the constitution was rejected is given as 7½ by Hilty, *Die Bundesverfassungen der schweizerischen Eidgenossenschaft*, p. 407, and also by Curti, p. 294, *Geschichte*, and De Salis in *Le droit fédéral Suisse*, 1892. They reckon Ticino as one of those accepting. The Federal Council, when submitting the constitution to the popular vote, accompanied it by a manifesto in which they said that a second rejection would be a national misfortune, and they implored the people to put aside private prejudice and vote only in the best interests of the country.

The report on the popular vote of the 19th of April was presented to the committee of the Council of States by Herr Kappeler, and in it he called attention to three features of the vote—

(a) The unlimited discussion preliminary to the vote, to which no opposition was offered by any party or local authority.

(b) The large percentage of voters who went to the polls. About five-sixths of the entire electoral body went to the polls, or about 85 per cent. of the registered voters.

(c) The quiet and dignified way in which the election was conducted. Throughout the entire country there was no trace of trouble or violence.

He concluded with these words :—"And that is why this constitution has become not only formally *in law*, but in the most profound meaning of the word, *in fact*, the fundamental law of Switzerland, a law that no party will attack, because no party will be able to attack it, but still more because no party will wish to, so great is the respect which a legal majority inspires in this country." See Borgeaud, *op. cit.*, pp. 301-6.]

An important right has been conferred upon the people quite recently, but it is only concerned with the Federal Constitution, and does not affect ordinary legislation.[1] It is the popular initiative, which is now enlarged to include a partial revision of the constitution.

It will be remembered that the Constitution of 1848 gave the people the right of demanding a revision of the Federal Constitution. In the discussions which took place in the Diet, it was understood that this right would include partial as well as total revisions.[2] However, subsequent demands for a partial revision were laid aside by the Federal authorities, who, basing their decisions on the letter of the constitution, declared that demands for revision could only take a general and indeterminate form.[3]

Thus when, in 1880, 56,526 electors demanded that Article 39 of the Constitution should be replaced by a new article, the electors had to resign themselves

---

[1] [The popular initiative was only intended to apply to the revision of constitutional articles, but in practice it has really the same effect as if it were expressly introduced for matters of ordinary legislation. Any proposition, of whatever nature, may be submitted to the people if it is presented in the form of a constitutional article. There is no clause in the Federal Constitution defining a constitutional article. Thus any citizen, if supported by 49,999 others, may provoke the vote of the Swiss people on any proposition whatever, as long as they demand at the same time that their project be incorporated in the constitution. The effect in practice has been to introduce an article regulating the mode of slaughtering cattle. Ordinary legislation moves within certain fixed limits determined by the constitution, but there is nothing to determine the limit of a constitutional revision. The new amendment covers the ground of ordinary legislation and a great deal more.]

[2] Curti, *Geschichte der schweizerischen Volksgesetzgebung*, p. 185.

[3] Blumer, *Handbuch des schweizerischen Bundesstaatsrechtes*, vol. iii. pp. 241-46.

to seeing their demand for a partial revision taken as a demand for a general revision and submitted to the people in this form.[1]

In order to free the people from this troublesome restriction, some of the deputies of the Right

[1] [In 1848 the constituent assembly inserted a declaration in the minutes that in the opinion of a majority of its members a partial revision might be undertaken under the same conditions as a total revision. The Councils in 1865 undertook to insert some amendments, the fate of which we have already noticed. The Assembly, therefore, was quite prepared to exercise *its* right of initiative in partial revision. In 1879 a petition containing more than the requisite number of signatures was received, demanding that the Confederation be invested with the monopoly of bank notes, and the text of the article was subjoined. The Federal Council declared that, according to Article 120, only the question of a total revision should be laid before the people, and they submitted the demand to the country in this form : "Ought the present Federal Constitution to be revised?" The reasons given for taking this step are quoted and severely criticised by M. Borgeaud, *op. cit.*, p. 309, &c.

It was clearly illogical that if the people could demand a revision of the whole, they should be constitutionally incapable of demanding the revision of a part of the whole without imperilling the whole constitution in order to insert a clause.

M. Droz, writing in 1894, gives the following reasons for the expediency of not admitting partial revisions by the people. He points out that the Federal Constitution is a compromise between the central and local sovereigns. Its aim has been to respect as far as possible the different languages, customs, institutions, and interests of those states which form part of the Confederation. If such a constitution could be demolished bit by bit by temporary coalitions varying according to their object, where would be the security of these interests? Either German Switzerland would be able by sheer majority to swamp Romance Switzerland, or the Catholics would be oppressed by the Protestants. If the people are invested with the right of demanding partial revisions, then under the influence of any special event or fleeting emotion 50,000 citizens could demand the revision of any article without giving a thought to its connection with other dispositions, or its place as part of a whole " (*La démocratie en Suisse*). See *Études et portraits politiques,* pp. 469–70.]

demanded that the right of the people to claim
the revision of specified articles of the constitution
should be formally recognised.   The Federal Council
was ordered to consider and report on the proposals,
and declared itself favourable to the amendment.
"The question of deciding whether the Federal
Constitution ought to be revised," they said, "is an
altogether different matter for the people than deciding if such and such an article ought to be
repealed, modified, or amplified.   The uncertainty
attending the probable results of a revision, combined
with the inevitable dissolution of the Chambers in
the case of an affirmative answer, always makes the
balance incline decisively towards rejection.   It is
therefore practically impossible to discover by means
of the popular initiative, as regulated in Article 120,
either the true feeling of the people with regard
to the modification of the constitution, or to do it
justice when discovered.[1]

The debates on the proposal commenced in the
Federal Assembly in September 1890. They were
carried on all through December, and taken up again
and brought to a close in April 1891.[2]

All the interest of the debates centred round the
form in which the popular initiative should be exercised.   The Federal Council presented the following
scheme:—"The repeal or modification of particular

---

[1] Message of the Federal Council to the Federal Assembly concerning the revision of the third chapter of the Federal Constitution, 13th June 1890, p. 5.

[2] One of the newspapers of Berne, the *Bund*, has given a report
of the debates almost in full. See the numbers of the 25th and 26th
September and of the 18th, 19th, and 20th of December 1890, and
of the 9th and 10th of April 1891.

articles of the Federal Constitution, as well as the insertion of new constitutional clauses, may be demanded through the medium of the popular initiative. As soon as 50,000 Swiss citizens, having the right to vote, shall present a demand of this kind, the question whether such a revision shall take place will depend upon the majority of the citizens taking part in the vote. Should it be in the affirmative, the Federal Assembly shall proceed with the revision."

To some of the deputies the great defect of this proposal was that it left the hands of the Chambers too free. As long as the power of giving effect to the demand was vested in the Chambers, the door was always left open for them to tamper as they liked with the expression of the popular will. These deputies, who included among their number the members of the Right, the democrats, the socialists, and some Radical democrats, proposed to confer on 50,000 electors the right of presenting a fully drafted bill, which should be submitted to the people in its original form, and should be inserted as it stood in the Constitution were it adopted.

It was urged against this "that it would be most dangerous to allow a bill framed by an anonymous committee to become part of the constitution without giving any opportunity for modification. The least important of laws are not made by the Federal Assembly without a great deal of work, careful study, and public discussion on both sides. The initiative by formulated bill allows a small group of persons to encroach on the rights of the Federal Assembly, a consummation which ought to be prevented."

A Radical deputy naïvely gave the true reason for

his opposition to the formulated bill ; he considered
that it would be furnishing a weapon to the minority.
" The fear is," said he, " that the people will take too
many *reactionary* measures. Surprises ought to be
avoided at all costs, for there is no knowing, when
once the proposals of the minority have been accepted,
whether they might not proceed to demand a referendum on the law of civil status or on that of
marriage itself. It is dangerous to go too far, for
it is possible that the people, in moments of anger,
passion, or ill-humour, may do very foolish things.
The people is sovereign, but it is not a legislator."

What appeared to this speaker the great evil of
the popular initiative appeared to others to be its
greatest merit. " The popular initiative," a democratic deputy said, " is the best kind of proportional
representation that we can get. It is an instrument
ready to the hand of any minority, and is the quickest
and most legal means of bringing before the people
those questions that have arisen among the different
sections of the nation. Thanks to the initiative, it
will no longer be possible to stifle ideas that have a
popular origin. The minority thus obtains the right
to appeal directly to the highest power in a democratic republic, the sovereign people. The popular
initiative respects the rights of minorities more
efficiently than all the so-called systems of proportional representation, which always leave some groups
unrepresented." The initiative by a fully drafted bill
—the " formulated initiative," as it is termed [1]—which
had already for some time past obtained a sympa-

---

[1] [The idea of the " formulated initiative " was taken from the
canton of Zürich, where it had been in use since 1869.]

thetic reception in the Council of States, was adopted in the National Council on the 8th April 1891 by 71 votes to 63.[1]

The Federal decree of the 8th of April 1891, modifying the constitution, and enlarging the sphere of the popular initiative to include partial revisions as well as total, was adopted on July 5, 1891, by the people and by the cantons. The result was that 181,882 Ayes and 120,372 Noes were recorded. In four cantons only was there a majority against the amendment, in the two half cantons of Rural-Basle and Appenzell (Outer Rhodes), and in the cantons of Aargau, Thurgau, and Vaud—all cantons that were intensely Radical.[2]

[1] [M. Borgeaud, p. 315, thus describes the way in which the new amendment became law : " A mass of individual propositions came to the surface, and amendments to every plan. The last days of the session had begun. Work was still accumulating in the committees, and the Council soon tired of these discussions of complicated propositions and abstract political theories. After debates which, considering their importance, were too short, and so confused that the newspapers gave up reporting them, a vote was hastily brought on, and, in spite of the efforts of the government and the committee, the formula of the Council of States was adopted by 71 votes to 63."]

[2] [It is a curious change of front for the Radicals to oppose the initiative, since they were so anxious to extend popular rights in 1874. The fact is, that though they have been in power the whole time, their work has been so often rejected by the referendum that they are not now anxious to extend the popular rights, though they do not like to openly oppose them. It will be noticed that, since 50,000 citizens can now initiate by means of a bill drafted by themselves, any 50,000 citizens of the same opinion are, in matters of legislation, equal to the two houses of the Federal Assembly.]

CHAPTER II

THE MODERN ORGANISATION OF "LEGISLATION BY THE PEOPLE"

In the first chapter of this book we have examined the different forms which *direct legislation by the people* has assumed in Switzerland during the course of the centuries. In this rapid survey of the various developments of the one fundamental idea, we have only superficially touched upon the modern forms of democracy.

The second chapter will therefore be devoted to the detailed study of *the Referendum* and *the Popular Initiative*. We shall examine carefully the rights which the initiative and the referendum confer upon the people in the Confederation and in the cantons, both with regard to the constitution and with regard to legislation generally, and attempt to describe these institutions in such a way as to show their practical working. We shall also point out their defects where they exist, and the expedients suggested by way of remedy.

SECTION I.—THE "RIGHTS OF THE PEOPLE" WITH REGARD TO THE CONSTITUTION.

1. § *In the Confederation.*

The rights of the people with regard to the Federal Constitution are set forth in Articles 118–123 of the Constitution of the 29th of May 1874, as recast by the Federal decree of the 8th April 1891.

The articles relating to the revision of the constitution are as follows :—

Art. 118.—The Federal Constitution may at any time be *wholly* or *partially* amended.[1]

Art. 119.—A *total* revision is effected through the forms required for passing federal laws.

Art. 120.—When either house of the Federal Assembly passes a resolution for the *total* revision of the constitution and the other. council does not agree, or when 50,000 Swiss voters demand a *total* revision, the question whether the constitution ought to be amended is in either case submitted to the Swiss people, who vote Yes or No.

If in either case the majority of the Swiss citizens who vote pronounce in the affirmative, there shall be a new election of both councils for the purpose of undertaking the revision.

Art. 121.—*A partial revision may take place by means of the popular initiative, or through the forms prescribed for ordinary federal legislation. The popular initiative consists in a demand by 50,000 Swiss voters for the addition of a new article to the constitution, or the repeal or modification of certain constitutional articles already in force.*

When the popular initiative is used for the purpose of amending or inserting various articles in the Federal Constitution, each modification or addition must form the subject of a separate initiative demand.

The demand by initiative may be presented in the form of a proposal in general terms, or as a bill complete in all its details.

When a demand is couched in general terms, and the Federal Assembly approves it in substance, it is the duty of that body to draw up a partial revision in the sense of the petitioners, and to refer it to the cantons for acceptance or rejection.

If the Federal Assembly does not approve the proposal, then the question whether there shall be a partial revision or not must be submitted to the vote of the people; and if the majority of Swiss citizens taking part in the vote express themselves in the affirmative, the revision shall be undertaken by the Federal Assembly, in conformity with the popular decision.

When a demand is presented in the form of a bill complete in all

---

[1] The passages in italics are the new clauses introduced by the Federal decree of the 8th April 1891.

*its details, and the Federal Assembly approve it, the bill shall be re-
ferred to the people and the cantons for acceptance or rejection.*

*In case the Federal Assembly does not agree, that body may draft
a bill of its own, or move that the people reject the demand;. and it
may submit its own bill or proposal for rejection to the vote of the
people at the same time as the bill emanating from the popular
initiative.*

Art. 122.—*A federal law shall determine more precisely the
manner of procedure in the case of demands by popular initiative
and in the votings on amendments to the Federal Constitution.*[1]

Art. 123.—The revised Federal Constitution, or *the revised
part thereof,* shall take effect when it has been adopted by the
majority of Swiss citizens who take part in the vote thereon and
by a majority of the states.

In making up the majority of the cantons the vote of a half
canton is counted as half a vote.

The result of the popular vote in each canton is considered to
be the vote of the canton.

The distinction made by the constitution between
a total and a partial revision is not, as a matter of
fact, a scientific distinction. At what point does a
revision cease to be partial and become total? There
is a lack of precision in the classification. Generally
speaking, a revision is looked upon as "total" when
the whole of the constitution is overhauled, and as
partial when it is confined to certain articles specified beforehand. But, as a deputy of the Council
of States lately remarked, this is by no means an
infallible criterion.

"Suppose," he said, "that it was proposed to suppress the Council of States, or to vest the executive
power in the hands of a president elected for life, no
one would call this a partial revision, but an impor-

[1] [This law, which was not voted when M. Deploige wrote, has
since been passed. For its contents see notes on following pages,
and also Appendix on the Popular Initiative.]

·tant fundamental change, although only one or two articles would be affected by it. It is therefore impossible to give an exact definition of a partial ·revision, or to draw any precise distinction between a total and a partial revision." [1]

In reality the distinction simply recalls a stage in the evolution of democracy when the Federal Assembly tried to prevent the people claiming a revision of specified articles of the constitution, and obliged them to make the demand in general terms without specially indicating the articles on which a revision was desired.[2]

[1] Session of the Council of States, 17th December 1891. The *Bund* reports it in its issue of the 20th December.

[2] [M. Borgeaud considers that there is in the amendment a confusion between the plural initiative and the popular initiative, *i.e.* between the initiative of a certain number and the initiative of the whole people. The popular initiative is only exercised when the majority of the people—in practice, the majority of those voting— command that a revision shall be undertaken.

The amendment says that "the popular initiative consists in a demand by 50,000 Swiss voters for the addition of a new article, or the repeal or modification of certain articles already in force."

This M. Borgeaud considers to be technically wrong, for the initiative of 50,000 persons, *i.e.* of one-fourteenth of the present voting population, is not the same thing as the initiative of the whole people, which is exercised when they are asked, "Do you wish for a revision of the constitution?" and answer "Yes." The 50,000 citizens may make a demand for the popular initiative, and do so when they ask in general terms that the constitution be revised. The question then goes to the people, who take the initiative and give their commands to the Legislature. The 50,000 voters can rouse the popular initiative to action ; they are not then exercising the popular initiative themselves, but the plural initiative; and when they initiate by means of a complete bill, the people, instead of being the starting-point of the revision, do not vote on the question until it is brought before them in its final shape. There is therefore no question of the popular initiative in this case. It is the plural initiative. See *op. cit.*, p. 321.]

Since the federal law of April 1891 has come into force, the distinction between a partial and a total revision has lost much of its importance. Nevertheless, as the procedure in the two cases is not the same, we shall retain the distinction made by the Federal Constitution.

I. The total revision of the Federal Constitution may be brought about in three different ways:

1. The revision can be undertaken by the Federal Assembly and carried out by the agreement of the two councils (Arts. 84 and 85, No. 14), as in the case of an ordinary federal law. The proposal for a revision may be brought before the Assembly either by the initiative of the members (Art. 93), or by a message from the government of a canton (Art. 93), or by a message from the Federal Council (Art. 102, sec. 4). The two councils debate separately, and the bill passes from one to the other until an agreement is arrived at. It is only when the two houses have come to an agreement on the subject of a new constitution that the procedure begins to differ from that adopted in the case of an ordinary federal law. The constitution as drawn up by the councils must, firstly, be always submitted to the popular vote; and secondly, cannot come into force unless it has been adopted by a majority of the people and by a majority of the cantons.

2. If one Chamber has voted for a total revision and the other does not give its assent, it is the people who are called upon to intervene as sovereign, and they decide if a revision shall take place or not. They do not indicate, however, in what sense the

revision shall be undertaken, nor what it ought to aim at, nor how far it shall extend. The question put before the electors is the general one: Do you wish the constitution to be revised; yes or no? This intervention of the people is contrary to Article 119, by the terms of which a total revision takes place, according to the forms laid down for federal legislation. Should the two houses differ in the case of an ordinary law, the bill is simply dropped, and that is an end of it.

This modification of Article 119 is only explained by regarding Article 120 as having been levelled at the Council of States, and due to the fear entertained by the authors of the constitution that the second Chamber would systematically oppose the proposals for revision which might originate in the National Council. The framers of the constitution were actuated by the same motive when they excluded the cantonal vote on the general question of revision or no revision, and made the vote of the people alone decisive. (Art. 120.)

If the majority of the electors taking part in the vote support a revision, the two Chambers are thereby dissolved, and the work of revision devolves upon the new Federal Assembly.

The appeal to the people, when made in such general terms, leaves the Assembly entirely unfettered in drafting the new constitution. It has received the order to revise, but it can carry out that revision as it judges best. What would happen, then, if the two Chambers could not agree upon the scheme? Would the old constitution remain in force, or would the people be again consulted, and would the Federal

Assembly be again dissolved in the case of an affirmative answer? The case is not provided for by the constitution, although it might easily arise. The division of the constituencies is so arbitrary that it not unfrequently happens that the opinions of the majority of the deputies do not reflect the opinions of the majority of the electors.

3. Should 50,000 citizens sign a demand for a total revision, the procedure is the same as in the preceding case. The same preliminary question is put to the electoral body, and if the majority decide for a revision, the two councils are renewed to carry out the popular wish. It is difficult to see why there should be a preliminary referendum in this case. The framers of the constitution probably considered that when the partisans of a revision had recourse to such an extreme measure as the popular initiative, it would probably mean that all other methods of bringing pressure to bear upon the Legislature had been tried and failed, and that the Federal Assembly then in existence would be openly hostile to any constitutional change. The appeal to the people will show whether the revision has their support, and if the answer be in the affirmative, it would be as well to elect a new revising assembly. It is, however, theoretically possible that the Chambers might agree with the demand of the 50,000 petitioners. In such a case, a dissolution occurring as the result of an appeal to the people would be useless, because the Federal Assembly has the power to undertake a revision of the constitution "at any time," on its own authority (Art. 85, sec. 14, and Art. 118 of the Federal Constitution.)

II. A partial revision which embraces one or more articles of the constitution can take place:

1. According to the forms prescribed for federal legislation, that is to say, by the two Chambers in the ordinary process of law. The articles so revised must always be accepted by the people and the cantons.

It should be remembered that when the Chambers disagree on the subject of a partial revision, the diffi culty cannot be solved by an appeal to the people as in the case of a total revision. When one Chamber takes the initiative in the case of a partial revision and the other refuses its consent, the only result is that the question of revision is shelved until a more favourable time.

2. A partial revision may also take place by means of the popular initiative, which is defined by the constitution as follows: " A demand presented by 50,000 Swiss voters for the adoption of a new article, or the repeal or modification of certain specified articles of the constitution then in force." [1]

When 50,000 electors make use of their right of initiative, they cannot include in the same petition propositions concerned with different subjects. They must make as many distinct demands as there are subjects to be revised (Art. 121, paragraph 3). The message of the Federal Council of the 13th of June 1890 gives the reason for this regulation: " This separation of subjects has the advantage of giving more liberty to the citizens. A demand by initiative should not be drawn up in such a way that

---

[1] [By the law of January 17, 1892, all signatures which are more than six months old are invalid. The names, therefore, cannot be collected gradually.]

a citizen who wishes for a revision on one of the subjects mentioned, and does not wish for a revision on others, is nevertheless obliged to sign for all or not sign at all. This method affords, moreover, the only effective guarantee to the great body of electors, who go to the polls upon the initiative of a relatively small proportion of their number, that a revision has really been demanded by the regulation number of qualified voters on each separate subject." The electors who wish to bring about a partial revision of the constitution can do so by one of two methods. They may demand in general terms that a certain article should be revised in a certain sense, or that a new article should be inserted in the constitution. They may also draft the new article themselves. They are then said to make use of "the formulated initiative." [1]

(A) When the demand is drawn up in general terms, two courses are open to the Assembly:

(a) If it agrees with the petitioners, it proceeds to effect the revision without further preliminaries, by framing the articles which shall embody the popular proposals. [2]

(b) If, on the other hand, the Federal Council does not hold the same views as the 50,000 petitioners, then

[1] [There is no provision made for the cantons as such to use the "formulated initiative." They can only initiate "in the forms required for ordinary legislation."]

[2] [By the law of January 17, 1892, the Assembly must decide within a year whether it agrees with the petition or not. They may, however, take their time about drafting the law proposed, as no time limit is fixed in which it must be ready. If the Assembly does not decide within the year whether it will accept or reject the proposal, then the popular suggestion is submitted by the Federal Council to the vote of the people, as if the Assembly had rejected it.]

the electoral body settles the dispute and decides by means of a referendum whether the partial revision demanded shall take place or not. If the reply is in the negative, the revision is dropped. If, however, the people decide in its favour, the revision demanded must be carried out by the *existing* legislative assembly, because no provision is made either for a dissolution or a renewal of the Chambers, as is the case when a total revision is demanded by the popular vote.

This method of procedure quite changes the character of the Federal Assembly. It ceases to be a parliament, and becomes merely a drafting committee. As a rule, the members of the Federal Council vote according to their personal convictions, and on their own judgment. Even the Federal Council expressly guarantees their liberty of thought and action, for Article 91 enacts that "the members of the two councils shall vote without instructions." In direct opposition to this principle, they are obliged by Article 121 to vote in accordance with the laconic order of an anonymous body of citizens, which forces them to contradict their public declarations by their actions.

They have given their reasons for their attitude; they have thought over and studied the matter, they have made it the subject of lengthy debate. But when the contents of the ballot-box have been counted the result becomes law, and whatever may have been the opinion of the deputies, they have to acquiesce in the decision and say "Yes," although only a few weeks ago they may have advanced the most potent reasons for saying *No*. Their final vote is, therefore, the expression of an opinion which is not only not theirs, but one of which they actually disapprove.[1]

The passive rôle imposed by the Federal Constitution upon the Swiss deputies will doubtless scandalise the citizens of a country which has adopted the representative system. In Switzerland, however, this is considered highly democratic. In other countries the initiative comes from above; the parliament and the king are together the legal sovereign. In Switzerland it comes from below, for the legal sovereign is the electorate. It gives its commands, and does not attempt to justify its orders.

(*B*) When 50,000 electors draw up a bill complete in all its details, it cannot be amended by the Federal Assembly, but must be submitted to the referendum in the form in which it has been received, either without comment or accompanied by a counter proposal. The Federal Assembly, as a matter of fact, examines the popular proposal, and then as a result may take any of the following courses :—

(*a*) If it agrees with the petitioners on all points,

---

[1] [Two further points should be noticed about this demand in general terms. The fact that the Assembly may decide within a year, merely whether it will accept or reject the popular proposal, means that it may practically take its own time to draft the law should it decide to act upon the demand. Should it refuse it, however, and the people decide in favour of it, then it may also take its own time to act upon the mandate, and thus may considerably delay the amendment by mere inertia. Then when they have finally drafted the law in "the sense indicated," it has to undergo the final test of being voted on. They are, moreover, left to interpret what the petitioners actually meant by the demand.

Again, if the project drawn up by the Federal Assembly be rejected, it is not stated whether the Assembly must go on making new schemes, or whether the question of a revision is to be considered at an end.]

it can simply submit the proposal to the popular vote.

(*b*) If it disapprove of either the principle or the details of the popular proposal, it may present a counter-project of its own.[1]

(*c*) If it consider that it is not a fitting opportunity for revision, the Assembly may simply propose that the people shall reject the proposal of the 50,000. In the two last cases, the counter-proposal or motion for rejection is submitted to the people at the same time as the popular proposal.[2]

III. Whatever form the revision takes, or whatever its aim may be; whether it be undertaken by the Federal Assembly of its own accord, or 50,000 citizens make use of their right of initiative; whether it be a question of a fundamental change in the constitution,

---

[1] [By the law of January 17, 1892, the Federal Assembly must decide upon its course of action within a year, and if they decide to present a counter proposal, must also have that ready within the year. There is no possible means of delay open in this case as in the preceding one.]

[2] [M. Hilty, Professor of Law at Berne, and one of the best known of the Swiss constitutional writers, proposed a scheme to the National Council in which the distinction between a partial and a total revision was abolished, the same procedure being made applicable to both. The cantons were given the same share as the people in proposing or vetoing a law or preliminary proposal. The initiative could only be exercised by means of a bill complete in all its details ; but whenever a demand was received, the people were to be asked first of all, "Do you wish for a revision on this particular point ?" In case of an affirmative answer, the popular bill, accompanied by a counter-proposal at the option of the Assembly, should be laid before the people for their vote. Owing to the stress of business and the rush at the end, this proposal did not obtain the consideration it deserved. Both M. Borgeaud (p. 316) and M. Dunant (*Législation par le peuple en Suisse*, p. 123) characterise it as preferable to the scheme adopted.]

or of the modification of a single article, there is always a final popular vote on the new constitution or on the new article. In other words, in constitutional matters the referendum is obligatory.

Moreover, the revised constitution or the revised articles cannot come into force unless they have received a double majority. In the first place, half the electors plus one who take part in the vote must have voted "Yes;" and in the second, in half the cantons plus one the majority who vote must have voted "Yes." The revision falls to the ground if it does not obtain this double majority.[1]

In a unitary republic it would be sufficient if the majority of the people should sanction a revision of the constitution. In a federal state like Switzerland, in which national and cantonal sovereignty coexist, a modification of the fundamental law is not possible without the assent of both the people and the cantons.

2. § *The "Rights of the People" with regard to Constitutional Changes in the Cantons.*

The rights of the people, in so far as the cantonal constitutions are concerned, are contained in Article 6 of the Federal Constitution of 1874, which is a literal reproduction of Article 6 of the Constitution of 1848.

"The cantons are obliged to obtain the guaranty of their constitutions from the Confederation. This guaranty is given provided that these constitutions have been previously accepted

---

[1] [Only one constitutional amendment has ever failed to get a majority in the majority of the cantons when it had obtained a numerical majority in the country. This was the amendment on weights and measures brought forward in 1872.]

by the people, and that they may be revised when an absolute majority of the citizens demand it." [1]

Therefore, according to the principle laid down in this article, the electors of a canton have in constitutional matters—(1) the right of initiative; (2) the right of approval.

If we leave the cantons with Landsgemeinden out of account, we find that a minimum number of signatures is fixed by the constitution of each canton, and that those who desire to bring about a revision must collect at least that number before their demand can obtain official recognition. [2]

The number is fixed at 1000 in Basle-City, Schaffhausen, and Zug, at 1500 in Rural-Basle, at 2000 in Schwyz, at 2500 in the canton of Thurgau, at 3000 in Neuchâtel and in Solothurn, at 5000 in the cantons of Aargau, the Grisons, Lucerne, and Zürich, at 6000 in Fribourg, Vaud, and Valais, at 7000 in Ticino, at 8000 in Berne, and at 10,000 in St. Gall. [3]

[1] [This clause was due to the fact that a great many of the constitutions made after 1830 declared that the revision of the constitution could not be mooted until a certain time had elapsed. In several cantons the people went beyond the law, and illegally revised their constitutions in spite of the statutory delay. In other cases the Council had the exclusive right to the initiative, and often refused to use it. The result was that outbreaks occurred and new authorities were created. Hence the insertion of Article 6 in the constitution. See Borgeaud, p. 176.]

[2] [All the Landsgemeinde cantons except Glarus and Appenzell (Inner Rhodes) fix a minimun number of signatures for a constitutional revision. See Appendix II.]

[3] [The proportion of these numbers to the voting population is given in the Appendix. The number in Berne was raised in 1893 to 15,000. Several of the cantons fix a lower number for ordinary legislation, which will be seen by comparing the figures here with those given on p. 173.

The cantonal constitutions have undergone so many important

A revision may now be undertaken "at any time," either on the initiative of the people or on that of the legislative assembly[1] (Great Council or Cantonal Council). About 1830, on the other hand, a certain time had to elapse after the making of the constitution before it could be altered. At the end of this period, which varied in length in the different cantons, the people decided if the constitution should remain in force or if it should be amended. To-day

changes since M. Deploige wrote, that this chapter has practically had to be rewritten. (See Appendix.) The details here and in the Appendix have been taken from the official collection of the cantonal constitutions, a supplement of which appears every year.

There were ten revisions in 1892, three in 1893, seven in 1894, six in 1895, and four in 1896. Five of these were total revisions. The dates of the present constitutional articles relating to revision are as follows:—Geneva, 1847 and 1894; Obwald, 1867; Neuchâtel, 1858; Thurgau, 1869; Zürich, 1869, 1891, 1893, and 1894; the Valais, 1895; Nidwald, 1897; Appenzell (Outer Rhodes), 1880 and 1892; Appenzell (Inner Rhodes), 1880 and 1883; Schwyz, 1884 and 1891; Aargau, 1885; Vaud, 1885; Fribourg, 1885, 1893, and 1894; Solothurn, 1885 and 1887; Schaffhausen, 1891 and 1892; Uri, 1891 and 1892; City-Basle, 1891; Ticino, 1891 and 1892; the Grisons, 1892; Rural-Basle, 1892; Glarus, 1892 and 1894; Berne, 1893; and Zug, 1894. Thus no less than fourteen of the cantons have altered the articles relating to revision in some way or other between 1891 and 1895.]

[1] [It would seem that in Ticino the Legislature has no initiative in partial revision. It belongs to the executive. In the case of a total revision it belongs to either the executive or the Legislature. (See Appendix.) M. Borgeaud considers that the popular initiative is only exercised when the people are asked the general question, "Do you wish for a revision?" and answer in the affirmative. In the case of a revision brought about by a demand in the form of a complete bill, he considers that the initiative proceeds from a fraction of the people merely, as neither the Legislature or the electorate have any say until the matter comes before them in its final form. (See Appendix, where the constitutions are classified according to this distinction.) The extent of the initiative by the citizens and of the initiative by the Assembly is given at length in the Appendix.]

there are only two constitutions which still retain the practice of periodical revision. They are the constitutions of Rural-Basle and that of Geneva.[1] "Every fifteen years the question of a total revision of the constitution shall be laid before the general council" [electorate] (Art. 153 of the Constitution of Geneva).

In the majority of the cantonal constitutions partial and total revisions are expressly distinguished, and the electors have the right to demand either the one or the other.[2] There are, however, certain differences of procedure in each case, just as there are in the Confederation.[3]

[1] [Rural-Basle in its new constitution (1893) no longer admits the principle of periodical revision. Its last constitution dated from 1863. In 1875, at the end of the regulation twelve years the people were asked if they desired a revision. The answer was, No. In 1887 they were again asked, and by a small majority answered, Yes. In 1889 the newly revised constitution was negatived by the people; a second one was drafted and again rejected. Then the people were asked if they still wished for a revision, and answered, No. Four years later we get a total revision. This periodical consultation was an expedient borrowed from the United States. In New York the people are consulted upon the necessity of a constitutional convention every twenty years, and also in Ohio, Maryland, and Virginia. In Michigan it is sixteen years, and in Iowa ten years. In New Hampshire the people decide every seven years. M. Borgeaud says that it would be wiser to adopt the Swiss system, which allows a revision to be brought about when the need is really felt for a constitutional change. It is now left to the chance of dates chosen arbitrarily. See Borgeaud, *op. cit.*, pp. 182, 183.]

[2] [All the cantons now make the distinction. The last two to adopt it were Berne in 1893 and Solothurn in 1895.]

[3] [Certain cantons now recognise the right of the electors to initiate by a bill complete in all its details. These cantons are given in the Appendix. For the differences in procedure when the demand is for a total revision, for a partial revision by a motion,

When the requisite number of electors demand a
revision, the people are first of all consulted on the
question whether there shall be a revision or not.[1]
This is the general rule except in City-Basle. There
the preliminary voting takes place only if the Great
Council does not agree with the demand.[2]

The people decide at the same time whether the
revision shall be undertaken by the ordinary legislative assembly or by a constituent assembly in
City-Basle, Berne, St. Gall, Neuchâtel, Schaffhausen,
Ticino, Thurgau, Vaud, and Valais; and in the Grisons
whether the Great Council shall be dissolved and
another be elected to carry out the revision.[3] As an
example we may cite the text of the Bernese Constitution on the matter :—

Art. 91.—"As soon as a demand is made (for a
revision), the Great Council shall submit the following questions to the decision of the political
assemblies :—

or for a partial revision by a bill, see Appendix. There are also
certain differences of procedure when the initiative for a total or a
partial revision emanates from the Legislature. See Appendix.]

[1] [In the case of a total revision; not always in the case of a
partial revision, and never if the demand is by bill and not by
motion. See Appendix.]

[2] [The preliminary voting always takes place in City-Basle in the
case of a total revision (Article 54 of the Constitution of December
1891); in the case of a partial revision only if the council does not
agree. This is, however, the case in several other cantons. See
Appendix.

In some cases the councils must draft the revision required
without consulting the people, whether they agree with the demand presented or not.]

[3] [There are other differences of procedure, according as the
demand for revision proceeds from the people or from the Legislature, and also in the case of a partial and a total revision. See
Appendix.]

(1), Shall a revision of the Constitution take place? And in the case of an affirmative answer—

(2) Shall the revision be undertaken by the Great Council or by a constituent assembly?[1]

In this preliminary referendum it is the majority of the electors who actually vote who decide. Lucerne is an exception. By the terms of Articles 31 and 33 of the Constitution, a revision cannot be proceeded with unless a majority of the *registered* electors give their assent. The Constitution of Fribourg, though not so clearly expressed as that of Lucerne, has been interpreted in the same sense. By the terms of Article 79,[2] the question of deciding whether the constitution ought to be revised is submitted to the vote of the people, and if an absolute majority of the active citizens pronounce in the affirmative, the revision shall be undertaken.

In 1884 the Radicals of Fribourg collected 10,000 signatures to back a demand for a revision, with the object of making the mayoralty of the communes an elective office.[3] The Catholic party decided not to

[1] [In Berne there was no express provision made for the case of a partial revision. This has been altered now, and the text quoted above only applies to the case of a total revision. A partial revision is carried out in the same way as an ordinary law. The electors either draft the law, or demand that it shall be drafted. The Great Council in the latter case undertakes the drafting.]

[2] The electors who were prevented from attending, and who excused themselves, in writing, to the president of the commune before the vote took place, are left out of account. [This has been altered by the constitutional amendment of November 1890, and the majority required is the majority of those who actually vote.]

[3] In the state of Fribourg the mayors are nominated by the government; in all the other cantons they are elected by the electors of the commune. [The mayors are now chosen by the people. See Hilty, *Politisches Jahrbuch der Schweiz*, 1894, vol. ix. p. 398.]

take part in the preliminary vote; which took place on the 25th of January 1885. The result was that only 6000 electors presented themselves at the polls in support of the Radical demand. The government of Fribourg, basing its decision on the text of the constitution, declared that the verdict of the referendum was directly opposed to the revision, since only one-fourth of the electors had recorded their vote in favour of the change.[1]

In the cantons of Aargau, Rural-Basle, Fribourg, Geneva, Lucerne, Schwyz, and Solothurn the revision is always undertaken by a constituent assembly.[2] In consequence, only the question of revision or no revision is put to the electors. The preliminary referendum is also confined to the one question in Zürich and in Zug, but in Zug the revision is undertaken by the existing Cantonal Council, whilst in Zürich the Great Council is dissolved as a matter of course, and is renewed to work at the revision.

The revised constitution, or the constitutional amendment, is always submitted to the people in every canton, and does not come into force unless

[1] There are about 28,000 electors in the canton of Fribourg. [This has been altered by the constitutional amendment of the 14th of January ₁1894. The requisite majority, as in Lucerne, is that of the electors who actually vote.]

[2] [Only in cases of total revision (see Appendix). In Rural-Basle the people decide whether it shall be by a constituent assembly or not, even in the case of a total revision, and also in Zug. In all the other cantons quoted, the Great Council carries out a partial revision (see Appendix). Rural-Basle, Solothurn, Zug, and Geneva (probably) recognise the right of the people to draft their own amendment.]

the majority of the electors decide to accept it.[1]
This majority is that of the electors who take part in
the vote. Zug, however, is an exception. There the
constitution (Article 33) declares that the majority
shall be that of the *registered* electors.[2]   In the
cantons of Aargau and St. Gall, if the revision is only
partial, the people do not vote upon the new articles
as a whole, but upon each one separately.[3]

Many of the cantons do not make special regulations to meet the case of a rejection of the constitution.

In City-Basle and in Lucerne the old constitution
remains in force.   In Schaffhausen the constituent
assembly or the cantonal council drafts a new proposal.   In the canton of Aargau the people are asked
whether the revision shall be undertaken a second
time, and, in the case of an affirmative answer,
whether it shall be by the existing or by a new
constituent assembly.   At Fribourg and in Solothurn,
if a revised constitution is rejected by the majority of
the active citizens taking part in the vote, the same
constituent assembly draws up a second scheme, and
if this second scheme is again rejected, a new constituent assembly is elected in Fribourg, but in Solothurn, after the second scheme is rejected, the people
are consulted as to whether the revision shall be

---

[1] [The constitution bears the date of its adoption by the people,
not of its ratification by the Confederation, in Zürich, Lucerne,
Uri, Schwyz, Unterwalden, Glarus, Solothurn, Appenzell, St. Gall,
Thurgau, Vaud, Neuchâtel, Geneva, Fribourg, Berne, and the
Grisons.]

[2] [This is now altered. It is the majority who actually vote.
See Constitution, 1894, sec. 83.]

[3] [Also in some other cantons.   See Appendix.]

proceeded with, and if the answer be in the affirmative, a new constituent assembly is then nominated.[1]

SECTION II.—THE "RIGHTS OF THE PEOPLE" WITH REGARD TO THE ORDINARY LAWS.

1. § *In the Confederation.*

We have seen in Chapter I. by what means the optional referendum was introduced into the Federal Constitution of 1874. We are now going to study the working of the institution in detail.

This right is contained in Articles 89 and 90 of the Constitution, which are as follows:—

"Federal laws, decrees, and resolutions can only be passed by the agreement of the two councils. Federal laws are submitted to the people, to be accepted or rejected by them, if a demand be made by 30,000 active citizens or by eight cantons. Federal decrees which are of general application, and which are not specially urgent, are likewise submitted upon demand" (Art. 89).

"The Confederation shall by law establish the forms and suspensory intervals to be observed in the case of the popular votes" (Art. 90).[2]

The two councils of whom mention is made in the first paragraph of Article 89 are the National Council and the Council of States. They meet in ordinary session as the Federal Assembly each year at Berne, on the first Monday in June and the first Monday in

---

[1] [For further details see Appendix.]

[2] The law of which mention is made above was passed immediately after the Federal Constitution came into force. It is *the Federal Law concerning the popular votings on laws and federal resolutions*, dated June 17, 1874. It was amplified later by a decree of the Federal Council dated May 2, 1879.

December.   They can be summoned on extraordinary
occasions by the Federal Council, or upon the demand
of a fourth of the members of the National Council,
or of any five cantons.   The ordinary sessions last,
as a rule, about three weeks.   The right of initiative
belongs (1) to each of the two councils, and to any
one of their members; (2) to the Federal Council;
and (3) to the cantons, who may exercise their right
by correspondence.   Every bill, from whomsoever it
originates, must pass through the hands of the Federal
Council.   Before each legislative session the Federal
Council prepares a list of so-called *tractandas*, which
serves as a basis for the division of the business
between the two houses.   One-half of the *tractandas*
are discussed first of all in the National Council, and
the other half in the Council of States.   The two
Chambers debate separately, but neither council can
debate at all unless the deputies present are a majority
of the total number of members.   Divisions are decided by the majority of those who vote.   When the
council that has first discussed the affair has finished
its examination, it communicates the result to the other
council within forty-eight hours.   If the other council
is of the same opinion, it sends a message to that
effect to the first council, who sends the bill on to
the Federal Council to be carried into effect.   If the
second council does not agree, however, it states the
points of disagreement to the first council, and they
form the subject of a new debate.   In this second
deliberation there is no debate on those clauses of a
law or decree on which the councils are agreed.   The
result of the second deliberation is again communicated to the second council, and this goes on until all

matters in dispute are settled, or until the Chambers declare definitely that they cannot see their way to reconciling their divergent opinions. In this latter case there is nothing more to be done, and the question remains unsolved until it be again put on the order of the day. In practice, the two Chambers habitually make reciprocal concessions, and a final agreement is the general rule.[1]

II. The discussions of the Federal Assembly have, as a rule, only a provisional character.[2] Neither their

---

[1] [For further details on the Federal Council and the Assembly see Preface.]

[2] Art. 85.—The subjects within the competence of the two councils are the following :—

1. Laws on the organisation and election of federal authorities.

2. Laws and ordinances on subjects which by the constitution are placed within the federal competence.

3. The salaries and compensation of members of the federal governing bodies and of the Federal Chancery, the creation of permanent federal posts, and the determination of the salaries connected therewith.

4. The election of the Federal Council, of the Federal Tribunal, of the Chancellor, and also of the Commander-in-chief of the federal army. The Confederation may by law assign to the Federal Assembly other powers of election or confirmation.

5. Alliances and treaties with foreign powers, and also the approval of treaties made by the cantons between themselves or with foreign powers; nevertheless, the treaties made by the cantons shall be brought before the Federal Assembly only in case the Federal Council or another canton protests.

6. Measures for external safety, and also for the maintenance of the independence and neutrality of Switzerland; the declaration of war and the conclusion of peace.

7. The guaranty of the constitution and of the territory of the cantons; intervention in consequence of such guaranty; measures for the internal safety of Switzerland, for the maintenance of peace and order; amnesty and pardon.

8. Measures for the preservation of the constitution, for carrying

vote on federal laws or on federal decrees is necessarily final. Both the laws and the decrees—these
latter provided only that they are of general import
and are not urgent—are submitted to the people for
their sanction if a valid demand for a referendum
be received within three months from 30,000 active
citizens or eight cantons.

Federal decrees differ from federal laws in that
they escape the referendum in two cases; and it is,
therefore, of importance to know what distinguishes
a law from a decree, and when the decrees are urgent
or "not of general import."

There are no definitions in the Federal Constitution to help us, nor are there any in the law of the
17th June 1874 which regulates the popular votings.
In the message which accompanied this law the
Federal Council asked "whether it would not be
advisable to give an exact definition of a *law* and
a *decree*,[1] in order that there might be in future
some *method* in the classification of the decrees of

out the guaranty of the cantonal constitutions, and for fulfilling
federal obligations.

9. The power of controlling the federal army.

10. The determination of the annual budget ; the audit of public
accounts, and federal ordinances authorising loans.

11. The superintendence of federal administration and of federal
courts.

12. Appeals against the judgments of the Federal Council in
administrative disputes.

13. Conflicts of jurisdiction between federal authorities.

14. The revision of the Federal Constitution.

[This translation has been adopted from Vincent, *State and Federal
Government of Switzerland*, in which the whole of the Federal
Constitution is translated into English.]

[1] [The French word is *arrêté*, which means the decision of an
administrative authority.] .

the Federal Assembly, and in the absence of which the Federal Assembly might be tempted to give a legislative decree an arbitrary interpretation, and order its immediate execution, thus removing it from the sphere of the optional referendum ? " " We have not thought it necessary, however," the authors of the message continued, " to follow out this idea by inserting in the law itself a theoretical definition of a law. We do not think that such a definition would constitute any guarantee against proceedings which are arbitrary or opposed to the spirit of the constitution ; for, however good it be, a definition can always be differently interpreted, especially when it becomes a question of applying it in a doubtful case. The necessary guarantees are to be found in the Federal Assembly itself, in the fact that both councils must be in agreement, and in the public opinion of the Swiss people."

Finding it impossible to establish any satisfactory test, the Federal Council proposed that the Federal Assembly should settle in each case whether a bill were a law or a decree, and also if a decree were "general" in its character, and whether the measures and orders contained in it were urgent or not. The Chambers approved this proposal, and the result is embodied in Article 2 of the Law of the 17th of June 1874.

"The right of deciding that an order is urgent, or that it is not general in its application, belongs to the Federal Assembly, and the resolution to that effect must in each case be formally attached to the order itself." [1]

[1] [M. Berney (*L'Initiative populaire*, p. 11) criticises the distinction as vague and arbitrary, and shows that in practice curious

The Swiss jurists are unanimous in the opinion that the existence of such discretionary power in the hands of the Federal Assembly is anti-democratic.

results have been obtained. "In theory one understands by a law, general abstract rules which are applicable to all cases, and which are in force for an unlimited time; and by a decree, a decision in a concrete case." He then goes on to show that persons born before 1855 have been exempted from military service by a law, and that grants to the Alpine railways have been made by a law. On the other hand, the investment of the funds of the Confederation and the bounty on sugar have been regulated by decrees. The post of engineer of public works has been created by a decree, a similar post in the statistical department by a law. The meteorological station was established by a decree, the Polytechnic School by a law.

The words "general in character" are also criticised by him. The French words are *d'une portée générale*, which are a translation of the German *allgemein verbindliche Beschlüsse*, which were taken from the Constitution of Basle, and mean resolutions binding on the majority, or which are intended to apply to the whole country; resolutions, in fact, which apply to all, and which must be observed by all.

Basle-City, however, did not consider this clause precise enough, and has substituted for it in the new constitution the words, "resolutions which have not a personal character."

One would have thought that a loan would certainly be regarded as general in character. We find, however, that an order of the 26th June 1889, changing the equipment of the infantry and authorising a loan of sixteen millions, was said to be "not general," as well as another in the same year giving the Federal Council a credit of seven and a half millions. The price of stamped envelopes was, however, fixed by a law, and a grant of 10,000 francs to the legation at Washington was considered "general in character," and was voted on by the people at a referendum.

Again, resolutions are apt to be considered "urgent" in rather a curious way. The situation of the National Museum was settled by a decree, and was characterised as urgent, it being undesirable to submit the question to the referendum on account of the cantonal jealousy. The purchase of a drill-ground at Frauenfeld was also withdrawn from the popular vote on account of urgency.

' Those laws and orders which can be submitted to the referendum have a special "referendum clause" attached.]

By a mere majority of the members present the Assembly is able to decide that such and such a resolution shall not be submitted to the people, but shall come immediately into force. There is no means of appeal against this decision, and the people have no legal means by which they can defend themselves.

. "There ought to be a more exact definition of the cases in which the referendum can be exercised," wrote M. Numa Droz, one of the members of the Federal Council. "As little margin as possible should be left for arbitrary decisions by the Federal Assembly. For instance, it is admitted that neither the budget nor international treatises come within the scope of the referendum, although the constitution is not at all explicit on the subject. Nevertheless, more than one attempt has been made to apply it to these subjects also. The debates which have taken place in the Federal Assembly on more than one occasion and on more than one subject have shown that there is a tendency among a considerable number of members to submit everything without exception to the referendum. There are many deputies who dare not oppose this course, lest their popularity should suffer. Let us profit, therefore, by the experience we have gained, and replace an ambiguously worded article by a clear text, in which it shall be intelligible to every man what are the rights of the people and what are the powers of the Federal Assembly."[1]

---

[1] Numa Droz, *La révision fédérale*, in the *Bibliothèque Universelle*, XXV. p. 30.

[M. Droz, writing in 1894, ten years later, still regrets the

M. Numa Droz wrote these lines in 1884. Nothing has been done, however, since that time by way of substituting a clearly worded provision for the ambiguous text of Article 89. The uncertainty as to what can or can not be submitted to the referendum continues therefore to exist.[1] Until such uncertainty be removed by definite legislation, the following are the subjects

deficiencies of the law, but does not now seem to consider it advisable to alter it. A list of subjects would have to be drawn up, he thinks, on which the referendum might be demanded, and it would be very difficult to exclude anything from the popular vote. Any attempt to do so would be characterised as undemocratic, and there would be a great outcry. He considers, however, that everything ought not to be submitted to the people, and that under the circumstances it would be better to let the text of Article 89 stand. In practice he thinks that it has not worked badly, though there have been a few anomalies. See *Études et portraits politiques*, pp. 465, 466.]

[1] I have a clear recollection, while I am writing this, of being present during June of last year at a very lively debate in the National Council on this subject of the application of Article 89. A federal decree of amnesty to the revolutionaries of Ticino of September 11, 1890, was before the house. The Federal Council held that, as it applied to a concrete case, the decree had no general application. A member of the Right, M. Python, from Fribourg, objected to this interpretation. He argued that the decree ought to have a clause attached permitting the referendum, on the ground that it suspended a law which all citizens were bound to observe. I am sorry that it is impossible for me, owing to the absence of Swiss parliamentary reports, to give the reader the text of M. Python's logical sequence of arguments.

I may say that the amnesty was not voted, and that the revolutionaries of Ticino came up for trial at the federal assizes of Zürich in the following July. The prisoners were acquitted, but the result gave rise to much scandal. One of the principal witnesses in the trial, M. Respini, who had been president in the government which the revolution overturned, told me that he hoped to throw some light upon the events which had occurred in Ticino of late years. His book, which will appear shortly, will certainly be an interesting episode in Swiss Radicalism.

which have been regarded as outside the sphere of the referendum according to the practice followed since 1874:—

1. Treaties with foreign states.

A vote took place on this question when the Federal Constitution of 1872 was being drawn up. The National Council then decided, by 67 votes to 31, that treaties should not be submitted to the referendum. The objections were that the omnipotence of the Federal Assembly in this matter gave it power to favour foreigners to the detriment of their own countrymen. This actually happened as a matter of fact when the Federal Assembly concluded the treaty of 1864 with France. The French Jews were thereby given the right of free settlement, a right which up to that time had been withheld from the Swiss Jews.[1]

2. Resolutions which are only intended to apply to special cases, such as those which guarantee the cantonal constitutions, and the decisions given in administrative disputes.

---

[1] [M. Droz says, in his article on "Swiss Democracy and the Popular Initiative," that it was solemnly understood at the time of the federal revision that neither the budget nor international treaties should be submitted to the referendum. To do so would be a continual peril to the internal and external welfare of the country, a menace to her very existence.

M. Hilty also says that before the compulsory referendum can be introduced into the federal domain it will be necessary to find a formula by which not only the resolutions of slight importance, but also diplomatic affairs, international treaties, decisions on peace and war, may be withdrawn from the popular vote.

Thus two of the greatest Swiss statesmen are of an opinion that it would on no account be advisable to submit these questions. They are submitted in the cantons, but the limits with which the cantons may conclude treaties, either with foreign countries or with one another, are very narrow, and the Federal Government can always quash any treaty which contravenes the Federal Constitution.]

3. Financial matters. These include the annual budget and state estimates, and the appropriations voted for the purpose of acquiring war material.[1]

4. Federal resolutions granting subsidies for the diking of rivers and construction of roads.[2]

III. The two classes of legislative decrees mentioned in Article 89, *i.e.* laws and orders of universal application and which are not urgent, are forwarded to the Federal Council immediately after they are passed. The Federal Council proceeds to publish them in the official Gazette (*Feuille Fédérale*), and sends, at the same time, a certain number of copies to the cantonal governments, who then distribute them among the communes. The object of thus publishing the law is to bring it before the people, and a certain period has been fixed during which bills and decrees of general application are suspended, and during which demands for the referendum may be sent in.

---

[1] [Certain expenses are sometimes incorporated with the budget to prevent their going to the referendum, as the grant to the St. Gothard Railway.]

[2] "It has been argued from this that the financial referendum is not to be found in the Confederation. It appears to me that those who speak thus have formed a false idea of our referendum. Owing to its purely optional character, there is no need to specially mention the financial referendum. The decrees on financial questions are bound by the same rules as all other decrees. As subsidies can only be granted by means of laws or decrees which are binding on all, all subsidies are subjects for the referendum by the ordinary rules of law which permit any federal decree to be submitted to the people provided that it is concerned with public and not with private interests. I cannot understand the distinction which the Assembly has been pleased to make between grants for improving the waterways and subsidies to the railways."—Dubs, *Le droit public de la Confédération Suisse,* vol. ii. p. 153.

This period has been fixed by the law of the 17th of June 1874 at ninety days, reckoned from the day of publication.[1] (Law of the 17th of June 1874, Art. 4.)

IV. The referendum may be demanded during these ninety days by 30,000 active citizens, or by eight cantons (Art. 89 of the Federal Constitution). It may be said at once, that since the Federal Constitution of 1874 came into force the cantons have never made use of their right. This will easily be understood when we think of the complicated procedure which is connected with such a demand. The federal law requires, as a matter of fact, that the demand shall emanate from the legislative authority of the canton. Assuming, first of all, that a preliminary understanding exists between the opposition in eight different states, it would be necessary, as a rule, to summon an extraordinary session of the Landsgemeinde or Great Council. That is the first difficulty. Then if the Great Council, in each case, should decide on claiming the referendum against a federal law, the next step would be to get its decision approved by the majority of the electors within the canton (Law of the 17th of June 1874, Art. 6).[2] All this would have to be done within three

---

[1] [The period is really ninety-two days. It is counted as beginning on the day after the publication of the law; and a demand posted on the last day, which reached the office the day after the delay expired, would nevertheless be counted. It is not necessary, however, to wait until the expiration of the delay if the necessary figures are collected sooner.]

[2] [I do not understand from Article 6 that the decision of the Council must be approved by the people to be valid. It seems to

months, in eight cantons at the least. Within the same time it is evidently much easier to collect the signatures of 30,000 electors all over Switzerland.

Let us now examine the regulations affecting the demand for a referendum made by 30,000 active citizens.

The law lays down as a principle that a citizen who makes or who backs a demand must sign it personally (Law of the 17th of June 1874, Art. 5). It follows that (1) he is forbidden to sign for a third person, even if he add to the signature the words "by order," or "with assent"; (2) if the electors of a commune decide in the communal assembly [1] to claim the referendum, and forward a demand to that effect to the Federal Council, only the number of signatures which actually back the written demand will be taken into account, and not the number of electors who have voted for the demand in the communal assembly. It is a doubtful question whether the elector must actually sign his name himself. The law is not precise

me that if the cantonal constitutions choose to enact that such decisions shall be approved by the people, the federal law recognises their right to do so. Certain cantons, such as Berne, Basle-City, Aargau, and Vaud, do not seem to recognise any necessity for an appeal to the people. In Zürich a decision of the Great Council to demand the referendum is subject to the optional referendum upon the demand of 5000 citizens, or one-third of the members of the Legislature. This would seem also to be the case in Schaffhausen, the number of citizens being 1000.]

[1] The electors of the communes of German Switzerland are in the habit of assembling in *gemeinde* to settle all local affairs of importance. The communal assemblies are not peculiar to Switzerland. Many existed in the Middle Ages in different countries, in Italy, in Spain, in England, and in the province of Liège. (De Laveleye, *Le gouvernement dans la démocratie*, ii. pp. 312, 329, 338, 365).

on the point, and the inference is that illiterates can sign with a cross or some sort of a mark.

The law only makes one stipulation, that individuals who demand the referendum should be in enjoyment of their political rights; and illiterates enjoy these rights as well as others. A case in point arose in 1885, on the occasion of the demand for a cantonal referendum in Ticino. The government of Ticino had cancelled more than 600 signatures which had been given in the form of a cross. The question came before the Federal Council, who reversed this decision, and from that time crosses have been considered as valid signatures. As the power of demanding the referendum belongs only to active citizens, signatures have to be attested by the communal authorities of the locality in which the demand is signed, in order to certify that those who sign are in possession of their political rights. This attestation has to appear at the foot of each list, and is somewhat as follows ·

"The undersigned, president (*or other title*) of the commune of ......, certifies the right to vote of the ...... (*number*) persons who have signed the above list, and declares that they are in full enjoyment of their political rights in this commune."

The date and the signature of the president follow. No charge is made for his attestation.

It is obvious that 30,000 signatures do not collect themselves. Who, then, is it that takes the initiative in a movement for the referendum, and how do the agitators obtain the necessary number of signatures? In practice this varies according to circumstances. When a party law is in question, the deputies of the Catholic opposition are naturally singled out to inaugurate the campaign. As a rule they obtain great support from the *Berner Volkspartei,* and sometimes also from the *Eidgenössische Verein.*

The *Berner Volkspartei* is the Conservative opposition in the canton of Berne, and is composed mostly of peasants. The *Eidgenössische Verein* is mainly composed of the Conservative Protestants of Zürich, Basle, and Berne. When the three groups work together they nominate a committee, which sees to the printing of the sheets to be signed. These sheets are sent at once to trustworthy persons in the communes. Sometimes it is thought better to carry on the campaign more or less secretly. In that case election agents present the sheets at the houses of men of whom they are certain, and individual persuasion between man and man is the important feature.

At other times the lists are deposited in public places. For instance, while I was passing through Geneva, a referendum was being organised against an excise law, and I saw placards in the beer-shops with these words, "The demand for the referendum may be signed here."

When those in favour of a referendum thus openly organise a campaign, there is no reason why they should keep silence, and they make a good deal of stir. They get up public meetings, issue circulars, cover the walls with placards, and make use of all the newspapers they retain. The localities or classes of citizens specially affected by a law such as the excise law which I have just mentioned, organise the opposition. Those interested in the rejection of the law band themselves together without distinc-

tion of party, and committees are set on foot to
spread their views and collect signatures. These
coalitions and committees have merely an ephemeral
existence, and they dissolve and disappear as soon
as they have effected their purpose.

When the campaign is conducted by men who
understand their business, the necessary number of
signatures has been collected in a month. As a
general rule, however, they aim at considerably exceeding the 30,000. It makes a good impression on
the electorate at large.

A well-known agitator in the canton of Berne, M.
Dürrenmatt, who thoroughly understands the working
of the referendum, has told me that he proposed in
his paper to found a *Referendum Society* to demand
the referendum on every law voted by the Federal
Assembly. This society would include 3000 members,
each of whom would undertake to find ten signatures.
Even with an opposition less well organised, it ought
not to be difficult to find 30,000 men ready and willing
to sign all demands for a referendum that are presented to them. Among a body of over 600,000
electors, there are always a certain number who are
discontented, and who are perhaps on the side of the
opposition owing to certain peculiarities of character,
temperament, or even caprice. Many sign by conviction because they are democrats, and wish the
people to legislate on every subject. Others good-
naturedly sign to please their friends.[1]

[1] [M. Hilty says: It is quite certain that the signatures for the
referendum are not always obtained without the help of agents
paid for their trouble. I remember very well asking a sturdy peasant
why all the men in his village had signed a demand for the
referendum. He told me that a native from his valley had come

M. Chatelanat, formerly chief· of · the . statistical department at Berne, has drawn up a list of the cantons, and has classified them according. to the tendency to demand the referendum. The Catholic cantons head the list, Fribourg being the first. Then come Uri, Valais, Upper Unterwalden, Geneva, and the canton of Vaud. On the other hand, the Radical cantons of Thurgau, Solothurn, Glarus, and Zürich furnish the smallest number of signatures. The statistics of M. Chatelanat are only based on the experience of five years, but compared with the figures that I have been able to collect in Switzerland, they are correct for the years that follow.

V. Before the ninety days have expired the signed

from the capital of the canton to collect signatures. "He told us," the man continued, "that he should receive ten centimes (1d.) per signature, which was a very good thing for him, whilst it was·all the same to us whether the law passed or not. And so we signed."

M. Hilty goes on to say that this would not be the case when the people thoroughly understood the meaning and aims of the law, but he says "the history of the optional referendum proves that it is not always the worst laws that are attacked" (*Le Referendum et l'Initiative en Suisse, Revue de Droit internationale*, 1892, p. 397).

When the socialists were getting up the initiative petition known as "the right to work," their agents obtained 2d. per signature (Signorel, p. 333). M. Droz, when criticising Mr. MacCrackan's book, *What is the Referendum? Swiss Solutions of American Problems*, says : "Far from the referendum having got rid of professional politicians, it has rather encouraged them. It has favoured the development of a school who are systematically negative, the *neinsager*, led by all the discontented spirits, who only think of spreading that discontent among others which is seething within themselves" (*La Suisse jugée par un Américain*). See also "The Referendum in Switzerland," *Contemporary Review*, 1895, p. 328.

·· It is worth noticing that there have been only six demands which did not obtain the necessary number of signatures. They are given by De Salis, *Le Droit fédéral Suisse*, i. p. 457, &c.]

lists have to be forwarded to the Federal Council, who has them examined to see if they meet the requirements of the law.[1] If there is no attestation by the president of the commune at the bottom of the list, all the signatures in it are considered null and void. If the attestation is inexact, or there is no declaration as to the right to vote, or of the domicile of one or more of the citizens who sign, the signatures in question are cancelled as null and void. If several signatures on the list are evidently written in the same handwriting, all these signatures except one are also declared to be null.

It is not at all uncommon to find that two or three thousand names are thus cancelled, and these figures would probably be considerably increased if the Department of the Interior could spend more time in verifying the signatures.[2]

When the examination of the signatures is concluded, the Federal Council informs the cantonal

---

[1] Chatelanat, *Die schweizerische Demokratie in ihrer Fortentwicklung*, Berne, 1879, p. 12. [The demands may be posted on the ninetieth day.]

[2] [In the message of the Federal Council to the Federal Assembly concerning the popular voting of the 4th of October 1896, the following are the number of cancelled signatures:—On the first law, on the punishments for breach of discipline in the army, there were 64,025 valid signatures, 5361 doubtful, and 676 invalid; on the guarantee to be given with cattle, 43,964 good, 2018 doubtful, 350 bad; in the law on railway accounts, 3293 were doubtful and 513 bad. In 1898, on the purchase of the railways by the State, 3082 were doubtful and 723 bad; out of these 374 were rejected because they were written in the same hand. Two representatives of the Ultramontane party in 1882 proposed that the signatures should be kept secret after reaching the Federal Chancery, in order to avoid any intimidation. They were told that in public affairs publicity was the rule.]

authorities of any glaring irregularities, and they punish the guilty parties according to the penal laws.[1]

If no demand for a popular voting has been drawn up during the ninety days which follow the publication of a law or a federal order in the *Feuille Fédérale*, or if the official scrutiny prove that the demand sent in is not signed by 30,000 citizens, then the Federal Council decrees that the said law or resolution is to come into force, and makes provision for carrying it into effect, and it is then added to the official collection of the laws of the Confederation.

The exact number of signatures collected in each canton and commune is published in the *Feuille Fédérale*, and the Federal Council communicates the figures to the Chambers at their next session.

Should the petitions, when duly counted and examined, prove that the demand is supported by the requisite number of electors, the Federal Council organises the popular voting. It first of all informs the cantonal councils, and takes the necessary steps to ensure the prompt and general publication of the law or order which is going to be voted on.[2]

The day on which the voting shall take place is fixed by the council, and announced at the same time. It is the same day for all Switzerland.

---

[1] All the legal regulations as to the signatures for a referendum demand are also in force in the case of the signatures to a demand for a revision of the Federal Constitution, except that the number of signatures to be collected is larger.

[In the case of a partial revision the signatures must be collected within six months, and each sheet must contain the text of the law to be inserted or altered, so that each elector may know what he is demanding.]

[2] [Sometimes three laws are voted on at once. The Federal Council arranges matters so that there shall only be one voting.]

The voting may not take place until four weeks at least have elapsed after the law or order has been sufficiently published. This publication is carried out by sending a copy of the law to every voter.[1]

A proposal has been made in the Chambers that an explanatory message should be drawn up by the Federal Council or by one house of the Federal Assembly, and be sent round with the law. This suggestion was, however, negatived.[2] The result is, that the electors have to form their opinion of the law from its bare text. They have no official document to guide them, and there are no reports of the debates.

Thus, while the deputies only decide after studying the question at length, whilst they have in their hands all the useful documents, reports of commissions, and messages of the Federal Council; while

---

[1] [The Federal Council publishes the fact that a voting will take place, and the date, in the *Feuille Fédérale*. It sends a message to all the cantons, directing them to see that a copy of the law is sent to every elector, and that the decree as to the voting is posted up. It reminds the governments that the law must be in the hands of the electors four weeks before the vote takes place, and that each commune must be furnished with the official paper, on which the result shall be reported. It further states that the result must reach the Federal Chancery at latest within ten days after the poll, and that the canton must seal and keep the tickets. The results are to be telegraphed, so that there may be as little delay as possible.

The Federal Chancery prints all the laws and voting tickets, and sends them to the cantonal governments for distribution.

The time it takes to vote on a law may be seen by the threefold voting which took place in October 1896. Three laws were passed in March; the referendum respite expired on the 17th of June, and the demands had been duly sent in. They were examined, and the Federal Assembly, who announced the result, fixed the date by a decree dated the 10th of July. The voting took place on the 4th of October. The day fixed is nearly always a Sunday.]

[2] Hilty, *Das Referendum*, p. 382.

they discuss the bill from every point of view, and not only the principles involved, but also the minute details; the electors have, on the contrary, only the letter of the law put before them, an abstruse document in which experts themselves can hardly find their way about. It seems to me that the non-existence of any means by which the electors may receive positive information or have the matter impartially explained is one of the greatest shortcomings of the federal referendum. No doubt there is the press, and a federal councillor writing lately thus describes the influence of the press: "When I consider with what passion, or rather with what bad faith, certain questions are presented to the people in the press in spite of its almost unique opportunity for obtaining correct information, I consider, thorough democrat as I am, that in our federal state, with the influence of the state governments often opposed to the central power, the compulsory referendum in the case of all laws would be a mischievous institution."[1]

With the optional referendum, it is true, the press has fewer opportunities of misleading the people and of tampering with the popular judgment, but the

---

[1] Numa Droz, *La Révision fédérale*, in the *Bibliothèque universelle*, vol. xxv.

[The question was debated in 1875, 1885, and again in January 1892. The reason why it has always been unsuccessful is that the message has always been looked upon as a complement of the compulsory referendum, when a vote is certain to take place. When the referendum is optional, it is impossible to decide at what time the council ought to address the people. Shall it be issued when the law is just passed, and when no one dreams, perhaps, of demanding a referendum; or shall it be issued when the voting is to take place? In this latter case the message would not seem impartial, but rather a defence of the law attacked. See Hilty, *Revue de Droit internationale*, 1892, p. 404.]

ardour with which the newspapers enter into the contest is all the greater when the occasion arises.

This was the only reason which led James Fazy, of Geneva, to oppose the introduction of the federal referendum in 1891. "You are only making a laughing-stock of the people," he said, "when you make them vote and at the same time withhold from them the means of doing so intelligently. How can the Swiss people, who never obtain any accurate account of the debates of their federal representatives through the scanty reports of the press, be expected to vote reasonably when whole codes are presented to them? Is it fair to give the people the right of voting on the laws without giving them the opportunity of reading the debates upon those laws? I would not deny the right of the people to vote on the laws which their representatives prepare, but what I do ask is that the process should not be a mere farce."[1]

The plan on which the referendum is now organised is not calculated to assist the majority of the electors in forming a judicious and discriminating opinion on a law that is at all complicated. Most men vote from prejudice rather than conviction, or according to the word of command "accept" or "reject" given by the party leaders, or according to the advice of men in whom they have confidence. As for the independent and conscientious electors who have no time to study the law, they refrain as a rule from voting.

VI. The voting takes place on the same day throughout the whole of the Swiss Confederation.

---

[1] J. Fazy, *De la révision de la Constitution fédérale*, Geneva, 1871, pp. 90–92.

The right to vote belongs to every Swiss citizen who is twenty years of age and who is not deprived of his political rights by the law of the canton in which he is settled. There is no federal law which determines when electors ought to be deprived of the franchise. The absence of such a law is due to the referendum itself. Two attempts have been made since 1874 to codify the electoral legislation of the cantons. The first was the law of the 24th of December 1874, which was rejected by the people on the 23rd of May 1875 by a majority of 4680 votes ; the second, a law of the 28th of March 1877, was rejected on the 21st of October following by a majority of 81,673 votes. The result of the two appeals to the people is that very different regulations prevail in the different cantons as to the causes which suffice to deprive a man of his political rights. For instance, in the German cantons paupers and insolvents cannot be electors, and a debtor is made bankrupt for the smallest sum. In the Romance cantons, on the other hand, paupers have the franchise, and only persons who are declared to be fraudulent bankrupts are deprived of their political rights.

Before the vote takes place each elector receives a voting paper, on which the following question is printed, and which he is expected to answer: " Do you accept the law (or order) of the......(*date*) concerning (*the title of the law or resolution*), Yes or No ? " The elector writes his answer, Yes or No, in the blank space to the right of the question. He has to accept or reject the law in its entirety. He has to pronounce on all the articles and contents of a law at once, and cannot separate or amend them. The

press has already demanded that the minority of the
Federal Assembly, if it attains a certain figure, should
be allowed to submit a counter-proposal to the people,
to be voted on at the same time as the bill passed by
the majority. If this innovation were adopted, the
electors would have a little more freedom of choice.
However reasonable the suggestion may appear, it
has been put aside for the present, because it would
make the voting complicated, and would only confuse
the electors.

Another intrinsic defect of the referendum is that
whenever a law is rejected it leaves the federal
authorities in ignorance of the real feelings and
wishes of the people. That they do not want the
law is a fact to which the figures curtly testify. But
what is it that has caused these thousands of legislators, intelligent and interested men for the most
part, to form an opinion which has proved fatal to
the work of the Federal Assembly? What are the
premises from which the people reach those conclusions which they demonstrate so forcibly ? In what
direction shall the legislators next proceed, since they
have already made a false start ? To all these questions no answer is given. When a law is rejected the
result of the referendum is purely negative.

M. Dürrenmatt once proposed that the electors
should state the reasons which actuated them when
giving their vote. " The more intelligent, at any rate,"
he said, " would be able to do this, and it would prove
a valuable guide to Parliament as to the state of public
opinion when a legislative vote has taken place."

M. Dürrenmatt has even gone so far as to print
some voting papers in the *Berner Volkszeitung* which

might serve as models, and in which the reply was
followed by a few words summing up the reasons of
the electors. This scheme has had no result, however. The task of the elector, in such a case, would
not be so easy as might be thought at first, and the
handwriting, moreover, would make secrecy in voting
impossible.

We ought to notice yet another attempt to modify
Article 89 of the Constitution as regards the question
to be brought before the electors, proposed by a member
from Zürich, Herr Vögelin, in 1884. " To submit to the
people the complete draft of a bill which the deputies
themselves scarcely understand is to make a fool of
the people," he said. " I own frankly that I should
prefer no referendum at all to that caricature of it
we possess to-day. In the Middle Ages the questions
put to the people were simple, clear, and easy to
understand, and they summed up the fundamental
principle of a law. Then, after the vote had taken
place, the government drafted the law in accordance
with the expressed wishes of the nation. Why not
return to these ancient traditions ? The first objection that will be urged is that the legislators may
not always faithfully interpret the thoughts of the
people. Well then, let us give the people the right
of initiative. They will then be able to modify laws
which have been made against their will. I would
propose to give 50,000 electors the right of initiative,
and to substitute the following provision for Article
89: ' Each federal law will confine itself to expressing
some principle or fundamental proposition, and will
be submitted to the referendum in this form. If
the people accept it, a federal decree will supply the,

details.'"[1] Since 1884 the motion of Herr Vögelin has been often under consideration.

VII. When the votes have all been given, a report is drawn up in each commune or electoral district, which consists of four columns, in one of which the number of registered electors is entered, in another the total number of voters, in the third the number of those who have accepted the law or order in question, and in the fourth the number of those who have rejected it.   The cantonal governments correct the reports of the communes, and forward them to the Federal Council within ten days. They keep the voting tickets, however, in case the Council should wish to see them.   The Federal Council calculates the result of the vote from these reports.   If the majority of the electors who have taken part in the vote have written "Yes" on their voting paper, the law or resolution is considered as having been accepted, the Federal Council takes the necessary steps to bring it into force, and it is inserted in the official collection of the laws of the Confederation.

If it appear that the majority of voters have rejected the law or resolution which has been submitted, this law or resolution is considered to be null and void, and does not become law.   In both cases the results of the voting are published in the *Feuille Fédérale*, and the Federal Council informs the Chambers of the result at their next session.

[1] Herr Vögelin presented his motion to the National Council.   I found his speech in a Zürich journal, the *Züricher Post* of the 12th of July 1884, which M. Curti kindly sent me.

VIII. There is one last question in connection with the referendum which is especially interesting to the head of the financial department, and by which also the tax-payers are indirectly affected, and that is the financial outlay in the case of a popular vote. The necessary cost of printing a law on the recovery of debts and on bankruptcy amounted to 47,696 francs. With the other expenses, the voting on this law alone cost the Confederation about 130,000 francs, and this is by no means exceptional.[1]

IX. In conclusion, let us sum up the differences between the referendum on a revision of the Federal Constitution and one which is merely concerned with federal laws or ordinary federal decrees.

(1) The constitutional referendum is *compulsory* —that is to say, the vote is enjoined by the constitution, and takes place as a regular part of the procedure, no demand being necessary.

The legislative referendum is *optional*. The right of demanding it is vested in any 30,000 electors or eight cantons, and the popular voting only takes place if a demand be made in accordance with the rules laid down by law.

(2) A federal decree revising the constitution does not become law unless it obtains a numerical majority

---

[1] Adams, *La Confédération Suisse*, Basle, 1890, p. 98.

[M. Hilty says that more than 600,000 copies of the law have to be printed in different languages, and are, of course, distributed gratis to the citizens. The expenses depend on the length of the law. He gives the printing expenses of the first law against bank notes, which was rejected, as 14,425 francs 95 cents; the expenses of the law on military taxation as 14,485 francs; and the three laws which were voted on in October 1877 cost 20,843 francs. See *Revue de Droit*, &c., p. 405.]

in the country at large, and also a numerical majority in the majority of the cantons.

An ordinary federal law which has been voted on by the people can come into force as soon as the bare majority of the Swiss electors accept it, without any reference to the fact that the electors in the majority of the cantons may have rejected it. For instance, the law on marriage of the 24th of December 1874 only obtained a majority in nine and a half cantons, but in the whole country it obtained 213,199 votes to 205,069. In the same way, the bankruptcy law passed on the 17th November 1889 by a majority of 26,396 votes, although it only obtained a majority in eight cantons. The argument used to justify the disregard of the cantonal vote in the case of ordinary laws is the following: By the constitution certain powers have been given over to the central government, and this surrender has been made with the assent of the majority of the cantons. By that act of cession the cantons have lost their right to interfere in these matters, or in the legislation affecting them. The supporters of the cantonal sovereignty answer this argument by reasoning as follows: The Confederation is a community. There can be no question of any individual surrender of powers, when they belong to the community as a whole. It is inherent in the very idea of a confederation that those who compose the community should be able to make themselves heard on all questions.

2. §. *The "Rights of the People" with regard to the Ordinary Laws in the Cantons.*

I. *The Optional Referendum.*

The optional referendum has been adopted by the cantons of Lucerne, Zug, Schaffhausen, St. Gall, Vaud, Neuchâtel, Geneva, and the half canton of Basle-City.[1]

We have just discussed the federal referendum so fully that it will be unnecessary for us to enter into many details here, for the optional referendum is organised on much the same plan everywhere.

The following matters may be submitted to the popular vote:—

1. The laws in those cantons we have just mentioned.

2. Certain decrees. In Basle-City and in Neuchâtel they are decrees which are of general import and which are not urgent;[2] in St. Gall, decrees which are general, not urgent, and which the constitution of that canton does not declare to be within the exclusive jurisdiction of the Great Council.

---

[1] [Schaffhausen has now adopted the compulsory referendum; Ticino also has the optional referendum. Certain cantons have the optional referendum on certain subjects. It is optional in Schwyz for treaties, decrees, and orders, but is compulsory for laws. In the Grisons it is optional in the case of resolutions which are not urgent. Vaud, it may be mentioned, has a compulsory financial referendum. In Basle-City all laws and resolutions which the *people* initiate are subject to the compulsory referendum.]

[2] [In Basle-City the words used are "*nicht persönliche natur*" (not of a personal nature). In Neuchâtel "urgency" requires a majority of two-thirds of the Council.]

In Lucerne, Zug, and Schaffhausen, decrees which grant money over a certain sum are also subject to the optional referendum.[1] In the canton of Vaud "any law or decree passed by the Great Council," in Geneva "laws and decrees which are not of an exceptionally urgent character," are within the sphere of the referendum. The cantonal law of Geneva expressly excludes "the annual law for expenditure and revenue as a whole," but special provisions of this law can always be submitted to the referendum if (1) they impose a new tax, or increase a tax already existing; or (2) if they propose an issue of stock, or a loan in some other form.[2]

3. Treaties in the cantons of Lucerne, Zug, and Schaffhausen. By the Federal Constitution the cantons have the right of making treaties with one another about subjects for legislation, or on administrative and judicial matters (Art. 7). In some exceptional cases they have the right of concluding treaties with foreign states in matters which concern the public economy and questions of local relations and police (Art. 9). Treaties which come under either of these two heads are submitted to the optional referendum in the three cantons quoted above.[3]

---

[1] The sums are 200,000 francs in Lucerne, 40,000 francs in Zug, and 150,000 francs in Schaffhausen.

[2] [In practice the budget is never submitted in any state.]

[3] [In Schwyz also they are subject to the optional referendum, but now in Schaffhausen to the compulsory referendum.

The treaties between the cantons can always be submitted to the Federal Council, should that body desire it or another canton raise a protest; and if they contain anything contrary to the articles of the Confederation, or if they injure the rights of the other cantons in any way, they are annulled by the Council.

Treaties with foreign countries on subordinate questions mentioned above are also submitted to the Council, and are annulled

The number of signatures necessary to bring about a popular vote are 500 in Zug, 1000 in Basle-City and Schaffhausen, 3000 in Neuchâtel, 3500 in Geneva,[1] 4000 in St. Gall, 5000 at Lucerne and in Ticino, and 6000 in the canton of Vaud. Moreover, the demand for a referendum must be presented within thirty days after the publication of the law, resolution, or treaty in the *Feuille officielle* (Gazette).[2] In Lucerne and Zug laws are only published at the end of the legislative session. In the other cantons a law or decree is published immediately after it has passed the Great Council.[3] In Schaffhausen all the legislative acts which come within the scope of the referendum are sent to the electors, with an explanatory message, within eight days after their publication.[4]

in like manner if they contain anything contrary to the Confederation or the rights of other cantons. On important matters the cantons can only treat with other countries through the Federal Council, and the Federal Council concludes treaties with other countries in the name of the canton, as in the case of the treaty between France and Geneva in 1858, and between Great Britain and Vaud in 1872.]

[1] [It is now 2500 in Geneva.]

[2] In Neuchâtel and Lucerne the referendary respite is forty days, in Basle-City six weeks. The laws and legislative decrees do not come into force until the expiration of the respite, and, if a referendum be demanded, not until the people have pronounced. [In many cantons provision is made that the voting must take place within the next forty or fifty days after a referendum is inevitable.]

[3] [In Neuchâtel, if a law is too long to send around to the electors, the title is printed and sent round, with the intimation that the law itself can be studied in the communal Chancery. In Lucerne and Zug the laws are deposited in the communal Chanceries at the end of every session for perusal.]

[4] [In Schaffhausen the voting now takes place once a year, in spring.]

The electors who claim the referendum put their signatures at the foot of a written demand, as in the case of a federal law. In Ticino the signature must be given by the elector in person in the communal offices, in the presence of some delegate of the Chancery. In Neuchâtel and Geneva, the electors who support the demand for a referendum must sign personally. In the two former cantons he must give his christian name, surname, address, age, and profession. In the cantons of Lucerne, Zug, and Schaffhausen the Great Council has power to divide up a law in certain exceptional cases when a referendum has been demanded, and may submit the different provisions separately to the popular vote.[1]

In Schaffhausen voting is compulsory, and the penalty for not voting is a fine of two francs.

Everywhere except in Zug the majority of those voting decides whether a law shall be accepted or rejected. In this canton a law is not considered as rejected unless the majority of registered electors have voted "No."[2] This is a survival of the old popular veto, when the principle was applied that *qui tacet, consentire videtur.*

The name *optional referendum* is also given sometimes to the popular voting on laws and orders, which takes place at the instance of the Great Council itself or at the request of a group of

[1] [Also in Zürich, Solothurn, and Aargau, where voting is compulsory.]

[2] [This is now altered in the new Constitution of 1894, and Zug is no longer an exception.]

deputies. This referendum at the option of the Legislature exists in some of the cantons we are now considering.

In Lucerne and Zug the Great Council has power to consult the people on a resolution it has just passed. Moreover, in the canton of Zug, laws, treaties, and financial decrees are submitted to the people if one-third of the deputies demand the referendum, as soon as the final vote on a law, treaty, or decree has been taken by the cantonal council.

In Rural-Basle laws and resolutions when general in character are submitted to the referendum upon demand of 4000 electors, or in consequence of a decision of the Great Council to that effect.

Finally, in St. Gall there is a referendum when 4000 electors claim it, or if one-third of the Great Council demand it directly the law is passed. In this latter case the majority of the Great Council can always insist that the popular vote shall be taken on the separate provisions of the law and not on the law as a whole.[1]

The referendum at the option of the Great Council is an institution which is scarcely ever used, and to which the Swiss democrats do not attach any particular value. It has been criticised as follows by M. Hilty, a National Councillor and a Professor of Law in the University of Berne :—

"This form of referendum cannot be highly recommended, for it does not seem right in principle

[1] [In. St. Gall the Great Council may also consult the people during the making of the law, and ask them whether certain provisions shall be put in or not.]

that the representatives of the people should be able arbitrarily to submit or withhold laws according to their will and pleasure. The real danger is that the questions referred will be those which are certain to be accepted, and on which the government does not run the risk of rejection, or those for which the government does not wish to take the responsibility, or perhaps those in which many members have voted against their inclination and wish to raise the question again by bringing it before the people." [1]

II. *The Compulsory Referendum.*

The compulsory referendum has been adopted in the cantons of Zürich, Berne, Schwyz, Solothurn, the Grisons, Aargau, Thurgau, the Valais, and in the half canton of Rural-Basle. [2]   In all these states the laws, and at least a certain number of legislative decrees, do not come into force until they have been expressly ratified by the people. A popular voting always takes place on all matters which are not placed exclusively within the province of the Great Council by the constitution.   There is no need for a fraction of the electoral body to demand the referendum.   It takes place as a matter of right, *ipso jure*, and no one can prevent it without violating the constitution.

M. Hilty considers that the organisation of the

---

[1] Hilty, *Das Referendum im schweizerischen Staatsrecht*, p. 415.   The criticism of M. Hilty seems only directed against the referendum which may be demanded by the parliamentary majority.

[2] [Also Schaffhausen since 1895.]

powers of the state differs essentially according to the form of referendum adopted.[1] To that we cannot, however, assent.

Under the optional, as under the compulsory referendum, the Great Council ceases to be the sole legislator and sovereign of the country. In both cases its duty is to prepare the laws, and these laws do not come into force until they have received the popular sanction. The distinction between the two institutions is that in the cantons where the compulsory referendum is in force the popular sanction is always expressed, in the optional referendum cantons it is sometimes expressed and sometimes tacit, according to the inclination of the electors. The difference is, therefore, obviously merely external. In practice it may be important; as a matter of right there is no difference at all.

Before describing the machinery of the compulsory referendum, let us see, first of all, what are the subjects upon which the people have to regularly give their opinion.

In one of the cantons with the compulsory referendum, the Valais, the influence of the people is reduced almost to a minimum. " Every decision of the Great

---

[1] Hilty, *Das Referendum im schweizerischen Staatsrecht*, p. 411. [He there says that in the optional referendum the fundamental idea is not that the legislative power should be exercised through the people, but that they should have a more or less restricted control or power of criticism, a kind of justified opposition to the Legislature, and that their intervention in legislative work is an exceptional occurrence. A state that has the optional referendum is always a representative democracy in which certain concessions have been made to the people.]

Council which entails an extraordinary expense of 60,000 francs, or during a term of three years an average expense of 20,000 francs, has to be submitted to the people for their approval or veto, if this expense cannot be covered by the ordinary revenue of the budget" (Art. 15). This is merely the financial referendum (*Finanz Referendum*).

But the electors enjoy much more extensive rights in other cantons. They pronounce—

(1) Upon the laws.

(2) On the treaties which the cantons may conclude within the limits assigned by Articles 7 and 9 of the Federal Constitution. In the canton of Aargau treaties are said to belong exclusively to the Great Council.[1]

(3) On certain orders or decrees passed by the Great Council.[2]

It is worthy of notice that several of the cantonal constitutions, those of Aargau and Zürich for example, have put an end to the irritating uncertainty which exists in public federal law between the rights of the people and the duties of the Chamber. They have solved the difficulty, not by making abstract definitions of a law or a decree, but by drawing up a list of

---

[1] [In Schwyz treaties are subject to the optional referendum, and also in Berne, in so far as they are not of a legislative nature. In some of the Landsgemeinde cantons, it is worth noticing,—Uri, Obwald, and Appenzell (Inner Rhodes),—treaties also belong exclusively to the Great Council.]

[2] [In the Grisons all orders creating new officials or bodies are subject to the compulsory referendum. The optional referendum applies to all resolutions which are not urgent, upon the demand of 3000 voters. Schwyz, Aargau, Thurgau, and Berne do not seem to recognise a referendum on decrees and resolutions other than finaucial ones.]

the subjects upon which the Great Council can legislate without consulting the people.[1]

Financial decrees deserve special mention, for they
always require the popular approval. All estimates
voted by the Chamber which exceed a certain sum
must be approved by the people.[2] In the canton
of Solothurn, the state cannot borrow more than
500,000 francs without the consent of the electorate.
This sum is fixed at 1,000,000 in the canton of
Aargau.

From 1869 onwards even the state budget was
submitted to the referendum in the Canton Berne.
The clause ran as follows: "The budget containing

[1] [The Constitution of the Grisons also defines the laws that are
to be submitted to the people. They are—

(1) "Organic laws." These are said to be "civil laws, penal
laws, those that regulate the procedure in civil and criminal
matters, and also in matters of police."

(2) Administrative laws, especially those relating to excise,
education, keeping of the highways, forests, game and fishing
rights, sanitary matters, and poor law, as well as other matters
of administration relating to the public welfare.]

[2] 500,000 francs in Berne, 250,000 in Zürich, 50,000 in Schwyz,
100,000 at Solothurn, 100,000 in the Grisons, 250,000 in Aargau,
and 50,000 in Thurgau.

[These constitutions all provide also that the annual expenditure
shall not be increased beyond a certain amount without a popular
vote. The sums are 20,000 francs in Zürich, 10,000 in Schwyz,
15,000 in Solothurn, 20,000 in the Grisons, 25,000 in Aargau, and
10,000 in Thurgau.

M. Hilty says of the financial referendum, that of all the forms of
the referendum this is the one which is the least to be recommended.
Financial matters are the point in which the people are most wanting in insight and in foresight. They cannot have that grasp over
the whole financial question which is necessary for a right judgment. The most important state works which affect future generations may thus be crippled through the niggardliness of those
who will not sacrifice anything for posterity.—*Das Referendum im
hweizerischen Staatsrecht.*] .

the estimates, drawn up for a period of four years, shall be laid before the people for their approval or rejection. It shall not become law unless it has been accepted by the majority of those voting in the canton " (Law of the 19th May 1869, Arts. 3 and 4).

The people of Berne having refused several times to pass the budget, the government was forced in 1880 to abolish this species of referendum.[1] They encountered a great deal of opposition, but. they triumphed at last by a very simple expedient. They inserted the article abolishing this disputed right in a law of the 16th of May 1880 which was very popular with the people because it suppressed several public posts. The pill being thus gilded, the people swallowed it without hesitation.

We may take the canton of Zürich as a typical example of the way in which the popular vote is organised in cantons where the referendum is compulsory. After having discussed and passed a law the Great Council sends it on to the executive with the request that they will submit it to the referendum. At the same time it charges the government, or a special commission, with the task of

---

[1] [The budget was also submitted in Aargau, and there, too, the government was left without funds, and it was found necessary to give up the practice.]

Except in Berne and Rural-Basle the Great Council still has the right of consulting the people on decrees which do not come within the scope of the compulsory referendum. In Schwyz it looks as if the legislators had aimed at enumerating all the possible forms of referendum. First of all, the *laws* are subject to the compulsory referendum ; then the cantonal council, or 2000 electors, may claim a referendum upon *decrees ;* finally, the cantonal council may ask the people for power to bring a law into force at once. This last plebiscite is peculiar to this canton.

drawing up an explanatory message for the people. The government immediately organises the popular vote by a decree which is published in the *Feuille officielle*, and which is sent to the communal councils. The cantonal chancery is responsible for printing the laws, messages, and voting tickets, and must see that each elector receives a copy of the law and official message thirty days before the vote at the latest.[1]

This message is one of the special features of the compulsory referendum. Its object is to explain the law, its character, its advantages and disadvantages, and thereby to enable each person to weigh the pros and cons, form a reasonable opinion for themselves, and give an intelligent vote.

As a matter of fact, the message is unfortunately by no means the impartial comment it ought to be. I have read a great number of them in the different cantons. With one accord they all dwell upon the advantages of the law, they aim at prepossessing the electors in its favour, and advise them to give an affirmative vote.[2] The electors know so well the form which the message will take that they do not even trouble to read it. My informants are unanimous on this point.[3]

[1] In the canton of Aargau, when the law is a lengthy one, a few copies are sent to the communal chancery, and the electors may see it there.

[2] The message does not always recommend the law. A deputy from the canton of Thurgau has told me that his government once sent a message to the electors in which they were advised to vote No. The government of Thurgau can afford to be so independent, for it is elected directly by the people and not by the Great Council.

[3] It was thought probable that the electors did not read the explanatory messages because they were too long. It has now

We find thus in the cantons which have the obligatory referendum the same defect that we have already noticed in the case of the optional referendum in the Confederation; that is to say, there is no valuable means by which the electors may be instructed as to the value of the laws, a defect which becomes more serious in this case because the votings take place so frequently.

It is not in the least astonishing to find that M. Herzog, who is a thorough democrat, nevertheless considers the present form of the compulsory referendum to be absolutely detestable. "I am convinced," he says, "that posterity will wonder how we could possibly acquiesce in a system which is so obviously defective." But M. Herzog does more than criticise. He makes an ingenious suggestion by which the present system may be improved. He proposes that public meetings should be held between the first and second reading of a law, at which the deputies should be obliged by the terms of the constitution to inform the electors as to the object of the law, its contents, advantages and disadvantages. Attendance at these meetings would be compulsory for all the electors.

A whole series of arguments, so M. Herzog says, can be adduced in favour of this proposal.

(1) Every decision arrived at by associations, or by

---

become the custom to make them shorter. I have before me the Civil Code of the canton of Solothurn which was sanctioned by the people on the 5th of July 1891. This code contains 905 articles (175 pages in 12mo). The message which accompanies it covers five pages. I know a great many law students who would rejoice if their professors could summarise their explanations like the government of Solothurn.

communes, congresses, or commissions of any kind
whatever, has always been made the subject of abun-
dant discussion and debate.   The popular votings
on bills are the only exception to the general rule.
They are left to chance.   What should we say if the
constitution were to authorise Parliament to vote
laws offhand without discussing them ?   Yet debates
are less necessary in Parliament, because the members
who compose it are most of them intelligent men.
Let us, therefore, make the *discussion* as much an
integral part of the referendum as the *vote*.

(2) The electorate would be able to exercise a real
control over the parliamentary action of their deputies.

(3) It is not at all an uncommon sight at the present
day to see the citizens giving in their ballot-papers
without knowing what it is they accept or reject.   If,
however, all the electors heard the law commented on
by their representatives, who had studied it at the
first reading, this would no longer be possible.

(4) It will be an important means of completing
the political education of the people, and they will
learn to think and judge for themselves.

(5) These meetings held between the two readings
of a bill will enable the electors to take an active part
in legislation, and will give them an opportunity of
expressing their opinion on the law and of proposing
amendments.

(6) That systematic opposition, to some extent a
matter of instinct, which exists between the people
and the legislative assemblies will disappear.

(7) It will no longer be possible for deputies to
vote according to the orders of a party chief.

(8) The people will get to know their deputies

better, and will be able to judge whether they should
be returned at the next election.

As far as I know, the system of M. Herzog has never
been tried but once up to the present time. That
was on a recent occasion in the canton of Berne, when
an educational law was under discussion. During
the interval of three months between the first and
second reading of the law, the educational committees
of the communes were ordered to call together the
heads of families in public meetings, and to invite
their comments on the bill as it stood after its first
reading in the Great Council. A member of the
Great Council told me that if the attempt succeeded
he should propose to make those intermediate consultations compulsory in the case of all important
laws. In the cantons of Aargau and Thurgau the
constitution requires that a public meeting should be
held before the voting takes place, in which the electors may discuss the law to be voted on.[1] But in
these cantons the electors have no power to change
or amend the law; they can only accept or reject
the law as it is submitted to them.[2]

I have made inquiries in these cantons with a view
to ascertaining whether the electors obtain any advan-

[1] [In Aargau and Berne every law must be published before the
second reading, in order to give the people an opportunity to take
exception to it. In Thurgau all laws proposed must, as a rule, be
published four weeks before they come up for debate.]

[2] [According to Stüssi, *Referendum und Initiativ in den Schweizer-
cantonen*, p. 151, such meetings also take place in Lucerne and
Schaffhausen (Lucerne has the optional referendum, it will be
remembered). If several proposals come before the people to be
voted on, it is provided that a debate shall take place on each
separately.]

tage from the discussions which precede the vote. I have been told that a debate is an unheard-of thing, and that an exchange of opinions at these meetings never takes place. The mayor of the commune contents himself with asking at the meeting if any elector wishes to speak, but no one answers; the audience have made up their minds beforehand, and are anxious to vote at once.

The method of voting is the same whether the referendum be compulsory or optional. Every active citizen receives his voting-ticket and his elector's card during the week preceding the vote.[1] On the voting-paper the question is printed, "Do you accept the law, Yes or No?" The elector writes his answer to the right of the question. He always accepts or

---

[1] [Most cantonal constitutions, whether the referendum is compulsory or optional, provide that the voting shall take place on a Sunday. In Zürich the elector gets his card some days beforehand, and his voting-ticket, and fills the voting-ticket in at home and deposits it in the urn (*Stimmurne*) after giving up his ticket to the presiding official. The urn is generally set up in some public place, such as a school-house. When the poll is closed the urn is opened in some public place, often in an inn, and the votes are counted.

The electors do not seem to get their voting-ticket beforehand in every canton. In some cases they have to go to the polling-place and fetch it, and fill in the ticket there and then. In Lucerne the elector gets his ticket, fills it in in a private place, puts it in an envelope given him for the purpose, and gives it in again. This preserves the secrecy of the vote.

Again, according to another system, the electors collect in the communes, and the voting-tickets are dealt out, and people fill them in there, and they are then collected (Thurgau), or they have to meet in the communes and give their tickets up in alphabetical order, which they have filled in at home (Fribourg). See Stüssi, *op. cit.*, p. 150.]

rejects the law as a whole. In two cantons, however, —in Zürich and in Aargau,—the cantonal council can in exceptional circumstances order that the law shall be voted on in sections.

In Zürich the cantonal council has sometimes availed itself of this right.[1]

In the cantons of Zürich, Aargau, Solothurn, Thurgau, and Rural-Basle voting is compulsory, in that the constitution authorises the communes to fine the electors who stay away.[2]

In the canton of Zürich, and only in that canton, voting by proxy is permitted. An elector may place three voting-papers in the ballot-box—his own and those of two friends—provided that he shows their elector's card.[3] But he is not allowed to give in more than three voting-papers. The counting takes place immediately after the poll is closed, and each commune forwards a report of the result to the capital of the canton. The fate of the law is decided by the majority of the electors who have taken part in the vote. If the majority vote " Yes," the law is considered to be accepted ; if they vote " No," it is rejected. In Rural-Basle a law is not considered to be accepted unless it is supported by a majority of those voting ;

[1] Stüssi, *Referendum und Initiativ im Kanton Zürich*, p. 38.

[2] [A most interesting account of the compulsory voting is given by M. Deploige in the *Revue de Belgique* for March 1893, in an article entitled *Le Vote Obligatoire*.]

[3] [In some of the cantons voting by proxy is forbidden, under various penalties. In Valais there is a penalty of 50 francs. In some cantons other voting-tickets than the official ones are recognised as valid. They are generally printed by one or other of the parties. In St. Gall M. Stüssi says they must be on white paper, and contain the question exactly as it is stated on the official paper.]

and secondly, the total number of those voting either one way or the other must amount to an absolute majority of the registered electors.[1]

The foreign reader will no doubt inquire whether the citizens of those states which have a compulsory referendum are frequently called upon to exercise their legislative powers or not. The following are the provisions of some of the cantonal constitutions in the matter. In Zürich, Thurgau, and Aargau the popular votings take place twice a year—one in spring, on the bills passed during the winter session, and the other in autumn, on the bills passed in the summer session. In case of need, however, the Great Council may order an extraordinary voting. In Rural-Basle · two votings per annum are fixed as a maximum. In Berne, by the terms of the law of 1869, the vote takes place as a rule on the first Sunday in May in each year, also at any time that the Great Council may order an extraordinary voting.[2]

---

[1] [This is now altered in the Constitution of 1892. The reason is furnished by M. Deploige when discussing the results of the referendum in the cantons. Out of 102 laws voted on in the twenty years between 1864 and 1884, no less than twenty-six fell through altogether because a majority of electors did not take part in the vote. Between 1881 and 1884, out of seventeen laws submitted, nine failed through lack of attendance and five were rejected.]

[2] [M. Droz, writing in 1895, and speaking of Berne, says that he had been summoned to the polls no less than a dozen times during the past year to vote at various elections and on federal and cantonal laws. He says he received a dozen laws which he was supposed to study before voting, but he confesses that, although he is accustomed to public business and the wording of such laws, he has not always been able to go into the question, and has often voted on the strength of what he has been told about them. See *La démocratie en Suisse et l'initiative populaire*, p. 464, in the *Études et portraits politiques*.]

M. Stüssi, who has written an interesting monograph on the referendum in Zürich, remarks that the
article of the constitution which limits the number
of the ordinary votings to two is in reality a dead-
letter.   In 1870 there were three votings—one in
February, one in April, and the last in May; in 1871
three votings—in January, in June, and in October.
Between 1870 and 1886 there were thirty-seven
votings, and only one of these was formally called
extraordinary.

The points of difference between the compulsory and optional referendum in practice are as
follows:—

(1) Under the compulsory system, as we have
already seen, the popular voting takes place as a
matter of course, whilst under the optional system
it must be demanded by a certain number of
electors.

(2) In all the cantons where the referendum is
compulsory, the law is accompanied by an explanatory message.

(3) There is a marked tendency in the cantons
to make it compulsory for the electors to vote, to
convert the right into a duty in fact, by imposing
a fine on those electors who do not put a ballot-
paper in the box.

Schaffhausen occupies the unique position of being
the only canton with the optional referendum in
which the electors are obliged to vote, and in which
there is an explanatory message.[1]

---

[1] [It has already been pointed out that by a constitutional amendment of 1895 Schaffhausen has introduced compulsory voting. The
votings take place, however, only *once* a year. It may be useful to

III. *The Popular Initiative.*

While the referendum has been an object of great interest to jurists and constitutional writers generally, the popular initiative, on the contrary, has remained almost unnoticed, and has, in fact, been the least studied of the Swiss democratic institutions. It is a curious fact that it should be so, for it is a striking innovation, and one that is far more important in its consequences than the referendum.[1]

give here a table of the cantons according as they have adopted the system of optional or compulsory referendum.

ZÜRICH	Compulsory, 1869.
BERNE	Compulsory, 1867.
LUCERNE	Optional, 1869.
SCHWYZ	Compulsory, Treaties optional, 1848 and 1876.
ZUG	Optional, 1877.
FRIBOURG	Representative government, *i.e.* none.
SOLOTHURN	Compulsory, 1869. Optional, 1856.
BASLE (City)	Optional, 1875.
BASLE (Rural)	Compulsory, 1863.
SCHAFFHAUSEN	Compulsory, 1895. Optional, 1876.
ST. GALL	Optional, 1861 and 1875.
GRISONS	Compulsory, 1852 (federal referenda before).
AARGAU	Compulsory, 1870.
THURGAU	Compulsory, 1869.
TICINO	Optional, 1883 and 1892.
VAUD	Optional, 1885. Compulsory (for finance), 1861.
VALAIS	Compulsory (for finance), 1852.
NEUCHÂTEL	Optional, 1879. Compulsory (for finance), 1858.
GENEVA	Optional, 1879.]

[1] I only know one professorial work on the popular initiative. That is an inaugural dissertation by a doctor of law of Zürich. The

The principle is an old one. We find that it has already been recognised for several centuries in the cantons with Landsgemeinden, and its essential character has hardly changed at all in all those years. The form in which it is now exercised and the way in which it is organised are of comparatively recent date, and it may therefore be termed the latest conquest of democracy.

The reader will remember that Major Diog tried as early as 1831 to introduce it in St. Gall, but without success. From that time the popular initiative became a prominent feature in the programmes of speculative democrats, who advocated it as the most effective expression of popular sovereignty. Its introduction into the cantonal constitution was retarded for some time by the violent opposition of the partisans of the representative system, who looked upon it as an anarchical institution, and one calculated to introduce uncertainty and confusion into legislation, and generally overturn the whole order of things. The people, on the other hand, took a long time to fully grasp the power conferred by the new right. They understood perfectly that the referendum was a defensive weapon against the abuse of power by a despotic assembly, but they could not realise being called upon to make the laws themselves. To reject an unpopular decree of the Chambers is right enough, so they argued, but to legislate for oneself, no thank you! Moreover, what

title is, *Das Volksinitiativrecht nach den schweizerischen Kantonsverfassungen,* Zürich, 1889. [Herr Stüssi has written a very interesting account of the referendum and initiative in the Swiss cantons—*Das Referendum und Initiativ in den Schweizerkantonen,* 1893.]

they heard and read about the subject was not
calculated to rouse them to any great pitch of enthusiasm. The initiative was too often compared
to the right of petition, and not having derived
any particular benefit from this latter right, they
attached very little importance to the former.

The comparison which is often made even at
the present day between the popular initiative and
the right of petition is nevertheless radically false.
According to M. Keller, there are four points of
difference between the two institutions.

(1) A demand by initiative is a proposition made
to the people as the supreme legislative power. A
petition is a request which may be addressed to
any official body.

(2) A demand by initiative must be supported by
a certain definite number of signatures given by
citizens who are in full possession of their political
rights. A petition may be presented by one person
only, and he need not necessarily be an elector, and
may even be a foreigner.

(3) A demand by initiative is always concerned
with some question of legislation, either the making
of a new law or the repeal of one already in force.
Petitions may be presented on any subject.

(4) The representative assembly is not free to deal
with an initiative demand as it pleases. It may
examine the demand, discuss and criticise it, but
in the end it must go to the electorate. The fate
of a petition rests entirely in the hands of the
Chamber.[1]

---

[1] [The difference has been well stated by Mr. Lowell, who says ·
"A petition is merely a suggestion made to the Legislature, which

It is also quite as misleading to draw comparisons between the optional referendum and the popular initiative, as was once done by a speaker in the National Council. "There is no great difference between these two institutions," he said, "for they both give to a certain number of electors the right of provoking a popular vote on·a legislative measure." This deputy was wrong. The initiative has merely a superficial resemblance to the optional referendum for the following reasons :—

(1) By the right of initiative the electors can propose a new law, or demand the repeal of a law in existence. By the optional referendum they only have the right of making an appeal to the people on the subject of a bill which has not yet become law.

(2) A demand by initiative may be made at any time; a demand for the referendum must be made within a certain time fixed by law.[1]

may act upon it or not as it sees fit ; but the initiative takes effect without regard to the opinion of the Legislature, and even against its wishes" (*op. cit.*, p. 280).

M. Berney points out that the initiative is the right of provoking a decision of the sovereign, the referendum the right of ratifying the decision of an authority.]

[1] [Two other features may be pointed out :—

(1) That the people in the case of a referendum are part of the ordinary procedure ; their assent, tacit or express, is a necessary part of the constitutional machinery. The demand by initiative is not part of the ordinary procedure, but an exceptional occurrence. ·

(2) The initiative renders the optional referendum practically useless, because it can do all the optional referendum can do and more. It is only limited by the fact that nothing may be proposed which contravenes the Federal Constitution. By its means a law can be repealed once it has come into force ; it is bound to no fixed time in making its adverse decision known as in the case of the referendum. It may act at any time, and call in question decrees

The popular initiative is, therefore, quite distinct from the other political institutions of Switzerland.

From the legal point of view, the introduction of the popular initiative makes democracy enter upon a new phase. The result of the referendum was to establish a perfect equality between the two factors of legislation, the parliament and the electoral body. Neither of them could do anything without the other. No bill could be drawn up without the intervention of the Chamber, no law could come into force without the express or tacit assent of the people. The Chamber and the people were on the same footing, and both took an equal share in the work of legislation, the former by means of its right of initiative, the latter by its right of approval. The introduction of the popular initiative has disturbed this equilibrium and displaced the centre of political gravity. The Chamber has been forced to share with the electors its right of proposing the laws. It has ceased to be an indispensable part of the legislative machine. The people can from henceforward legislate without it, in spite of it, and against it. In all the cantons where it exists, the popular initiative has either accompanied, or more often followed the referendum, as a natural and inevitable consequence of the latter, its necessary complement, in fact.[1] We have already seen that when the referendum says No, it does not create, it destroys. The popular will has, therefore,

which are withdrawn from the referendum because they are urgent, not general in character, or because they belong exclusively to the Great Council.]

[1] Except in the cantons of Vaud and Aargau, where, as a matter of fact, it has hardly ever been used. *Cf.* Chatelanat, *Die schweizerische Demokratie*, p. 5.

N

no means of positive expression. Nevertheless, among the mass of electors who reject a law, there must be some who are not merely habitual malcontents. There must be men who know what they want, and who have a clear idea of the changes which ought to be brought about, and the evils to be remedied. The course of events is somewhat as follows. These men, or their representatives, are treated with indifference by a transitory parliamentary majority. They petition and express their wishes both in speeches and in writings, and all to no effect. The majority in the Chamber have already formed their opinion, and are not to be moved from the position they have taken up. After encountering defeat in the Chamber, the opposition then turn to the nation, and, by working upon the electorate, are finally successful in getting the law rejected.

They soon become desirous of doing more than this, however, and are fired with the ambition to triumph by means of the people, and that in spite of and in opposition to parliament. Once the idea takes shape, the result is the initiative.

The initiative figured for a long time in the programmes of certain speculative thinkers, but it would never have taken form and become law if the referendum had not already existed, and was found to be so imperfect a means of expressing the popular will that it required supplementing.

In order to make a systematic study of the popular initiative as it is organised in the Swiss cantons where there is no Landsgemeinde, we shall have to ask, firstly, by whom is the initiative organised? secondly, what subjects come within its range? thirdly, in what form must the popular proposals be made? fourthly, what are the rights of the Chamber with respect to the demand? and, lastly, what is the final result of a demand?

I. The right of initiative may be exercised by any active citizen who can induce a certain number of electors to sign their names to his demand. This number varies in the different cantons.[1] It is fixed at 1000 in the cantons of Zug, Basle-City, and Schaffhausen, at 1500 in Rural-Basle, at 2000 in Schwyz and Solothurn, at 2500 in Geneva and in Thurgau, at 3000 in Neuchâtel, at 4000 in St. Gall, at 5000 in Zürich, Aargau, and in the Grisons,[2] and at 6000 in the canton of Vaud.[3] In the canton of Zürich, and in that canton alone, does the constitu-

[1] [Only three cantons do not possess the initiative in ordinary legislation—Lucerne, Fribourg, and Valais.]

[2] [The Grisons has now reduced the number to 3000. Ticino and Berne have also adopted the principle, and the number is fixed at 5000 in the case of Ticino and 12,000 in the case of Berne.]

[3] In the canton of Neuchâtel every elector who signs a demand must do so in person, giving his Christian name, surname, address, age, and profession (Law of 19th November 1895 on the exercise of the right of initiative, Art. 2). In the canton of Vaud every demand to submit a proposition to the vote of the communal assemblies must be placed in the cantonal chancery before being sent round. Any signatures collected before this formality is complied with are null and void (Law of the 16th September 1885 on the exercise of political rights, Art. 66).

[In Basle-City, Ticino, Vaud, Aargau, and Geneva the person who signs must do so personally. Various penalties are imposed by these cantons if a man should sign for another or sign more than one sheet. In Vaud the offender is deprived of his political rights for two years. In Ticino he is deprived of his political rights altogether. In Zürich there is a fine of eighty francs.

A period is appointed in every case after which the signatures cease to be valid. In Zürich and Thurgau they are good for six months, in the Grisons and Neuchâtel for a year. In Aargau it

tion recognise both the individual and the collective initiative. A demand signed by a single elector is treated in the same manner as a demand signed by 5000, the moment it obtains the support of a third of the members of the cantonal council.[1]

II. The electors are entitled to make use of the initiative ·

(1) To propose a new law except in the half-canton of Rural-Basle.

(2) To demand the repeal or modification of a law in force, except in the canton of Schaffhausen. In the Grisons and St. Gall the revision of a law may not be demanded unless it has been in force

is forbidden to collect the signatures by going from house to house. The demand has to be given up to the mayor of the commune, and for a week he has to be present at a certain hour in case any one should wish to sign.

In Ticino, as soon as the demand has three signatures, it has to be given in to the state chancery, who publish it in the Gazette. The lists to be signed are placed in the communal chancery, and can be signed during the following week between nine and five, and also on Sunday. An official is there to witness the signatures. If signed in any other way, all signatures have to be witnessed by a notary or the president of the commune. See Stüssi, *op. cit.*, pp. 120–22.]

[1] [In 1893 it was proposed that if 500 citizens sign a demand for a law, the council should send it to the communal assemblies when the next periodical vote was taken. If the demand were then supported by 5000 people, it should be treated as a demand by 5000 citizens, and be considered by the council and treated as an ordinary initiative demand. It was not adopted. In Zürich the electors can meet together in a communal assembly and there and then state how many of them support the demand, instead of writing their names on the paper when it is brought round to them. In Zürich it is also open to any official body to make a demand by initiative, but such a demand requires the support of a third of the council. So that in Zürich the initiative is formally recognised as belonging to a single individual, a corporate body, and 5000 citizens.]

a certain time—two years in the Grisons and three years in St. Gall.

(3) To propose a decree or legislative resolution, except in the cantons of Schwyz, Aargau, and Schaffhausen.   By the terms of the Constitution of Rural-Basle decrees emanating from the popular initiative must be decrees of general import.   In the Grisons no initiative demand is valid which proposes the repeal of a decree which has been declared urgent by the Great Council.[1]

III. A demand by popular initiative may take two forms: it may either be a suggestion in general terms, or a bill or decree with all the details filled in.   This latter form is known as the "formulated initiative." The majority of the cantonal constitutions do not make this distinction.   They do not expressly exclude the formulated initiative, but they seem only to recognise the proposal in general terms (*die blose Anregung*). The only constitutions that formally mention the two are Zürich, Solothurn, St. Gall, and Geneva.[2]

---

[1] [In Thurgau the popular initiative can only be exercised on the subject of a new decree, not the alteration of one already in force ; and in Zürich, St. Gall, Geneva, and Ticino on all decrees which are not placed within the exclusive province of the Great Council by the constitution.]

[2] [Berne, Schaffhausen, the Grisons, Basle-City, and Ticino expressly recognise the two forms, bringing the number up to eight and a half.   In Neuchâtel it is doubtful whether the formulated initiative is recognised or not.   The phrase is, " *Droit de proposer au Grand Conseil l'adoption, l'élaboration . . . d'une loi ou d'un décret.*"   Aargau, Rural-Basle, and Schwyz do not admit the possibility of the formulated initiative.   The Constitution of Vaud directs that if the popular proposal be so drafted that the answer to it must be either Yes or No, then it is submitted to the people as it stands.   If it is more complicated, the Great Council drafts the alteration or new law required.]

The demand, whatever its form, must be addressed to the ordinary legislative assembly of the canton (Great Council or Cantonal Council).[1]   In the cantons of Zürich, Solothurn, Aargau, Zug, and Geneva, a statement as to the motives of the demand must be handed in at the same time as the demand itself.[2]

IV. To determine between the rights and duties of the Chamber when a demand for the popular initiative is backed by the requisite number of signatures, we must first distinguish between demands preferred in general terms and bills expounded in detail by their authors.

(*a*) *Demands in general terms.*—Three systems are in vogue.

(1) In the cantons of Schaffhausen and Thurgau the Great Council immediately drafts the bill required by those who sign the demand.[3]

(2) In Rural-Basle, in the Grisons, and in Vaud, the demand is at once submitted to the vote of the people, and they decide whether the Great Council shall consider the proposal or not.   If the majority of the electors decide against the proposal, it is simply dropped.   If, on the other hand, the people approve its tenor, the Great Council proceeds to draft the bill or resolution demanded.[4]

(3) In the other cantons the Great Council first of

---

[1] The demand is sometimes addressed to the government (Council of State), which then transmits it to the Chamber.

[2] [Also in St. Gall.]

[3] [In Ticino, also, the Council have to draft the law in the sense demanded, but it can make a counter-proposal.   In Schaffhausen, too, the Great Council has the same right.]

[4] [Also in Schwyz and St. Gall.]

all examines and discusses the demand.[1]   Then, if it approves it, it drafts the law.   If not, it submits the demand to the people, and they decide whether it shall be carried into effect or not.   If the answer be negative, the demand is laid aside; but if it is in the affirmative, the Great Council is bound to draw up the bill which it had previously declined to draft before consulting the people.

(b) *Demands made in the* '*form of bills already drafted.*—Where the formulated initiative exists, the bill drafted by a group of electors must remain intact.   The Chamber cannot alter it in any way.   It has merely the right of presenting a counter-proposal if it does not approve of the contents or the form of the popular proposal.[2]

It should be clearly understood that, whatever the form chosen by the electors, their demand is in reality a proposal made to the people.   The preliminary examination by the Great Council constitutes part of the machinery of the popular initiative at present, but this examination is by no means essential.   Even when the Chamber drafts the law itself, it merely

[1] In Zürich the author of a demand may come and defend his proposal in person before the cantonal council, if he obtain the support of a third of the deputies, or if twenty-five of them consent to his being present.

[2] [In Berne the Great Council is expressly commanded to state its views, be they favourable or unfavourable, with regard to the law, but has no right of presenting a counter-proposal.   The counter-proposal may take the form of a recommendation that the popular proposal be rejected, or may be merely an improved draft.

In Zurich, if the demand is made in the form of a bill, the council may decide by a resolution that the author may take part in the debate on the clauses of the bill.   The commission whose duty it is to consider the bill and report on it to the house can always summon the author to explain his meaning should it desire to do so.]

occupies the position of a drafting committee, and it could be replaced by any assembly of jurists. Again, when the popular proposal is already drafted, the Chamber is little more than a registration department. It receives and forwards to the people the written and printed documents addressed to them. The right given it by the constitution to present a counter-proposal is a privilege which is shared with others. Any new group of citizens, provided they are sufficiently numerous, can, in virtue of their right of initiative, draw up amendments to the proposals of the first group, and present them to the people at the same time.

V. As the initiative demand is essentially a proposal made by a certain number of electors to the whole body of active citizens, any proposal emanating from the popular initiative is necessarily submitted to the popular vote for acceptance or rejection. It is equally true of bills presented in their final shape as of those which are made in the form of general suggestions and which are drafted by the Great Council. It is also true of all the cantons, whether their form of referendum be compulsory or optional.[1]

As a result, every elector receives the text of the bill and also the text of the counter-proposal of the Chamber. In certain cantons the bill is accompanied by an explanatory message, which is a summary of the arguments given by the authors of the demand.[2]

[1] [In Neuchâtel, if the Great Council accept the proposal *purement et simplement*, it is treated as an ordinary law, and subject to the optional referendum.]

[2] [This is the case in Zürich and Solothurn. In Solothurn it is expressly stated that the arguments in favour of the law given by

If the Chamber presents a counter-proposal, it naturally has the right of attaching an explanation of its
own attitude.[1]

The popular initiative has not been made use of
frequently enough for us to criticise it by the light
of experience. It is interesting, however, to read
the views of M. Stüssi, a democrat of Zürich, who
comments on the result of the popular initiative.[2]
He considers that the actual organisation of the initiative is defective in two respects:

(1) " The author of a demand can only appeal

the initiants shall be sent round to every citizen at the expense of
the state.]

[1] [In Schaffhausen and Ticino the method of voting on the two
proposals is interesting.

In Ticino, if the demand is made as a complete bill, and the
council makes a counter-proposal, the two are voted on at the same
time. Then there is a second voting, at which the proposal that has
received the largest number of votes is submitted alone, the question
being, " Do you accept this proposal or not?" The alternative is
the *status quo.* In Schaffhausen the counter-proposal of the Great
Council is voted on first. If this is negatived, then the popular
proposal is submitted to the electorate.

In Zürich, Berne, Rural-Basle, Solothurn, the Grisons, City-Basle,
Ticino, Schaffhausen, Thurgau, Vaud, and Neuchâtel various time
limits are fixed during which the Great Council must discuss the
demand and resolve on its course. In Solothurn and Thurgau the
matter must be submitted to the people within two months, in
the Grisons within a year and a half. Other cantons fix periods
between these two. In Vaud the Great Council has to be summoned at once in extraordinary session.]

[2] [The results of the initiative in Zürich are interesting. The
right was introduced in 1869, and first made use of in 1871. Between 1871 and 1893 there were twenty-one demands by initiative.
The result has been summarised by Mr. Lowell. He points out that
the net result of twenty-four years of the initiative has been the
adoption of two laws of doubtful value. One of them established a
house of correction for tramps, and the other abolished compulsory
vaccination. See pp. 285–87.]

to the electors known to himself and his friends. In this narrow circle it is necessary to bring every influence to bear to collect the necessary signatures. Party interests are appealed to, personal persuasion is tried, friends are asked to prove their friendship, the case is pleaded before the ladies, and, as a last resort, they are asked to sign for their husbands or sons. People who refuse to sign are worried to such an extent that they sign for the sake of peace. As a rule, they hardly know the contents of the paper to which they affix their signature. Is *legislation by the people* worthy of the name, when the exercise of the right of initiative becomes the monopoly of such privileged persons as have the money, the leisure, or the taste for intrigue? Is there anything in it calculated to educate the people politically?"

(2) "The popular bill, if it be accepted by the electorate, becomes part of our code, without any modification or amendment being possible. This is an extraordinary proceeding when one thinks of it. When a department of the Council of State[1] sees fit to propose a law, it consults experts first of all; then the bill is prepared, after mature consideration, by competent men. It is sent to the Council of State, and goes through successive readings. Then the proposals of the Council of State are sent to a commission of the cantonal council, which can introduce amendments. A public discussion follows, in which the matter is thoroughly debated from different points of view in the cantonal council; and, finally, a special committee revises the bill for the last time, and cor-

[1] A ministerial department.

rects faults or obscurities in the draft. None of these precautions are taken when a bill is brought forward by the popular initiative. It is impossible that a few individuals unfamiliar with legislation and administration can succeed at once in drawing up a satisfactory law. Perhaps it might be said, 'If this is true, the remedy is to abolish the formulated initiative and restrict the right of the people to presenting general propositions.' I do not consider that this would be advisable. A mere proposal does not deserve the honour of a popular vote.

"The individual who wishes to be a legislator ought to know exactly what he wants, and also the form in which his ideas ought to be embodied—how they fit in with the system of laws already in force, and what changes would be produced were his proposal adopted. It is quite ridiculous to call upon the people to vote on a vague formula whose significance and scope there is no means of ascertaining."

After having thus criticised the actual system, M. Stüssi mentions with approval a scheme drawn up by the Grütliverein of Zürich several years ago bearing on the exercise of the popular initiative. The following are the main outlines of the scheme:—

"When a citizen shall make a proposal to the cantonal council, the proposition shall be immediately published in the *Feuille officielle*, with an invitation to all the electors to make amendments and communicate them to the office of the cantonal council within a month. The author of the demand shall be informed as to the amendments sent in.

"A special commission of the cantonal council

shall discuss the amendments within two months, with the assistance of the author of the demand.

"An additional two months shall be granted to the author to allow him to decide whether he will still maintain his proposition, either in its original or amended form; and if he shall decide to do so, he shall send it to the cantonal council, accompanied by a statement as to the motives which actuated him.

"The proposal shall be discussed at latest in the second ordinary session of the council held after the demand has been received.

"If the proposal is supported by one-third of the members of the cantonal council, the author has the right to demand that it should be submitted to the people on the occasion of the next popular vote.[1]

"If 5000 electors support it, it shall be submitted to a second vote for definite acceptance."

When the proposal was brought forward it was attacked with so much bitterness that the authors did not even succeed in obtaining the 5000 signatures required by the Constitution of Zürich to enable them to submit it by initiative demand to the people.

---

[1] "All the difficulties of the existing system with regard to the collection of the 5000 signatures are got rid of by this preliminary plebiscite," says M. Stüssi. "In the proposal of the Grütliverein the proposal of one elector is brought before all the citizens, its supporters have time to think, and are not forced to declare themselves. All the measures now taken against false signatures would become useless, as obviously only electors could vote for or against the bill."

CHAPTER III

THE RESULTS

IN the first chapter we summed up the arguments which were formerly adduced both for and against the introduction of the referendum. We described the fears of its opposers and the hopes of its supporters. Now that the referendum has been in force a certain number of years, we should like to know how far the apprehensions of the one or the confidence of the other were exaggerated, and whether the future has justified those who fought against legislation by the people or those who guided it to victory. These questions are, however, so difficult and complicated that I cannot pretend to give any decided answer one way or the other. To give a scientific judgment on the results of the referendum, it would be necessary to have an intimate knowledge of the history of twenty different states, their traditions, their needs, the character of the inhabitants, the impressionable nature of the electors generally, the organisation of parties, the action of the press, the influence of the authorities, the contents and defects of the laws which have been submitted to the people, and the circumstances which called them forth. Such historical, psychological, social, administrative, and judicial studies are an indispensable preliminary to a true estimate of the referendum; but where is the man who has made them? In

my opinion, those democratic fanatics who blindly
do obeisance to "His Majesty the Popular Will"
as no courtier ever bowed down before an oriental
potentate, only make themselves ridiculous. Neither
do I sympathise with those who condemn democratic institutions without examination, or after a
merely superficial one. It is, however, doubtful
whether the time has arrived for us definitely to
pronounce judgment. Switzerland has only just
begun her experience of direct legislation. We must
leave her at present to experiment, to develop and
perfect her institutions, which are rudimentary and
incomplete as yet. We must give the masses time
to become familiar with the new machinery of government. Some time must still elapse before we can
actually approve or condemn the system.

In writing these chapters on the results of the
referendum, my sole aim is to furnish some data for
criticism, which are, to my regret, only too incomplete. With this end in view, I propose to describe,
first of all, the principal legislative votes which have
taken place in the Confederation and in the cantons,
and then I shall quote some of the most interesting
criticisms of the Swiss themselves on the referendum.
Now and again it will be necessary to comment on
certain laws and the results of votes, and where this
is done, it is always based on information obtained
from good authorities. Exaggeration in these questions is, however, easy, for almost everything is relative, and therefore, in spite of all precautions, it is
quite possible that my views may be erroneous and
inexact. If this is so, I am ready to correct them,
and shall thank those beforehand who will have the
kindness to set me right.

TABLE OF THE VOTES ON FEDERAL LAWS SINCE THE FEDERAL CONSTITUTION OF 1874 CAME INTO FORCE.

Laws and ...	Date of Voting.	No. of Signatures demanding the Referendum.	Result of the Voting — Passed by	Result of the Voting — Rejected by	
1. Federal law on marriage and registry	My 23, 1875.	1. 106,560	209	205,069	A.
2. Federal law on the ... use of the Swiss citizens	pril 23, 1876.	2. 108,674	202,583	207,263	R.
3. Federal law on the issue and convertibility of bank notes		3. 35,886	120,068	193,233	R.
4. Federal law on the tax on exemption from military service	Ju y 9, 1876.	4. 80,549	156,157	184,894	R.
5. Federal law on labour in factories		5. 54,844	181,204	170,857	A.
6. Federal law on the taxation from military service	Oc 21 1877.	6. 63,300	170,223	181,383	R.
7. Federal law on the political rights of the Swiss		7. 40,207	131,557	213,230	R.
8. Federal law granting subsidies to Alpine railways	Jan. 19, 1879.	8. 37,805	278,731	115,571	A.
9. Revision of Art. 65 o the Federal Constitution (death penalty)	May 18, 1879.	9. Compu sry.	200,485 / 15 cant.	181,588 / 7 can cat.	A.
10. ... for the revision of Art. 39 of the Federal Constitution (bank notes)	O. 31, 1880.	10. 52,588	121,099 / 4½ ans.	260,126 / 17½ ans.	R.

TABLE OF THE VOTES ON FEDERAL LAWS—*continued.*

Laws and Orders submitted.	Date of Voting.	No. of Signatures demanding the Referendum.	Result of the Voting.		
			Accepted by	Rejected by	
11. Revision of the Federal Constitution (patents) . . .	July 30, 1882.	11. Compulsory.	141,616 7½ cantons.	156,658 14½ cantons.	R.
12. Federal law concerning measures to be taken against epidemics .		12. 8,320	68,027	254,340	R.
13. Federal resolution appointing a Federal Secretary of Education .	Nov. 26, 1882.	13. 180,993	172,010	318,139	R.
14. Federal law concerning the organisation of the Department of Justice and Police . .		14.	149,729	214,916	R.
15. Federal law concerning the tax and licence on commercial travellers . . .		15.	174,195	189,550	R.
16. Federal law concerning the introduction of an article into the penal code . . .	May 11, 1884.	16. 93,046	159,068	202,773	R.
17. Federal resolution appropriating 10,000 francs for the legation at Washington . .		17.	137,824	219,728	R.
18. Partial revision of the Federal Constitution on the manufacture and sale of spirituous liquors . .	Oct. 25, 1885.	18. Compulsory.	230,250 15 cantons.	157,463 7 cantons.	A.
19. Federal law concerning alcohol.	May 15, 1887.	19. 52,412	267,122	138,496	A.
20. Revision of Art. 64 of the Federal Constitution (protection of inventions) . .	July 10, 1887.	20. Compulsory.	203,506 20½ cantons.	57,862 1½ canton.	A.

TABLE OF THE VOTES ON FEDERAL LAWS—*continued.*

Laws and Orders	Date of Voting	No. of Signatures demanding the Referendum	Result of the voting — Accepted by	Rejected by	
21. Federal law on the procedure to be followed in ...es of ...bt and bankruptcy	Nov. 17, 1889.	62,948	244,317	217,921	A.
22. ...al revision of Federal Ch-...n on insurance against sickness and ...ts	Oct. 26, 1890.	1	283,228 / 20½ ...s.	92,200 / 1½ ...s.	A.
23. ...al law on ...ens for federal ...s	March 15, 98.	84,572	91,851	353,977	R.
24. Partial revision o the Federal ...(popular initiative)	July 5, 98.	...ny.	181,883 / 18 ...s.	19,372 / 4 ...s.	A.
25. Revision of ...t. 39 of the ...(monopoly of ...)	Oct. 18, 1891.	Compulsory.	228,286 / 14 ...s.	159,268 / 8 ...s.	A.
26. Law on ...e ...iff and customs		51,564	220,004	158,934	A.
27. Federal resolution concerning the ...e of shares of the Central Railway ...y	Dec. 6, 98.	91,698	130,507	288,956	R.
28. Initiative demand concerning the ...e of slaughtering ...ls	Aug. 20, 1893.	83,159	191,527 / 11½ ...s.	127,101 / 10½ ...n.	A.
29. ...t to the Federal ...stitution concerning the right of legislating for ...s	Mch 4, 1894.	1	135,713 / 8½ ...s.	158,492 / 13½ ...s.	R.
30. Initiative demand ...n the right to have adequate y ...d work ...l	June 3, 94.	52,387	...0 ...	308,289 / 22 ...s.	R.

O

Laws and Bills submitted.	Date of Voting.	No. of Signatures demanding the Referendum.	Accepted by	Rejected by	
31. Initiative on the disposal of the surplus from the customs	Nov. 4, 1894.	67,828	145,462 / 8½ cantons.	350,639 / 13½ cantons.	R.
32. Representation of Switzerland in foreign countries	Feb. 3, 1895.	37,040	124,517	177,991	R.
33. Revision of art. of the Federal Constitution (monopoly of match manufacture)	Sept. 29, 1895.	Compulsory.	19,174 / 7½ cantons.	184,109 / 14½ cantons.	R.
34. The revision of the military articles of the Constitution	Nov. 3, 1895.	Compulsory.	195,178 / 4½ cantons.	269,751 / 17½ cantons.	R.
35. The federal law on discipline in the federal army	Oct. 4, 1896.	69,386	77,162	310,938	R.
36. Law regulating the guarantees to be given in case of the sale of cattle		45,982	174,860	0 ,918	R.
37. Law on the accounts of the railways	Feb. 28, 1897.	,596	223,228	176,574	A.
38. The law establishing a state bank		79,123	195,764	255,984	R.
39. Revision of art. 24 of the Federal Constitution relating to forests		Compulsory.	19,102 / 15 cant. B.	8,961 / 7 cantons.	A.
40. Federal amendment on the question of the purity of edible commodities	July 11, 1897.	Compulsory.	162,250 / 18½ cantons.	86,955 / 3½ cantons.	A.
41. Law authorising the purchase of the railways by the state	Feb. 20, 1898.	85,505	386,634	182,718	A.

(It is a fact worth noticing that no law has ever been *accepted* by majority of the electors.)

I. *The Principal Votings on Federal and Cantonal Laws.*

The foregoing table gives the title of the federal laws which have been submitted to the people, the date of the vote, the number of signatures collected for the referendum demand, and the result of the poll. Between 1874 and 1891 the Federal Assembly has passed about one hundred and fifty laws and resolutions of universal application. Most of these legislative decrees have come into force with the tacit consent of the people; nineteen have, however, been submitted to the referendum on the demand of larger or smaller groups of electors. Out of this number thirteen have been rejected and six accepted.

Besides these legislative referendums, there have been eight compulsory votings on partial revisions of the constitutions, so that the people have pronounced on twenty-seven laws in all.[1]

Before a referendum can take place 30,000 signatures must be collected. The reader will see, on consulting the third column of the list, that the

[1] [The figures up to February 1898 are as follows :—There have been two hundred and eight laws which might have been voted on; twenty-six have been submitted to the people upon demand, of which seventeen have been rejected and nine accepted. There have been thirteen compulsory votings, by which five of the laws were rejected and eight accepted. In addition to these there have been three compulsory votings on initiative demands ; one of the proposals was accepted and two were rejected. The people have, therefore, decided the fate of forty-two laws altogether. Between 1892 and February 1898 there have been fourteen votings and five laws accepted.—*Referendums Tafel.*]

number of signatures is no certain indication of the result of the vote. Some laws have been accepted when there has been an immense petition against them; others have been rejected when the number of signatures demanding the referendum has been inconsiderable. The fourth and fifth columns contain the numbers of the electors who have respectively accepted and rejected the laws. The total number of citizens who have taken part in each vote will be obtained by adding the Ayes and Noes together. In comparing this number with that of the registered electors, which is now about 650,000,[1] it will be seen that there is a considerable discrepancy. It would seem that scarcely half the electors go to the polls.

According to the statistics published in 1879 by M.Chatelanat, 61 per cent. of the electors on an average took part in the federal vote during the first five years after the referendum came into force. It will be seen that the percentage of those who stay away has not grown much less since that time.[2]

---

[1] [According to the statistics given in the *Statistisches Jahrbuch der Schweiz* for 1896, the registered electors number 709,788, and are divided as follows : Zürich, 92,783 ; Berne, 120,673 ; Lucerne, 34,034 ; Uri, 4495 ; Schwyz, 12,891 ; Obwald, 3824 ; Nidwald, 2877 ; Glarus, 8323 ; Zug, 6207 ; Fribourg, 29,882 ; Solothurn, 21,800 ; Basle-City, 15,407 ; Rural-Basle, 13,272 ; Schaffhausen, 7993 ; Appenzell (Outer Rhodes), 12,214 ; Appenzell (Inner Rhodes), 3005 ; St. Gall, 51,695 ; Grisons, 22,599 ; Aargau, 43,145 ; Thurgau, 24,243 ; Ticino, 37,792 ; Vaud, 64,000 ; Valais, 27,744 ; Neuchâtel, 27,256 ; Geneva, 21,634.]

[2] According to the statistics given in the *Statistisches Jahrbuch*, 1896, it will be seen that between 1879 and 1891 the average number who went to the polls was 58.5 per cent., and that between 1891 and 1895 it has fallen to 53.9. In the case of the initiative demand with regard to the disposal of the surplus from the custom duties, the percentage rose as high as 71.9 per cent. It fell as low

M. Chatelanat also remarked that the chief oppositiou always came from the same cantons. This
conclusion, arrived at in 1879, has remained true
for subsequent votes. The states which exhibit the
most striking tendency to reject laws are: Appenzell
(Inner Rhodes), Uri, Valais, Fribourg, Unterwalden.
Then follow Vaud, Schwyz, Lucerne, and Zug. On
the other hand, Schaffhausen, Zürich, Basle, Thurgau, and Glarus are the most inclined to vote
" Yes."[1]

It is important that the reader should notice this,
in order that he may not attach an exaggerated importance to the reasons which may seem to have contributed to the rejection of any particular law. It is
clear that the leaders of the opposition will not invoke
the referendum against laws which are irreproachable
in tenor, because they themselves will lose in the
end both in reputation and prestige. It is, however,
none the less true that a law which is merely unob-
jectionable, or does not rise above the level of medio-
crity, will be judged more or less severely according
as it comes before electors who share or oppose
the political opinions of the parliamentary majority.
The majority of the Federal Assembly is composed
of Germans, Centralists, and Free-thinkers. It is not
astonishing that a prejudice against federal laws
should exist among those groups in the nation who
are opposed to one or other of the three characteristics of the majority; nor is it surprising that the

as 43.5 per cent. in the case of the constitutional amendment on
small industries. In the three votes in October 1896, 56.3 per cent.
took part.]

[1] [The figures of the voting of October 1896, given in the *Statistisches Jahrbuch* for 1896, still bear this out (p. 295).]

Romance cantons, which dread the excessive influence of the great German cantons, should oppose any new encroachment by the Confederation, or that the Catholic cantons, which were the victims of a factious coalition in 1874, should take their revenge when they find an opportunity, or that the inhabitants of the small primitive cantons, who retain an excessive love of independence, should show a dislike to innovations which attack their secular institutions, and object to laws which restrict their liberties, disturb their habits, and make life more complicated.' To estimate the real influence of these prejudices, which are always at work in the different groups in different parts of the country, and to attempt to fathom the exact degree to which these three or four hundred thousand minds have been affected by *a priori* argument, is an impossible task. The reader should, however, never lose sight of the fact that the imperfections of the laws we are going to examine have not been the only factor in determining their fate at the hands of the people.

The first law which had to face the popular vote after the introduction of the federal referendum was *a law on marriage and the civil rite*, of the 24th of December 1874. By the terms of this law, " the civil rite and the custody of the registers which refer to it are a matter for the civil authorities throughout the whole territory of the Confederation. The officers who perform the civil rite must be laymen, and are the only persons competent to make entries of the civil rite in the registers" (Art. 1). Before 1874 the registers were kept by the clergy in the majority of the cantons.

"No conditions in restraint of marriage may be imposed founded on differences of creed or the poverty of one or other of the parties" (Art. 25). Before this, the Church on one side, and the cantonal and communal authorities on the other, restricted the right of marriage—the Church prohibiting mixed marriages, the communes the marriage of paupers, with the aim of preventing the propagation of pauper families whom they would have to support.

"A religious ceremony cannot take place until after the legal celebration of marriage by the civil official, and upon the presentation of the certificate of marriage" (Art. 40). "A fine not exceeding 300 francs shall be imposed upon all clerics who act contrary to the dispositions of Article 40. In the case of a second offence the fine is doubled."

In paragraph 5, after enumerating a certain number of reasons which form sufficient grounds for a divorce, the law continues: "If none of these grounds for divorce exist, and nevertheless the circumstances are such that the conjugal relations are severely strained, the court may give judgment for either a divorce or a separation." "A separation cannot be effected for longer than two years. If no reconciliation takes place between husband and wife during that time, a divorce may again be sued for, and the court may then freely give judgment according to its convictions" (Art. 47).

This law was the inauguration of the policy of centralisation and secularisation which was foreshadowed in the Federal Constitution of 1874. It encountered a great deal of opposition in Parliament, especially the clauses relating to marriage and divorce. When it was finally passed, 106,560 electors, Catholics and conservative Protestants, signed a demand for a refereudum. The opposition were defeated in their campaign, and the law was accepted by the people by a small majority. The Catholic writers regard this first law as one of the most mischievous results of the referendum. "The effect of this unfortunate law," says M. Ernst, "has been to confer upon Switzerland the doubtful honour of heading the European divorce statistics." [1]

M. Ernest Naville, an eminent Protestant, whose labours in philosophy reflect lustre on his country, is also among those who deplore the result of this first popular vote. He explains the favourable majority as follows: "We have in Switzerland a law on marriage and divorce which has an injurious effect on family life, and this law has been ratified by a plebiseite. At the same time it is probable that if it had been submitted alone to the popular vote, it would have been rejected. To think otherwise would be to do the Swiss people an injustice. The fact was that the proposals with regard to marriage and divorce were contained in the same law as other clauses relating to the civil ceremony for which the need was obvious. It was necessary, however, to adopt or reject the whole, and it is my firm conviction that a great many citizens who voted Yes for the law as it stood did so reluctantly, and would have voted No

---

[1] Ernst, *Die Volksrechte im Eidgenössischen Bunde*, in the *Monat Rosen*, 1883-84, p. 399. "It is only fair to say," wrote a Protestant pastor, "that in the Catholic cantons the percentage of divorce is smaller than in the Protestant states. This fact is easily understood by any one who knows the nature of the Catholic creed" (Marsauche, *Confédération Helvétique*, Paris, 1891, p. 205).

on the question of marriage if it had been submitted
separately."[1]

On the same day that the people accepted the law
on marriage they rejected a law relating to the *right
of the Swiss citizens to the franchise.* Before 1874
the cantons were sovereign in this matter, and each
of them determined the grounds on which its citizens might be deprived of their political rights. The
result was a great diversity in the laws, especially in
the matter of the franchise of bankrupts and paupers.
These two classes of citizens were treated much more
favourably in the Romance cantons than in the German cantons. The new Constitution of 1874 authorised the Chambers to reduce the laws on the franchise
to uniformity. Accordingly they at once proceeded
to draft an electoral law. This law was rejected by
the people on the 23rd of May 1875. It was presented again at a later date, and this time was not
only rejected, but rejected by a much larger majority,
This repeated refusal has left the cantons in enjoyment of their ancient independence, and the franchise
is still regulated by each canton according to its own
will and pleasure.

It would be somewhat difficult to say why the
people pronounced against the law of the 18th of
September 1875 on the issue and repayment of
bank notes. I asked a member of the National
Council about it, and he told me that the experts
did not agree. Some wished that the issue should
be absolutely unrestricted, others wished for a mono-

---

[1] E. Naville, *À propos du Referendum* in the *Représentation proportionnelle,* vi. p. 58, Brussels, 1887.

poly. The bulk of the electors, however, had no
opinion one way or the other. They were in the
same position as the Ephesians mentioned in the
19th chapter of the Acts of the Apostles, " The
assembly was confused ; and the more part knew not
wherefore they were come together." A new law on
the subject which placed the banks of issue under
the control of the Confederation came into force in
1881, and it does not seem to have occurred to any
one to demand a referendum on this occasion. A
short time before, on the 31st of October 1880,
the people had pronounced against the demand for
a constitutional revision the aim of which was to
create a monopoly of issuing bank notes in favour
of the Confederation. The proposal was started by
means of the popular initiative, but was rejected
finally by the enormous majority of 139,027 votes.
Ten years later, on the 18th of October 1891, the
question came before the people again, and this time
they gave a quite different verdict, for by 228,286
votes to 150,268 they bestowed the monopoly of
bank notes on the Confederation.[1]

The two federal laws on the subject of *the tax
on exemption from military service* of the 23rd of
December 1875 and the 27th of March 1877 imposed

---

[1] The question now is whether the monopoly shall be given to
a state bank, or whether it shall be exercised by a national bank
created by the issue of shares and having an independent administration. The new constitutional provision leaves the way open for
either to be established. In whatever way the matter is finally
settled there will be another demand for the referendum. [The
proposal took the form of a state bank, and the law was voted
down in February 1897.]

an annual tax on every Swiss citizen capable of bearing arms who did not personally perform his military service. The tax was graduated according to the income of those liable. In estimating the income of the person exempted, the fortune he would inherit from his parents or other relatives was taken into account. It had always been possible for the cantons to levy this tax, but only some of them had done so. The federal law therefore appeared in the disagreeable light of a fiscal law imposing a new tax on a large number of citizens. A third edition of the law (28th June 1878) at last escaped the referendum. " It seems to me," wrote M. Naville, " that this result was due not so much to the modifications introduced into the original bill as to the indifference of the people, who felt that the matter must be settled." [1]

By this law every Swiss who, from any reason, fails to perform his service is obliged to pay an annual tax. This tax comprises, firstly, a capitation tax of six francs ; and secondly, a further tax of one franc fifty centimes for every thousand francs of capital or every one hundred francs of income. This graduated tax is paid until the person liable reaches the age of thirty-two. Between thirty-two and forty-four the amounts are reduced by one-half.[2]

The votes of the 21st of October 1877 and the 19th of January 1879 are two which are worth recording. By the first the people accepted *the law regulating labour in factories*—an excellent law, which

[1] An attempt was made, chiefly in Geneva, to get up a petition for a referendum, but only 5513 signatures were obtained.

[2] The military tax yielded 2,670,000 francs in 1886, and 2,470,000 francs in 1887. The receipts from this source are divided equally between the Confederation and the cantons.

triumphed in spite of the opposition in the industrial centres.[1] By the second the federal law
granting subsidies to the Alpine railways was also
accepted.[2]

The Swiss people had already proved their hostility
to the Federal Constitution and to centralisation
several times, but they had only been able to express
it by negative votes. They could only vote down the
laws prepared by the Chambers in virtue of the
powers given them by the constitution. By the
referendum of the 4th of April 1879 they were able
to assert their attachment to cantonal independence
in a positive manner by restoring to the cantons the
right to inflict capital punishment, which had been
entirely abolished by Article 65 of the Federal Constitution of 1874. Whether rightly or wrongly, the
abolition of capital punishment was said to have
caused a fresh outbreak of crime. A popular agitation was organised, and a deputy of the Council of
States proposed that Article 65 should be revised.
The Assembly were afraid of seeing the demand for
a revision supported by 50,000 signatures, and afterwards approved by the majority of the people, the
result of which would have been the re-election of
the two Chambers. They therefore yielded to the
popular outcry and passed the amendment. A great
many members who voted for it hoped nevertheless
that the people would reject it. But the people dis-

---

[1] [See Lowell, "The Referendum in relation to Labour," in *The
International Journal of Ethics*, vol. vi. ; also *Governments and Parties
in Continental Europe*, vol. ii. pp. 265–69].

[2] Of the 37,803 electors who signed the demand against this law,
32,308 belonged to the canton of Vaud.

appointed them. The revision was ratified by fifteen cantons to seven, and by 200,485 votes to 181,588. As a result of this vote the cantons are now free to re-establish the death penalty for crimes at common law. Many have already done so, but the penalty has in no case been exacted as yet.[1]

During the period between 1881 and 1884 not a single law submitted to the referendum found favour with the people. The Federal Assembly gave great dissatisfaction to the Conservative minority by passing a law, towards the end of the year 1881, which was intended to increase the Radical majority in the National Council. Ticino was divided into two electoral districts, one of which contained five Conservative subdivisions and the other two. The latter district was carved out in such a way as to make it possible for Radicals to be returned. They also created a new district in the canton of Fribourg, with a purely fancy boundary, in order to still further increase their party in the Chamber by the addition of two Radicals from that canton.[2] When the minority demanded that the Bernese Jura, Aargau, Neuchâtel, and Geneva should be similarly divided, their demand was refused, for in those cases the minority might possibly have won some seats. The injustice of these proceedings

---

[1] In the canton of Lucerne two death sentences have been commuted to imprisonment for life—the one in 1885, the other in 1890. [The other cantons which have re-introduced capital punishment are Uri, Schwyz, Obwald, Zug, Appenzell (Inner Rhodes), St. Gall, and Valais.]

[2] The Radicals of Ticino have succeeded in holding their own in the constituency which was constructed to suit them, but those of Fribourg lost their seats in the second election of 1884.

made the opposition furious, and they decided to avail themselves of every opportunity of retaliation. The referendum was the natural means at hand, and they made use of it several times, and always with success. ·

Two measures were submitted to the people on the 30th of July 1882. The first was *a law respecting the measures to be taken for the prevention of epidemics,* and the other *a federal decree on patents.*

The law on epidemics was rejected by the immense majority of 254,340 votes to 68,027. Vaccination was made compulsory, and the most stringent regulations were laid down to ensure .isolation in case of illness. These were the principal reasons which caused the law to be rejected. The feeling against the law was so irresistible that the federal resolution on patents was involved in the ruin. Had it been presented by itself it would probably have been accepted. It was laid before the people again on the 10th of July 1887, and received 203,506 affirmative and 57,862 negative votes, and a majority in 20½ cantons to 1½. Nor was the law on epidemics given up. Compulsory vaccination was dropped, and being thus modified, the law came into force on the 1st of January 1887, without a referendum being even demanded.

Of all the popular votes which have taken place since the introduction of the federal referendum, that of the 26th of November 1882 is unquestionably the most notable, both from the importance of the question voted on and from the large number of electors who went to the polls. The people were called upon to approve a federal decree passed by the Chambers in pursuance of the terms of Article 27 of the Constitution. By that article, "the cantóns shall make provision for elementary education, which must be adequate, and placed exclusively under the direction of the civil authority. Such instruction shall be obligatory, and in the public schools free of charge. The public schools must be so organised that they may be frequented by those belonging to all denominations without prejudice to their freedom of belief or of conscience. The Confederation shall take such measures as may seem necessary against cantons who do not fulfil their obligations in this matter."

Since 1874 no steps have been taken to enable the Confederation to exercise its right of control over elementary education. The entire organisation, administration, and supervision of the public schools were left to the cantonal councils, and the provisions of Article 27 as to non-sectarian teaching were nowhere observed. In deference to the wishes of their citizens, the state had continued religious teaching within the schools, and in a great many of the communes of the Catholic cantons the teachers were members of recognised religious associations.

Such a state of things seemed intolerable to the Radical majority in the Federal Assembly. They envied the laurels gained by Liberalism in other countries, and, doubtless in obedience to cosmopolitan Freemasonry, they resolved to make education the field for religious warfare. To start the campaign, they voted an inquiry into the methods of teaching in the Swiss cantons by a resolution framed as follows:—

"Art. 1. The Federal Council are asked to make immediate inquiry, through the Department of the Interior, into the condition of the schools in the cantons, and to make the necessary investigations in order to ensure that Article 27 be fully carried out, and to collect evidence which may form the basis of future legislation on the subject.

"Art. 2. To enable the State Department to perform its task, a special Secretary is to be appointed (Secretary of Public Instruction), whose annual salary shall be 6000 francs (£240). His powers shall be determined by a special order of the Federal Council.

The proposed inquiry was bound to reveal that Article 27 had been disregarded in many places, and the immediate result was bound to be a new law on elementary education.

The lines upon which this law would be framed was clearly indicated by a federal councillor when called upon for an explanation from the platform. Elementary education would be made either non-sectarian or secular. The staff would be laymen, the subjects secular, the methods secular, the school-houses secular. Education would be secular down to the most minute details, even in the purely Catholic communes.

The publication of the federal resolution was the signal for a general outcry in protest. "God in the schools" was the motto adopted by Catholics and orthodox Protestants throughout the whole of Switzerland. A vast petition was organised within a short time, to which 180,995 signatures were appended. No demand for a referendum had ever been so strongly supported before. It is easy to imagine the energy with which the campaign was conducted up to the day of voting. The authors and partisans of the resolution used every means in their power to ensure success. They raised a bogus cry against Catholicism, denounced the danger of clericalism, and, as a supreme argument, represented the Jesuits as waiting to enter the country. It was all in vain. The common-sense of the country asserted itself, and could not be exploited as in 1874. All these intrigues were estimated at their real worth, and on the 26th of November the federal resolution was rejected by 318,139 votes to 172,010.

Catholics, Federalists, orthodox Protestants, and religious people generally, united to vote "No." The minority was composed of German Radicals, Freethinkers, and Socialists. The referendum on this occasion did good service for Switzerland. It checked the advance of anti-religious Radicalism at the very first step, and saved the country from the educational struggle and its deplorable consequences.

The following year the referendum was claimed on no less than four laws which had been passed in December 1883. They were :—

(1) A law organising the Federal Department of Justice and Police.

(2) A federal resolution on licences to commercial travellers. This resolution enabled Swiss travellers to take orders on samples without special licence, an immunity which foreign travellers already enjoyed by means of treaties.

(3) A federal resolution granting a subsidy of 10,000 francs to the Swiss Legation at Washington for the expenses of its secretariat.

(4) The law of the 19th of December 1883 which

contained an addition to the federal penal code, framed as follows:—

"When the independence or impartiality of the cantonal tribunals are likely to suffer in consequence of political agitation, the Federal Council may remove a criminal case from the cantonal jurisdiction to the federal tribunal, which shall hear and determine the case."

This last law was the only one which gave rise to serious complaint. Its object was to make an exception in favour of the Radicals of Ticino, who had been the cause of the disturbances in Stabio, and thereby to remove these voters from the jurisdiction of the courts of Ticino. Many of the electors, and especially the Federalists, disliked the idea of placing the honour and reputation of the cantonal tribunals at the mercy of the political authorities. The other measures were indeed subjected to a searching criticism.[1] Although in ordinary times they would certainly have been accepted, and no one, as a matter of fact, would ever have thought of a referendum.[2] But the majority in Parliament had been carrying matters with a high hand, and had alienated the sympathies of a considerable number of electors. The people therefore rejected all four laws by large majorities without making any distinction. It is a question whether the laws were really unpopular, but the people dis-

---

[1] For instance, the law dealing with the legal system was characterised as an attempt to start a costly and superfluous bureaucratic institution by creating a special department for justice and legislation. Again, the decree relating to the Washington Embassy was said to involve the country in useless expenditure, &c.

[2] [The law on commercial travellers came into force in January 1893 without a referendum being demanded.]

liked the general policy of the government, and took this means of showing their discontent.

The general elections for the National Council took place in the following October. It would be only natural to expect that the people, who had so energetically disclaimed the policy of the majority of the Federal Assembly, would disavow their representatives as they had their politics, and would confide the power to other hands when they had the chance. But nothing of the sort happened, and a Radical majority almost as large as that of 1881 was returned to the National Council. The people may perhaps have thought that the lesson of the 11th of May was sufficient, and that it would produce the desired result. It is impossible to say what the reason was, but this is by no means the only case in which the Swiss electorate have rejected Radical laws and, to the general astonishment, have nevertheless soon afterwards re-elected the very deputies who passed these laws.[1]

I have made many inquiries among political men in Switzerland in order to solve the enigma. I was told by one that when the elector is confronted with the text of a law, he does not think of the legislator who is behind it, but concentrates his attention on the law itself. When he has a ballot-paper before him, then he will vote according to his personal preferences and sympathies, and, in considering the good or bad qualities of the man, he forgets all about the legislator and his past history. " It would be very foolish for us to excite ourselves about elections as you do in Belgium," said another. " It makes no great

[1] [See also the last elections in October 1896, in Preface.]

difference to electors who are not fanatics whether
Mr. X. or Mr. Y. is seated on the parliamentary bench,
as long as the Chambers can take no important decision against the will of the people, and as long as
we have the referendum by which we can reject the
laws we do not like.   It is really of no matter to us
whether the Chamber is composed of this or that
party, for it does not govern us.   We ourselves are
the sovereigns of the country."

The supporters of proportional representation and
the men who have dabbled in electoral intrigue
generally attribute the difference between the result
of the referendum votes and the result of the elections to the gerrymandering of the constituencies,
which are always created on party lines.

"All these explanations," an old journalist told me
one day, "do not satisfy me at all.   I am utterly
at a loss when I think of the contradictions of the
electoral body.   If a fortune could be made at my
profession in Switzerland I would start a competition, and offer a prize to the man who should give
the most complete and satisfactory answer to that
question."

To us it appears quite as remarkable that a legislative assembly should be able to remain in power
after having received such a stinging rebuff from the
electors.   It is certain that, in a country with a
parliamentary system, a popular vote similar to
that of 11th May would have brought about the
dissolution of the Chambers within forty-eight hours.
In Switzerland the disagreement between electors
and elected does not produce such serious results.
"To submit to the sovereign and to obey him seems

to us more democratic than to resign," was the reply of a venerable National Councillor in answer to my queries. Then he added: "A party does not willingly give place to its adversaries, because it generally finds it to its own advantage to remain in power."

The popular vote which took place on the 28th of November 1885 was compulsory. It was an amendment of the Federal Constitution, the object of which was to invest the state with the monopoly of the manufacture and sale of distilled spirits. The revision was energetically opposed by the interested parties—a not very attractive company of schnaps drinkers, alcohol merchants, potato growers, and distillers. The Socialists also ranged themselves on the side of the opposition, saying that the government was going to raise the price of "the poor man's schnaps," and that it would be better to tax the wine and fine liqueurs of the well-to-do. Their argument was based on a false assumption, for the fine liqueurs and the wine had to pay the new duty according to the amount of alcohol they contained. The financial question was, however, a secondary matter compared with the great social importance of the revision, the aim of which was to mitigate the evils of alcoholism.

The revision was approved by the people and by the majority of the cantons, but *the law on spirituous liquors*, which was drafted soon after, again encountered the same opposition. A demand for the referendum was signed by 52,412 electors, the signatures including 18,000 schnaps merchants of Berne and 5000 absinthe dealers of Neuchâtel. At the referendum, however, the law was accepted by 267,122 votes to 138,496.[1]

The federal law on the procedure in cases of debt and bankruptcy is one of the most complicated that the Assembly has been obliged to draft in pursuance of the Constitution of 1874. During fifteen years this law remained under discussion, undergoing many transformations in the Chambers, and being consider-ably modified in parts by special commissions. It was no slight task to reduce the law to uniformity on so important a subject, especially when it had hitherto been regulated by the legislatures of twenty-five cantons on different and sometimes very divergent principles. The jurists say that the authors of the law, of whom M. Ruchonnet was one, have been entirely successful in their delicate and difficult task. In spite of its merits the law did not escape the referendum, which was demanded out of hostility to the parliamentary majority rather than from any rooted objection to the law. The Conservatives felt aggrieved at the interference of the federal authorities in Ticino on behalf of the Radicals in the canton. The majority were also accused of having given a biassed judgment in an appeal on an education question.[2]

---

[1] Before the law came into force the distilleries in Switzerland amounted to several thousand. They were for the most part small concerns with one still, and were frequented by the villagers.— Adams and Cunningham, *The Swiss Confederation*, p. 238.

[2] The case was an appeal from a commune in the canton of St. Gall. In this canton the schools were separated according to sects, and the Federal Council, basing its interference on Article 27 of the Constitution, suggested that the schools should be amal-

The opposition came chiefly from the cantons of Lucerne, Fribourg, Valais, and Ticino; and 62,948 signatures were soon collected. Oddly enough, though German Switzerland would have gained by the adoption of the law, which was much more lenient than the cantonal laws on the subject, yet the majority against the law came chiefly from the German cantons. The Protestant Romance cantons and the canton of Zürich gave an almost solid vote for the law, and thus carried the day. It was accepted by 244,317 votes to 217,921.

In the voting of the 26th of October 1890, the people and the cantons accepted an addition to Article 34 of the Federal Constitution. This new clause is as follows: " The Confederation shall introduce, by means of legislation, a system of insurance against sickness and accidents, taking into account the existing friendly societies. It can declare that all` persons shall compulsorily insure themselves, or may confine it to certain classes of citizens." [1]

The *federal law* of the 26th of September 1890, *con-*

gamated. The commune of Lichtensteg decided by a majority to pay no attention to this demand, but the minority appealed first to the government and then to the Great Council of St. Gall. Being unsuccessful there, they addressed themselves to the Federal Council, who gave judgment against them. Finally the case came before the Chambers, when a long discussion took place, with the result that the appeal was dismissed by eighty-eight to thirty-eight votes.

[1] [The law on the subject has been under discussion for some time. The commission has reported in favour of compulsory insurance in case of sickness and accidents, and the matter was discussed in the National Council in June 1897. The law has passed the National Council, and now (October 1897) has to pass the Council of States.]

cerning the officials and federal employees who have
become incapable of fulfilling their duties, authorised
the Federal Council " to pay a pension upon retire-
ment or non-reappointment to those officials who have
become incapable of adequately fulfilling their duties
through age, or infirmities contracted during their
period of service, and who have rendered at least
fifteen years' faithful and conscientious service to the
federal administration " (Art. I.).

Such a law was a novelty in Switzerland, for retiring pensions for officials are unknown in the Confederation and in the majority of the cantons.   But
they are unknown in name rather than in fact, for
the administration has been in the habit of keeping
on and paying their old employees as long as possible, their work being done for them by paid clerks.

The law, therefore, could not be accused of burden-
ing the budget with a new charge.   It was, however,
rejected by the largest majority ever known since 1874.
There were 353,977 Noes to 91,851 Ayes.   I was
in Switzerland shortly after this voting, when people
were still talking of the result.   One day I asked a
Bernese peasant why he had voted No.   "When I
am old and past work I do not get a pension," he
said.   "Then why should these gentlemen in the
federal offices get one ?   Their income is much
larger than that of many a citizen."   No doubt many
other people on the 15th of March reasoned like this
Bernese peasant.

On the 18th of October 1891 a large majority
accepted a new tariff, framed in an aggressive spirit,
with the object of bringing pressure to bear in the

matter of certain commercial treaties which were about to be renewed.[1]

The last federal vote that we must notice is that of the 6th of December 1891. The question was the purchase of the stock of the Central Railway by the Confederation. Although the principle of national-isation of railways had many supporters among men of all parties, the resolution to purchase the Swiss Central was rejected by an enormous majority.

The opposition appealed to the referendum for two reasons, the one political, the other financial. The purchase, they said, would result in the increase of federal bureaucracy ; it would strengthen the central power, by placing under its orders a whole legion of public servants. Financially they would, moreover, do a bad stroke of business ; for the Berlin Jews, ex-pecting a large profit, had bought up the shares of the Central some months before. They were quite ready to sell them now at prices thoroughly favour-able to themselves. The people showed great sense in not accepting the purchase under these conditions.[2]

---

[1] The signatures of the referendum were collected chiefly in Geneva. *A cheap-food league* (*Ligue contre la renchérissement de la vie*) was even formed in the town. As the centre of a district divided by the frontier, Geneva needs more than any other canton the power of free exchange with neighbouring states. In fighting for the freedom of export it was fighting for its economic existence.

[2] M. Welti, the President of the Confederation, resigned on account of the vote of December 6. As head of the Railway Depart-ment, he had been very prominent in the purchase question. He had defended the plan not only before the Federal Assembly, but also at public meetings held in the different towns. His resigna-tion, which he could not be persuaded to withdraw, was naturally deeply regretted by all parties. It is necessary to notice it here, because the decision of M. Welti has created a very important precedent. No federal councillor up to this time ever dreamt of

It is not possible as yet to record the results of the popular initiative in constitutional questions, as the electors have not had time to use their right. The *Berner Volkszeitung* suggests the following series of reforms that might be brought about by means of the formulated initiative[1] :—

(1) A fresh distribution of constituencies; electoral tickets containing only one name (*scrutin uninominal*), or proportional representation.

(2) The compulsory referendum.

(3) The election of the Federal Council by the people.[2]

resigning when the law for which he was responsible was voted down either by the Chambers or the people. In 1882, for instance, when the educational inquiry was rejected by the people, it never occurred to the federal councillor who openly avowed himself the author of the resolution that he was bound in any way to resign in consequence. The Federal Council has always been considered to be unanimous in its decisions, and only to be responsible to the Federal Assembly. If the example of M. Welti be followed, the chiefs of the department will become personally responsible to the people instead of collectively responsible to the Chambers.

[1] *Berner Volkszeitung*, July 8, 1891.

[2] In the *Basler Volksblatt*, one of the principal Catholic organs in German Switzerland, it is stated that a committee of deputies, composed of Radical democrats, has already been formed, with a view to provoking a popular movement in favour of the election of the Federal Council by the people. In a long article the *Basler Volksblatt* declares that the Catholics will support this reform on condition that the election of the Council shall take place by proportional representation (*Basler Volksblatt* of February 6, 8, and 9, 1892). In 1884, M. Vögelin, of Zürich, had already demanded that the minority should be represented in the Federal Council. "Seventy-two men," he said, "have passed through the Federal Council since 1848, but a Catholic has never been considered worthy to enter it. And you are surprised, gentlemen of the Federal Council, to see the people distrusting the decrees of the Federal Council and the laws voted by the Assembly that elects this Council. You are astonished when these laws are rejected as party laws. You should

(4) A reform in the law of marriage and divorce.

(5) The reduction of the salaries of federal public servants to sums not exceeding 5000 francs (£200).

(6) The reduction of the military budget.

(7) The suppression of costly and useless embassies.

(8) Free education.

Votes on Federal Laws and Initiative Demands from 1892 to December 1897 [Editor].

During 1892 no referendum took place, but in 1893 we get a voting on a constitutional article drawn up by 50,000 citizens. It may be said that the first use of this new right was not such as to encourage much hope of its value in the future. A certain group of persons (see Table) professing to be actuated by humane motives, but still more, it would seem, by a feeling of intolerance towards the Jews, drafted an amendment to the effect that animals should not be killed without having been previously stunned, thus rendering it impossible for the Jews to bleed their animals as enjoined by the Mosaic law. The agitation began first of all in Aargau and Berne. In both cantons the Great Councils forbade the Jewish practices, and declared that all animals must be slaughtered according to Christian methods. The Jews then appealed to the Federal Council, who investigated the matter thoroughly, and reported that the Hebraic mode of slaughter was not more cruel than the ordinary method, if anything perhaps less so. In any case, interference in the matter was contrary to the principles of religious liberty guaranteed by the

---

remember that your exclusiveness does not only injure your colleagues of the Right, but the whole Catholic party. You have lost the confidence of the people. You will not win it back till you make up your minds to render justice to all, and not only to your partisans" (*Züricher Post*, July 10, 1884). The first attempt in this direction has been made recently. One of the chiefs of the Right, M. Zemp, of Lucerne, has recently been elected a member of the Federal Council in place of M. Welti.

constitution.   The result was that the Federal Council quashed the order of the Argovian and Bernese Councils.   The Anti-Semitists then appealed to the Federal Assembly, who supported the decision of the Federal Council by a large majority.   The Anti-Semitic Committee next took up the new constitutional instrument, and drafted the so-called "slaughter-house" article, which was signed by 83,159 voters.   The Federal Assembly, when submitting the article to the referendum in August 1893, recommended that it should be rejected, but in spite of this advice a majority both of the people and the cantons voted in favour of the amendment, "thus placing Switzerland among the nations that oppress the Jews, and this by a method of petty persecution unworthy of an enlightened community."[1]   It may be noticed, however, that the particular kind of animal is not defined, nor is it stated what mode of stunning should be employed ; nor is there any punishment provided should these regulations be transgressed, which makes the article a dead-letter in those cantons which do not choose to enforce it.   The Federal Assembly has been petitioned to enact a law which shall provide a penalty, but it has always refused to entertain the proposal.

On March 5, 1894, a vote took place on the constitutional amendment giving the Confederation the right to legislate for small industries.   The Federal Government, under Article 34, has the right of legislating on the work of children in factories, on the length of the working day, and on the protection to be accorded to workmen in insanitary or dangerous industries.   The Factory Act passed in consequence of this was accepted by the people, and seems to have worked very well.   The government, therefore, proposed to add another constitutional article, in virtue of which they would have the right of legislating for small establishments.   The avowed object of the amendment was to permit the elaboration of a law which should apply the provisions of the Factory Acts to those employed in small workshops.   The clause, however, was so broad in its terms that it gave the Confederation the right to legislate on labour organisations, and they might even go so far as to pass a law compelling workmen to join in trades unions.   The debates brought this out very clearly.   The Council of States was quite willing to adopt the amendment, but would have nothing to do with compulsorily

[1] Lowell, *op. cit.*, vol. ii. p. 285.

forcing people to join in labour organisations. This was also the attitude of the majority of the National Council. It was said that many members voted for the bill merely in order to let it come before the people, when it was sure to be voted down. The law was not only unpopular on account of its socialistic tendencies, but it was regarded as bestowing fresh powers upon the central government, and as having a unifying tendency generally. This is often a fatal objection to a law in Switzerland, and so the amendment was rejected by 158,492 to 135,713 votes, and by $13\frac{1}{2}$ to $8\frac{1}{2}$ cantons. Only about 43 per cent. of the electors went to the polls.

The next popular voting took place three months after, in June 1894, on a constitutional amendment proposed by the popular initiative. It was of a socialistic nature, and originated with the Socialist party. The text of the demand ran as follows :—

" The right to have adequately paid work provided belongs to each Swiss citizen. Federal legislation and cantonal and communal laws are to render this right effective by every means possible. In particular the following measures are to be taken :—

" (a) The hours of work are to be reduced in the greatest possible number of branches of industry, with the aim of making work more plentiful.

" (b) Institutions such as workmen's exchanges are to be organised, in order to procure work gratuitously for workmen. Workmen are to be legally protected against unjustifiable dismissal.

" (d) Workmen are to be insured in such a manner that they shall be protected against the consequences of loss of work, either by means of a public insurance, or by insuring workmen in private institutions by the aid of public funds.

" (e) The right of meeting is to be efficaciously protected, so that the formation of associations to protect workmen against their masters shall never be prevented, nor the right of joining in such associations be interfered with.

" (f) An official board shall be established to which workmen might appeal against their masters ; and work in the factories and workshops is to be organised in a democratic manner, especially in the factories and workshops managed by the state and the communes."

This proposal was signed by 52,387 names, but when put to

the vote was defeated by the enormous majority of 232,409 votes, only 75,880 having been recorded in its favour.

The Socialists meanwhile had been preparing a second demand, on the subject of gratuitous medical attendance.

A law was under discussion in the Federal Assembly on the subject of the insurance of workmen in case of sickness or accident. The Socialists were not satisfied with this law, because both workmen and employers were to co-operate in the administration of the insurance funds. They wished to exclude the employer from all participation in the administration. To effect this they proposed that the insurance funds should only be used in case of loss of work, and should be supported and managed by workmen only. The Confederation should provide gratuitous medical attendance for all, and the masters should support and maintain an insurance against accidents. This project did not succeed in getting more than 40,000 signatures, and therefore had to be dropped. The Grütliverein was responsible for this attempt.

The third voting, which took place in 1894, created an enormous amount of excitement in Switzerland, and was known as "the Spoil's Campaign." In 1850 the custom duties yielded between four and five million francs. In 1894 they had increased to thirty-five millions. As a result there was a considerable surplus, which has been employed in subsidising railways, in vast works of fortification, in grants to native manufactures, and in erecting public buildings. Some cantons were thus subsidised at the rate of 1 franc 33 cents. per head of the population, while others obtained 154 francs. The mutual jealousy of the cantons was aroused, and an initiative amendment was set on foot signed by 67,828 citizens, by which the surplus was to be distributed among the cantons at the rate of 2 francs per head. The Swiss are always very chary of expenditure. Thus the amendment was specially calculated to appeal to them. Pamphlets were circulated giving an account of the salaries of the public officials, and brilliant schemes were propounded as to what the cantons could do with the money. The opposition were quite as active, for the initiative was an attack on the whole system of federal finance and administration. If an amendment could be thus incorporated into the constitution by which the people should be paid 2 francs a head, the cantons to spend the money as they liked, with no supervision from the central government, it was practically turning the Federation into a company for the distribution of dividends to the shareholders. After a period of great political agitation, in which 496,601 voters out of 700,000 registered electors went to the polls, the motion was lost by 205,177 votes. An act of religious intolerance, an extremely advanced socialistic measure, and the attempted pillage of the Federal Treasury to the tune of six million francs, have been the result of the latest experiment in direct legislation. The fact that the last two were rejected is not a guarantee that such things will always be rejected, and the new federal initiative has been the cause of great anxiety in Switzerland.[1]

The year 1895 was characterised, from the referendum point of view, by three constitutional amendments. The first vote was taken in February 1895, *on a law regulating the diplomatic and consular service.* Diplomatic posts, and the salaries attached to them, have always been dealt with in the Chambers by means of a decree. Consuls, on the other hand, have been appointed when necessary by the Federal Council, and the necessary expenses included in the budget. The Federal Council proposed to place the creation of diplomatic posts on the same footing as consular appointments.

The Federal Assembly amended this proposal, with the result that a law was passed declaring that no new post should be created by the Federal Council without the sanction of the Assembly, but that such appointments should not be submitted to the referendum. It is difficult for the ordinary citizen to judge of the importance of a diplomatic post, and the diplomatic representatives do not seem to be popular in Switzerland. They seem to be regarded as a set who get excellent salaries for doing very little. Those parts of the country which had few relations with foreign lands objected to the law on the ground that it would involve additional expense, and others objected to having such questions taken from the sphere of the referendum, and recalled how they had been able to put a stop to the extra 10,000 francs a year to the Legation at Washington. Thus jealousy of their own rights, fear of the encroachments of the central government, and the dislike of increased expenditure, were all sufficient

---

1 See Borgeaud, *Revue du Droit Public,* November–December 1894. Also Numa Droz, *Études et portraits politiques; Le Referendum et l'Initiative populaire en Suisse, La Suisse jugée par un Américain.*

to ensure the rejection of the law by a 50,000 majority. Only about 44 per cent. of the electors went to the poll, however.

The next voting was on *a constitutional article giving the Federal Government the monopoly of making matches.*[1] The object of this amendment was a purely humanitarian one. The operatives in the match factories, most of which were situated in Frutigen, in Berne, were in a most miserable condition owing to the prevalence of necrosis, a sort of cancer brought on by the effects of yellow phosphorus. Many attempts had been made to remedy this condition of things. Domestic work at matches had been forbidden, and in 1879 the manufacture of matches with yellow phosphorus was forbidden altogether. These precautions proved useless, as the matches were made and sold secretly; so the law was repealed. The masters were made responsible for every case of necrosis occurring in their factories, and there were stringent regulations as to the sanitary condition of the factories. Nothing, however, seems to have been of any use, and finally the Federal Council proposed to establish a monopoly. The particular objection to this course, apart from any objection that might apply to monopolies in general, were :

(1) If the principle is once recognised that the government should buy up a manufacture when it is dangerous, where will you stop ?

(2) The Factory Acts are sufficient to meet the case ; why not enforce them ?

(3) By buying out the masters the country is virtually paying them for the harm they have caused, and offering a direct inducement for laws to be neglected.

It is said that the opponents of this measure did not bestir themselves very actively against the law in the Assembly, *i.e.,* they voted for it in order to let the question be finally voted down by the people, who disliked it on account of the monopoly, because it was supported by the Socialists, who were unpopular at the time, and because it increased the power of the central government.

In November another voting took place, *on a constitutional amendment centralising the army.* By the Constitution of 1874

[1] See *Revue Politique et Parlementaire* for July 1894, p. 116.

the control of the army in time of peace was divided between the cantons and the Confederation. To the cantons were confided the duties of executing the military laws, and providing the clothing and rations of the troops. The various corps were composed, as far as possible, of men from the same canton ; and the composition of such corps, their efficiency, and the appointment and promotion of the officers, were all left to the states, subject to general rules to be established by the Confederation.

The new amendment placed the army almost entirely under the control of the Federal Government. It declared that "everything which concerns the army is within the province of the Confederation. For the future the Confederation shall not only make the military laws, but shall execute them, and shall make provision for the administration, the instruction, the clothing and subsistence of the army." The cantons still retained the right, under these new provisions, of disposing of the military forces in their territory, but they were no longer to appoint any but the under-officers, the principal officers being appointed by the Confederation. Special administrative districts were to be created for the control of the army by the central government, and each district was to coincide, as far as possible, with the boundary of a canton.

The object of these changes was to secure the greater efficiency of the army, and to introduce some sort of uniformity into the equipment and training of the troops. The appointment of the principal officers was to be placed in the hands of the Confederation, in order that men should not be appointed for merely local reasons. This law passed the Federal Council and the Chambers almost unanimously. The Radicals were in favour of the law, the Socialists against, and the Conservatives neutral. The press was on the side of revision. Appeals were made to patriotism. Europe was represented as waiting to take advantage of Swiss military weakness, and those who voted against the reform were denounced as traitors to their country. The law, however, was rejected. The people were afraid that the schools for recruits and the periods of annual training would be increased. Many military men argued in favour of a longer period of military service, and looked upon the revision as a means of bringing this about, and this naturally did not increase the popularity of the measure. The idea of administrative districts was also disliked. These reasons, joined to the diminution of the

Q

cantonal authority, and the increase of power to the central government, involved in the change, were quite sufficient to kill the bill.

Three laws were voted on at once in October 1896. The law that created the greatest amount of excitement was one which directed that the railways should prepare a statement of their accounts. This measure was strongly opposed in Romance Switzerland. It was said to be an insidious attempt to commit the people to the state ownership of railways. It was also accused of being an attempt to reduce the price at which the state would buy up the shares. Another argument urged against the law was, that it would frighten away capitalists from investing in Swiss railways, especially in the mountain lines of the Simplon, the Engadine, and the Splügen. Public opinion was so excited on the subject that it almost became a race conflict. The Romance Swiss were represented as enemies to federal progress, whose resistance must be broken down. The German deputies had nearly all voted for the law, and those that had voted against it dared not openly oppose it before the people on the eve of the general elections.

The law was warmly supported by M. Zemp, the federal councillor in charge of the bill, who had taken the place of M. Welti on the latter's resignation. He represented the Catholic party, who were opposed to the law ; but he defended it so well that he practically carried his party with him. He pointed out that this bill was only a step towards the elucidation of the question on which the people would be able to give judgment later, and a clearer judgment in consequence of the accounts being properly drawn up. It is said that the victory of the law was due largely to M. Zemp's exertions, for it was calculated that between 30,000 and 40,000 Catholics voted on his side, and the law was carried by a majority of 46,000. The bill is known as the " Zempacher Sieg."

The same day as the law on railway accounts was passed, the law on discipline in the federal army was heavily voted down, not one canton having pronounced in its favour. The objections levelled against it were that it increased the federal military authority, and that the general was invested with powers in time of peace which he formerly only possessed in time of war. The majority against the law was the large one of 232,676.

The law which regulated the trade in cattle was voted down by a small majority. It enacted that guarantees given with animals should not form sufficient ground for rescission of contract unless they were in writing. This was contrary to the custom in certain cantons, and the law was therefore defeated.

The question of a state bank, which was voted on in February 1897, is one which has been pending ever since the constitutional amendment of 1891 was passed. A great many persons then voted for it, thinking that it would be a mixed bank. The bank, however, that was proposed was a state bank. The cantons were invited to subscribe towards it, but were to have no part in the administration. The great argument against it was that a state bank of this kind would be at the mercy of politicians. It was said that if the law passed, the government could compromise the credit of the country at any time, and would, moreover, be incompetent in a time of crisis. The law was adopted in the National Council by a small majority, and nearly failed to pass the Council of States, so many members having stayed away in order not to have the responsibility of voting. The authors of the law threatened to make use of the initiative if the law were not passed. The opposition therefore gave in, in order to appeal to the referendum, and the result justified their expectations, the law was voted down by a majority of 60,220.

On the 11th of July 1897 two constitutional amendments were submitted to the people, both of which were accepted. One of these gave the Confederation the power to legislate on food-stuffs. A certain uniformity of regulation in the matter of the standard and purity and control of food sold is very necessary. Some people were afraid that this would involve protection under the pretence of hygiene, but the change was not really unpopular, and so was accepted.

The other amendment had to do with the regulation of forests. Those in the mountainous regions were already under the control of the Confederation. By this amendment all the forests were placed under the central government.

On 20th February 1898 a very important voting took place on the question of the purchase of the railways by the Confederation. The concessions granted by the government to the private companies expire on the 1st of May 1903, and this is regarded by many as a suitable time to effect their purchase by the state. Five years' notice to the companies was, however, necessary, and the question of the state ownership of railways had therefore to be settled by May 1898.

A demand emanating from the popular initiative was prepared in 1896, to the effect that the Confederation should take in hand the management of the railways for five years, and then should take over all the lines at twenty-five times the average annual value. The Federal Council was about to bring in a bill on the subject, and so the initiative demand was not presented, although the requisite number of signatures was obtained. All through 1897 the Assembly were occupied with the question, and the bill authorising the repurchase was passed on the 15th of October. A referendum was then demanded, and the measure was finally carried in February by 386,634 votes to 182,718. This is a very different result from that obtained in 1891, when a proposal to buy up only one of the great lines was rejected.

The Federal Council have been working towards this end for nearly half a century. The question came up in 1848, and the Council reported in favour of state ownership in 1852, but the Assembly could not then face the responsibility of developing the railway system. In 1883 the government brought the question up again, and suggested that the railways should be repurchased in 1888, but their efforts were unsuccessful. In 1887 the Council proposed that the Confederation should take over the lines of the North-Eastern, but again the Assembly would not support them.

In 1890, however, the Assembly seems to have changed its attitude, and purchased so many shares in the Jura-Simplon railway that they became entitled to a considerable voice in its management. Then they passed a bill in 1891 authorising the purchase of the "Central" by the state. The measure was, however, rejected by the people. The bill on railway accounts passed in 1896 had the effect of preparing popular opinion to receive the larger question favourably, so that in February 1898 the majority in favour of the state ownership of railways was double as large as the minority against. Public opinion has thus completely changed round since 1891.

It is proposed to divide the railway management up into five districts, corresponding to the five great lines, with a general directory above them. Only the five great lines are to be taken over at first; the St. Gothard cannot be bought up till two years later. The smaller lines and "funiculaires" up the mountain sides are still to be left to local management. The price of the repurchase is to be twenty-five times the average profits for the past ten years. The Federal Council has estimated that the cost will be about 962 million francs, and that a further 42 millions will be needed for new works. The companies are almost certain to object to this price as being too low, and the matter will finally be fought out before the Federal Tribunal. The immediate effect has been a fall in the price of Swiss railway stock.

The message of the Federal Council sent to the Assembly on the 25th March 1897, and which was circulated amongst the people before the voting day, set out both the history of the movement and the advantages of the proposal very fully. The Council stated the old argument, that whereas the rival companies are mainly concerned with dividends, the chief interest of the state was the convenience of the public. They also stated that all profits should go to the improvement of the service and the lowering of fares. They declared that one of the advantages would be unity of administration, involving a saving of labour and expense, and ensuring greater security of traffic. They promised a limitation of hours for the employees, and better arrangements for pensions and sick benefit. They dwelt on the cheapening of fares both for passengers and carriage of goods, and proposed the establishment of a sinking fund for the redemption of the original capital. Another advantage urged was, that there would be a freedom from foreign influence which may creep in with foreign shareholders.

It was urged against the law that the profits will not be such as to enable the Confederation to carry out these reforms. The railways have been paying 3.7 per cent. dividend on an average. If the Confederation borrows money at 3.5 per cent. as proposed, how are they to carry out the necessary reforms, such as the increase of stations, reduction of fares, the augmentation of salaries, and the reduction of hours worked by the officials on the 0.2 per cent. profit?[1]

---

[1] For a *résumé* of the arguments against the purchase, see the articles on Switzerland by M. Droz in the *Revue Politique*, &c., for June and December 1897.

But the people were sanguine, and of late years there has been a strong feeling in favour of state ownership. Every time a train was behind time, or a parcel went wrong, or anything happened, the cry always was, " Oh, if the state only owned the railways." The prospect of cheap fares and better service outweighed the objection to increased centralisation.

The Chambers have been very busy discussing the question of the unification of the law, and also the question of compulsory insurance.[1]

The unification of the law must be voted on by the people, since it is a constitutional amendment, and this will probably take place in 1898.

We see that on the whole the result of the referendum in Switzerland has been Conservative, and that it to some extent bears out the dictum of Sir Henry Maine, who says : "It is possible by agitation or exhortation to produce in the mind of the average citizen a vague impression that he desires a particular change. But when the agitation has settled down on the dregs, when the excitement has died away, when the subject has been threshed out, when the law is before him in all its detail, he is sure to find in it much that is likely to disturb his habits, his ideas, his prejudices, or his interests, and so in the long run he votes 'No' to every proposal." [2]

The Factory Act, the alcohol law, and the amendment on the compulsory insurance of workmen, are Radical measures that have been sanctioned by the people. The law on epidemics, on education, on state railways, on the state bank, the amendments dealing with legislation on trades and on matches, may be con-

---

[1] The only way to keep up to date in the Swiss votings is to follow the course of events month by month in the *Bibliothèque Universelle,* and to read up M. Droz's admirable summaries in the June and December numbers of the *Revue Politique et Parlementaire.* M. Borgeaud and other well-known Swiss writers also give an account of the political doings of Switzerland from time to time in the *Revue du Droit Public.* The Swiss Government publishes every year a *Jahrbuch für schweizerische Statistik,* which gives the statistics of the federal votings for the year. The text of the laws and the messages of the Federal Council are always given in the *Feuille fédérale.*

[2] Maine, *Popular Government,* p. 97.

sidered as Radical measures defeated at the polls. We have examined in detail the reasons why each law was accepted or rejected.

The results have, however, been summarised by several writers. Mr. Lowell points out that there is a tendency to reject measures that are in any way Radical, and he continues : "This is a very instructive fact, because it means that the people are really more Conservative than their representatives." He also remarks that the people object to laws which cover a great deal of ground, which are complicated, or try to effect too much at once. "The symptom," he says, "is a very healthy one, for it shows that the people want to understand the laws they are enacting, and cannot be driven or hurried into measures whose bearing is not clear to them." Another characteristic discernible in these popular votings is the dislike of spending money. "The fact is, that in Switzerland there are no great cities with an enormous proletariat class which does not feel the weight of public burdens, or realise that an increase of taxation affects its own comfort and prosperity; and, on the other hand, the peasants are in the habit of dealing with small sums, and do not see the need of liberal salaries for the men who do the public work." [1]

M. Hilty points out that it is not always the worst laws that are attacked, and says : "I consider that of all the laws and decrees rejected, only one, that giving retiring pensions, and perhaps the order creating a Federal Secretary of Education, have been really unpopular on account of their contents, and not on account of their form." [2] In considering whether the referendum is satisfactory or not, he thus describes certain elements of referendum politics [3] :—

In the first place, "nothing is more fatal to a law than the recommendation of the foreign journals. If the wind is in that quarter the cause is lost."

Secondly, he considers it very ill-advised to consult the people on several questions in the same voting when one law is especially doubtful. The hand which writes the first "No" easily repeats it a second time.

Thirdly, the season at which the voting takes place is not

[1] Lowell, vol. ii. pp. 269–72.
[2] Hilty, *Revue de Droit internationale*, 1892, p. 397.
[3] Ibid., p. 479.

without influence. When people are very busy in the fields, the rural population do not hasten to the polls.

"As for the campaign in the press, experience proves that it should not begin too early, and naturally also not too late. In all these affairs there is an advance-guard which engages first, but which does not decide the day. As the voting approaches one gets to know the way in which public opinion is being formed. It is at that moment that the real speaking and writing should be done. What happens later is labour lost."

M. Hilty considers that the speeches made by members of the government at public meetings in favour of the law only prejudice people against it. They say, "He must have his reasons for being infatuated with the law."

He accounts for the fact that laws have been rejected the first time and accepted the second time, by saying that the first time many people did not vote through sheer carelessness, thinking it all safe.

The Conservative result of the referendum has also been attributed by other writers to the fact that the opponents of the law go to the polls in much greater numbers than the supporters of a law.

M. Signorel considers that laws have been voted down, firstly, out of a real opposition to the views of the Federal Assembly ; and secondly, out of a dislike to the general policy of the government. He points out that there are two ways of getting people to accept a law :—

(1) By incorporating some popular provisions with the unpopular ones, so that one carries the other.

(2) By presenting the law time after time until it is accepted.[1]

The Conservative result is said also to be due largely to the fact that the federal referendum is optional. M. Droz says :[2] "In order to obtain signatures, the opposition has to create a sort of adverse current which is afterwards very difficult to control. It is to this fact that the defeats suffered by the Federal Assembly on very advanced measures, and also on some very insignificant ones, are mainly attributed."

M. Dunant says that in examining the results two facts may be noted. The first is, the attachment of the cantons to their

---

[1] *Le Referendum législatif*, p. 398.
[2] *Contemporary Review*, vol. lxvii. p. 337.

independence, which they regard as an historical right ; and the second is, a dislike for all expenses for which the people do not see the immediate utility. "The referendum has made the people Conservative," he says, "and it has often made laws fail which are very strongly supported and very cleverly defended. It is sufficient on these occasions for the different minorities to unite at the poll in order to obtain a compact and decisive majority."[1]

Nearly all the writers agree in saying that laws have been voted down more out of hostility to the government than out of hostility to the laws. All writers are unanimous in praising the Swiss for the great moderation they have shown. There have never been any troubles or acts of violence at any of the votings.

Let us now see what the results of the referendum have been in the different cantons, taking the German cantons first.

Herr Stüssi, in an interesting monograph on the referendum in Zürich, gives a description of the principal popular votes which have taken place in his canton from 1869 to 1885,[2] and although he makes no secret of his preference for direct legislation, he seems to have made an impartial examination of the facts. He sums up the result in the following words:—

"All the laws useful to the canton have been accepted, even those which demanded considerable money sacrifices from the people. No law which

[1] *Législation par le peuple en Suisse*, pp. 113 and 115.

[2] Stüssi, *Referendum und Initiativ im Kanton Zürich*, Horgen, 1886. It would be a good thing if the example of Herr Stüssi, Secretary of State for Zürich, were followed elsewhere. It has been impossible for me to obtain exact information in many cantons on the results of the referendum. The heads of the administration who have the necessary documents in their possession could easily draw up complete tables of comparative statistics on the subject of the popular votings.

would have really advanced either moral or material progress has been definitely laid aside.[1]

"In those rare cases which seem to contradict this conclusion the referendum has simply displayed its inherent ultra-Conservative character, and delayed an advance which would seem to most too rapid."[2]

---

[1] The author means by this that laws which have perhaps been rejected a first time have always been accepted by the people at a later date.

[2] [Mr. Lowell says that the tendency to reject measures that are in any way Radical is more noticeable in the cantons than in the Confederation. He says : "Strange as it may seem, the dislike of Radical projects applies to labour laws and other measures designed to improve the condition of the working classes, although laws of that kind are commonly believed to be highly popular with the vast majority of people." To illustrate this, Mr. Lowell quotes the canton of Zürich, which is largely devoted to manufacturing :—

"In 1870 the people rejected there a cantonal law which limited the duration of labour in factories to twelve hours a day, which protected the women who work in them, and forbade the employment of children during the years when they were required to go to school. In 1877 they voted against a federal factory law intended for a similar purpose. In the following year they rejected a cantonal law to establish a school of weaving ; and in 1881 they voted down another law providing for the compulsory insurance of workmen against sickness, regulating their relations with their employers, and making the latter liable for injuries to their employees caused by accidents. Moreover, they have repeatedly rejected measures for increasing the amount of education required in the public schools, and they have refused to provide free textbooks for the children. All this does not mean that the people are certain to reject laws intended for the benefit of the working classes ; on the contrary, they voted in Zürich heavily in favour of the recent amendment to the Federal Constitution giving the Confederation power to enact a statute on the compulsory insurance of workmen. But it does mean that they are less ready to sanction measures of this character than the Legislature is to pass them.

"Every law designed for the benefit of the working man involves, or rather is liable to involve, a present sacrifice on his part ; but the sacrifice is not evident so long as the principle of the law is merely

Herr Stüssi gives at the end of his pamphlet a list of the votes which have taken place during the fifteen years of which he treats. We find that 120 bills have been presented for the sanction of the people, and that of this number 80 have been accepted and 40 rejected. I was enabled to take some notes myself at the cantonal chancery, and find that between 1886 and 1890 there were thirteen

stated in general terms. Any working man, for example, can easily understand the wisdom of forbidding the labour of children of immature years, but it is not easy for him to see how he gains anything by losing the wages his son has been earning in the mill. Hence the same man may very well vote for a candidate or a party that proposes to enact a labour law, and yet find himself bitterly opposed to that very law when it is presented to him for approval. Moreover, the referendum places in the hands of the employers a means of exerting a direct pressure upon their operatives, which a secret ballot has not the slightest tendency to mitigate. The rejection of the first Factory Act in Zürich is said to have been largely due to the influence of the mill-owners, and a little reflection will show how they might bring about the defeat of a labour law. Suppose, for example, that an act limiting the hours of work in factories is passed by the Legislature, and that a demand is made for the popular vote. Then suppose the employers announce that if the law is ratified they will be obliged to cut down wages. In such a case many of the operatives, not caring to run the risk of a decrease in wages or a strike, will be likely to vote against the act and kill it."— *Government*, &c., pp. 268–69.

M. Curti says that a whole series of good laws have been adopted in Zürich—laws in favour of agriculture, laws reforming the penal system, laws on the construction of several large hospitals, on the contribution of the state to the expenses of communal poor-houses, and on grants to the construction of railways, as well as a great many other propositions concerning the administration of justice, police, education, and other questions of public administration. Quite lately, he says, the working day of those employed in shops and domestic industries has been limited to ten hours, and the bill was accepted by the people by 45,309 votes to 12,356. See *Revue Politique et Parlementaire*, August 1897.]

votes, four of which have resulted in the rejection of the proposed law or resolution.[1]

When the electors have to sanction all laws as in Zürich, the number of voters who go to the poll is a matter of considerable importance. M. Stüssi has calculated that, on an average, 74 per cent. of the registered electors have either deposited or sent their ballot-paper. The first thing that affects the size of the vote is clearly the law itself. If it is a party measure and rouses the passions of the bulk of the electors, or if it is a financial law and closely affects the material interests of the citizens, immediately a large majority of electors make use of their right. If,

---

[1] The figures are given from 1869–96 by M. Curti, *Le Referendum Suisse*, p. 232 of the *Revue Politique et Parlementaire* for August 1897. He says there have been seven votes on constitutional laws, 137 on laws passed by the cantonal council, two on treaties with other cantons, and twenty-five on initiative demands. He does not, however, give the results of the voting. These are given in Herr Stüssi's latest book, *Referendum und Initiativ in den Schweizer Kantonen*, for the years 1869–93. Of 128 measures passed by the council, ninety-nine were accepted and twenty-nine rejected. Of the thirty federal questions voted on, the people approved twenty-three, including the initiative demand on the Slaughterhouse Act, and voted against seven.

The popular initiative has been no mere formality in Zürich, for there were twenty-two initiative amendments in this period. It will be remembered that any 5000 voters can propose a law in this way and require it to be submitted to the people, and any one person can do the same with the consent of one-third of the cantonal council.

The petition of the single person has only been made use of twice between 1869 and 1893. In 1883 a bill that came before the people in this way was rejected. In 1871 two measures proposed in this way were accepted by the people, but they were adopted by a majority of the Council, and have therefore been classified by Stüssi as petitions. Four of the demands, made by 5000 citizens, were approved by the Council; of these two were accepted and two rejected.

on the contrary, the country takes little interest in the law, the number of citizens who will go out of their way to express their opinion will be inconsiderable. They will consist of public servants and employees of the state, certain fanatical believers in direct legislation, and sometimes malcontents who vote "No" out of pure opposition, and who, calculating on the numerous abstentions, hope to defeat the law.

There is an external factor which may contribute to increase the number of voters, and that is, the coincidence of the referendum with an election. Although elections have not the importance in Switzerland that they have in Belgium, since the representatives chosen by the people cannot pass legislation which is final, their laws being always amenable to the popular tribunal, yet it is an obvious and universal fact that the elections are better attended than the referendary votings. Probably politicians work harder to ensure their own success

In two other cases the Council prepared an alternative which was ratified, while of the remaining fifteen only three were adopted by the people. Of these one established a house of correction for tramps, another re-established the death penalty (but the people afterwards negatived the statute for carrying it into effect), and the third abolished compulsory vaccination. Only three laws opposed by the Legislature have therefore been adopted by the people during twenty-four years, and of these Mr. Lowell says : "One was of doubtful value, about another the people seem to have changed their minds, and in the opinion of most educated people the third was clearly bad." See vol. ii. p. 287.

M. Curti's criticism of the initiative is as follows : "It must be acknowledged that the initiative has not always been well directed. Those who have used the initiative have often propounded questions which were not urgent, or have drawn up their demands in such a way that they could not withstand criticism. But the institution has always had the advantage of acting as a safety-valve for political passions." See *Revue Politique et Parlementaire*, August 1897.

than the success of their laws. However that may
be, we can state as a fact that at Zürich, when there
is a referendum and an election on the same day,
the average number of electors who pronounce on
the law or decree submitted to the vote rises from
74 to 79 per cent.[1]

There is a third factor which contributes materially
towards filling the ballot-boxes, and that is, the power
of the communes to inflict a fine on the electors who
abstain from voting. Herr Stüssi gives some surprising figures on this subject. On the occasion of
the referendum on the 25th of June 1871, it was
calculated that 97, 94, and 59 per cent. of the electors voted in the communes of Uster, Horgen, and
Riesbach respectively, while in the communes of
Zürich, Glattfelden, and Aussersihl the percentage
was only 19, 14, and 10 respectively. In the first
three communes the vote was compulsory, in the
others it was optional. These figures were so remarkable that it was proposed to pass a cantonal
law which should introduce compulsory voting into
all the communes without distinction. The first bill
drafted for this purpose was rejected by the people,
and a motion on the same subject, made somewhat
later in the cantonal council, only obtained 50 votes
against 90. The communes, therefore, remained free
to establish compulsory voting or not as they liked,
and we are thus enabled to judge accurately as to
how far the threat of a fine increases the vigilance
of the electors.

On the occasion of the referendum of the 4th of

---

[1] In Zürich, for example, an average of 81 per cent. of the electors take part in an election.

May 1879, the average of electors voting was 90 per cent. in the 121 communes where the voting was compulsory, and only 70 per cent. in the communes where the voting was optional. On the occasion of the referendum of the 28th of April 1878, the proportion was respectively 86 per cent. and 55 per cent. Compulsory voting produces another result to which it is important to draw attention, namely, a marked increase in the number of blank ballot-papers. In the two votings we have just mentioned, there was an average of 21 and 24 per cent. of blank tickets in the communes where the voting was compulsory, and only from 17 to 20 per cent. in the communes where the voting was optional.

Voting by proxy, which is peculiar to Zürich, also tends to increase the number of blank ballot-papers. If the elector is obliged to go and give his vote in person, he likes, when he has exerted himself so far, to influence the result to some extent, and therefore fills in the ballot-paper. On the other hand, a man who, merely to escape the fine, sends the ballot-paper by a third person, takes little interest in the result of the voting, and will easily abstain from giving any opinion at all. However that may be, the proportion of blank ballot-papers to the whole number placed in the ballot-boxes has been 11 per cent. during the five years between 1869 and 1874. It rose to 19 per cent. in the following period, from 1875 to 1880. It has fallen to 18 per cent. from 1881 to 1885. Looking at these numbers, the conclusion is that on an average, from 1869 to 1885, 62 per cent. only of the registered electors have given a vote which is worth anything; and in that way it has happened that in 100 votes out of 120 the minority has given the law to the majority. "After all," says Herr Stüssi, "is not that preferable to submitting to a law voted by 150 or 200 deputies?" Yes, it is preferable, if votes only are counted. Perhaps it is not if it were a question of the worth of the vote.

In the canton of Berne sixty-eight laws have run the gauntlet of the referendum between 1869 and 1880. Of these fifty have passed safe and sound, and eighteen have not found favour with the people.[1]

M. Chatelanat published in 1877[2] some very detailed statistics about the Bernese referendum. We see from them that only 45 per cent. of the electors took part in referendary votings. This proportion has remained the same for the years after 1877; but of 110,000 active citizens only 48,000 on an average take the

---

[1] [M. Curti says that one hundred cantonal laws and initiative demands have been submitted to the vote between 1869 and 1896, and of these thirty-one have been voted down. The people, he says, have several times displayed their opposition to laws on salaries, pensions, and other fiscal questions. On the other hand, they consented to state subsidies being given to the railways, they increased the salaries of teachers in the elementary schools, and decided on the construction or enlargement of scholastic institutions and hospitals.

The popular initiative, introduced in 1893, has been twice used in Berne with success—firstly, to abolish compulsory vaccination; and secondly, to introduce a system of bounties for the rearing of cattle and horses. A law on this latter subject, prepared by the Great Council, had been voted down owing to the objection of the small farmers, who did not consider the subsidy fairly distributed. The popular law was accepted. The election of the Executive, the Great Council, and the deputies to the Council of States, by the system of proportional representation, was also claimed by the popular initiative, but was rejected by the people.]

[2] Chatelanat, *Die Wirkungen des Referendums im Kanton Bern*, in the *Zeitschrift für schweizerische Statistik*, 1877, p. 193.

trouble to drop a ballot-paper into the box when there is a law to sanction. On the other hand, when the Great Council is to be elected, immediately the number of electors that go to the poll is considerably increased. On an average they amount to 69,000. During the period of twenty years which have passed since the introduction of the referendum into Berne, an absolute majority of the electors has only nine times taken part in the votes. Of the sixty-eight laws submitted to the referendum only one has obtained more than half the votes of the registered electors. In all other cases the result has been decided by the minority.[1]

Herr Dürrenmatt, a member of the Great Council at Berne, considers that the considerable number of abstentions is partly due to the unwieldy size of the constituencies. He intends to introduce a motion that the vote should henceforth take place in the commune. If his preliminary proposal is adopted, he intends claiming compulsory voting, and the payment of a franc to those who come to vote. This last idea is not new. In olden days, at one period of the Athenian democracy, the citizens present at the meetings of the Ecclesia were also indemnified. There

---

[1] [Mr. Lowell (p. 272) points out that between 1869 and 1878 the percentage of those who took part in the vote varied from 81.6 to 20.2 per cent. "It is worth while to observe that the largest vote was cast on religious questions, the next on political ones ; then came railroad, then school, then financial, then economic ones ; whilst the smallest vote was polled on administrative regulations, no doubt because the people felt that they did not understand them. This list of subjects shows that cool, and sensible as the Swiss are, they are not exempt from the popular tendency, good or bad, to take more interest in sensational than practical matters."]

is only one kind of law which seems to have been able to arouse the Bernese from their habitual indifference. When it was necessary, on the 18th of January 1874, to vote on a religious law which placed the Church in absolute dependence upon the state and the people, then 69,478 electors thought it their duty to go and vote for its acceptance. The minority which voted "No" was composed of 17,133 votes. In all there were 86,611 votes given. The majority comprised the Protestants and Old Catholics, who assumed by this means the right of regulating the religious affairs of the Catholics.[1]

In the canton of Solothurn, from 1870 to 1891, fifty-one laws have been adopted, and fifteen have been rejected.

The laws which the people are most ready to refuse are in Solothurn, as elsewhere, those which concern the payment of public servants. The officials often suffer from the dislike which the peasant feels for a bureaucracy. Colonel Vigier of Solothurn has sent me the reports of the Central Department responsible for ascertaining the result of the ballots. It would appear from the results of the twenty-two votes contained in the reports, that out of 17,000 electors 8300 on an average appear at the poll. The smallest number that took part in a single vote has been 4998, the highest 12,620. On the other hand, when

---

[1] It should be remarked that this is not the only case in which democracy has been oppressive to liberty, and that it is not only at Ber   that the government of the people has been the domination of numbers, in which the minority has been disarmed and oppressed by a sectarian majority. The exact details are given by M. Woeste in his *Histoire du Culturkampf en Suisse*, Brussels, 1887, pp. 45, 59, 122.

an election took place on the 20th of November 1887, for the re-election of the Council of State, no less than 15,548 voted out of 17,591 registered electors.

In the half canton of Rural-Basle the people have been required to give their decision on ninety-four laws from 1864 to 1881. The net result has been that forty-five laws have been accepted and twenty-three have been rejected. Seventeen times the referendum has come to nothing because a majority of electors have not taken part in the vote.[1]

From 1881 to 1884, out of seventeen laws submitted to the people, three only have been accepted, five have been rejected, and more than half of the laws failed because an absolute majority of the electors did not go to the poll.[2]

I have not been able to obtain the statistics of the number of voters in the canton of Aargau. The number of laws rejected by the people there is considerable. Between 1870 and 1883 twenty-one laws out of forty-eight were rejected, and four out of ten between 1885 and 1889. The people have a special aversion to laws on taxation. From 1878 to 1885 they constantly refused to vote the state budget.[3] The majority has now succeeded by making some con-

---

[1] *Amtsbericht des Regierungsrathes des Kantons Basel—Landschaft vom Jahre* 1880.

[2] *Amtsbericht vom Jahre* 1884. [These figures show that the tendency to stay away has increased of late years. In the new Constitution of 1894 the majority of those who take part in the vote is decisive whether a majority of electors take part or not.]

[3] Aargau was the only canton besides Berne which was in the habit of submitting the budget to the referendum.

cessions to the opposition in striking the budget out of the list of subjects which must be submitted to the referendum.[1]

In passing to the French cantons we are at once struck with the fact that *legislation by the people* is much less developed there than in the German cantons. Three of them, Geneva, Vaud, and Neuchâtel, only possess the *optional* referendum. Fribourg has always adhered to the representative system pure and simple.[2]

I spent a long time trying to discover the reason

[1] [The particulars of the votings in the canton of St. Gall are given by M. Curti. Between 1831 and 1894 there were 336 laws passed, twenty of which have been submitted to the referendum. Of these two passed, eighteen failed. Therefore, whenever a referendum has been demanded, the law has nearly always been voted down. The laws rejected have usually been tax laws. The two laws accepted have a political-religious character; the first proposed to remove funerals from ecclesiastical influence, and the second imposed penalties on priests who attempted to stir up religious dissensions. Both were carried by a small majority of about 300.

The initiative has been made use of to introduce proportional representation, but it was negatived by 22,143 votes to 19,875. It has also been made use of to lower the rate of interest on mortgages from five to four per cent., which was accepted by 22,642 to 12,859 votes. Compulsory voting exists in this canton, but it is doubtful whether the fines are strictly enforced. They are, however, very political in St. Gall. There are 51,430 registered electors, and no less than forty political newspapers.]

[2] Politicians conclude from that that Fribourg is the most retrograde and reactionary canton in Switzerland. They would probably not express this opinion if Fribourg were not a Catholic canton. In fact, the representative system has not prevented the starting of a university calculated to become a scientific institution of the first rank, and subsidised by the Great Council in December 1886 to the extent of 2,500,000 francs.—Adams, *The Swiss Confederation*, French edition, p. 227.

of the difference between the German cantons and the French, a difference which is gradually becoming less marked in course of time, owing to what one might call the "contagion of example." I am inclined to believe that the difference is due to the fact that the citizens of Romance Switzerland were not brought up in the elementary school of liberty like those in German Switzerland. The citizens of the German communes have always been accustomed to meet in *Gemeinden* to discuss all important matters which interest the communes. They soon become ambitious to enlarge their sphere and to extend it to the domain of cantonal interests whenever they consider that these interests have been inefficiently dealt with by the Great Council. Their French fellow-citizens have not enjoyed this preliminary political training "In Romance Switzerland," wrote M. Dubs, "there is a general idea that communal life emanates from above, and we have no sort of communal assembly. Sometimes the communal electors merely have the right of electing the communal council,[1] which is responsible for nominating the municipal council or executive. This lack of communal life reacts on the political life, and the Romance peoples are much too ready to listen to those in power and wait for them to take the initiative." [2]

---

[1] A deliberate assembly.

[2] Dubs, *Le droit public de la Confédération Suisse*, vol. i. p. 282. [The difference is thus summed up by Mr. Lowell : "Among the Germans there is more jealousy and distrust of the government and more confidence in the direct action of the people, while the French are less democratic in the Swiss sense of the term and more inclined to follow the lead of the regular authorities. Hence the referendum is peculiarly a German institution."]

There can be no doubt, with our present information, that the Valais shares with the Grisons the honour of having been the cradle of the referendum. The referendum exists there in the *compulsory* form, which is considered more democratic than the *optional*; but the only laws upon which the people pronounce are those which involve an outlay of more than 60,000 francs. As a matter of fact, the electors never have the opportunity of using their right. " We always try," a member of the canton told me, "not to exceed the sum of 60,000 francs on any single occasion."

The referendum has existed in Geneva since 1879. It has only been used twice—once against a law ordering the construction of a railway from Geneva to Annemasse; and secondly, against a cantonal resolution granting a subsidy of 400,000 francs to a railway of local importance constructed by a private company. The law was accepted, the resolution rejected.

In Neuchâtel the referendum has only been set in motion twice since 1879—once against a law creating a state bank, which was accepted by the people; and secondly, against a law on the licences of inns—a good law, so I was told, but which was rejected.

The electors have twice made use of their right of initiative. In 1884 they demanded the purchase by the state of a little line of railway which was being mismanaged. The purchase was decided by 9358 votes to 6772. In 1888, the Conservatives, who are in a minority in the canton, but were assisted on this occasion by a group of Radicals, demanded that the law should declare it impossible for a man to be at the same time a National Councillor and an official in the cantonal administration. This proposal was supported by the people.

In the canton of Vaud the referendum does not seem to have been made use of at all, and the popular initiative has only been resorted to once, and that was in 1883. On that occasion the Conservatives demanded, like those of Neuchâtel, that a man should be declared incapable of being at the same time an official in the cantonal administration and a deputy to the Federal Chambers. The people accepted the law, but its authors paid dearly for their success. The Radicals sought for revenge, and introduced progressive taxation on capital in the cantonal constitution of 1885. They persuaded the people that the public revenue ought to be drawn almost exclusively ·from the leisured classes, and that the taxes paid by poor citizens would be reduced in consequence. When the constitution was submitted to the popular vote, it was accepted by 30,000 citizens and rejected by 20,000 out of 60,000 registered electors. The result of the adoption of progressive taxation is easy to imagine. M. Wuarin, without expressly mentioning the canton of Vaud, enables us to recognise it in the following passage in his interesting book *The Tax-payer*:—

"What has happened where the graduated tax has been directed with openly hostile intention against large fortunes? The holders of great fortunes who are not ready to bear much ill-treatment have been driven from the country. It has given rise to a certain number of family arrangements in order to divide up great fortunes so as to bring the higher classes of taxable capital within the range of lower taxation. Moreover, people living abroad, and possessed of a comfortable fortune, have lost all wish to enter a country so inhospitable to wealth, even though it be their own native place."[1]

The political editor of the *Revue Suisse* characterises the law of Vaud on graduated taxation as "absolutely monstrous." It not only levies an enormous toll on great fortunes, but it puts every one under a sort of inquisition, and subjects them to proceedings which are the negation of liberty and personal independence. The citizens, bound hand and foot, are practically delivered into the hands of commissioners named by the government or in its employ, and they are not even able to invoke the protection of the law courts.

The reason that the referendum does not work in the canton of Vaud is due to the fact that the oppositiou is numerically in a hopeless minority. The Radical party is supreme in the canton, for out of more than two hundred members of the Grand Council the Conservatives can scarcely count sixty, of whom eighteen come from the town of Lausanne. Under these conditions, the minority has no interest in making use of the referendum. For any appeal to the electoral body to be effective, it is necessary that those who make the appeal should not be opposed

---

[1] Wuarin, *Le Contribuable*, Paris, 1889, pp. 118–19. Also *L'évolution de la démocratie en Suisse*, in the *Revue des deux Mondes*, August 1, 1891. [See also Lowell, p. 267 and note. In the *Revue Socialiste*, 1894, pp. 567–88, there is a very interesting article by M. Henri Mayr on "Progressive Taxation in the Canton of Vaud."]

by an overwhelming majority which votes solid at the bidding of its leaders.

If, on the other hand, there are two parties in a state, both of whom are well organised and highly disciplined, and nearly equal in strength, then the referendum is bound to become a weapon of the opposition, and, as a matter of fact, this is what actually happened in the Italian canton of Ticino.[1]

For forty years the Liberals had been in power, thanks often to illegal and revolutionary means. In 1875, when the religious struggle had reached the stage of acute·exasperation, a violent reaction took place, and a Conservative majority was sent to the Great Council. As Ticino did not then possess the referendum, the Conservative leaders thought fit to introduce it in 1883. They might be turned out any day and a Liberal majority might return to power, in which case the persecution of the Church would begin. It was prudent when in power to make sure of having a weapon against the Radical laws of the future. Unfortunately they put their scheme into execution rather too soon. If the Conservatives had introduced the referendum on the eve of an election when they expected a reverse, it would have been excellent policy; but in 1883 their position was still too strong, and their new law reacted on themselves.

Shortly after the introduction of the referendum, the Great Council passed a law dealing with the

[1] At the elections of March 3, 1889, on the dissolution of the Great Council, the average poll of the Conservatives was 12,653, of the Liberals 12,018 (*La question électorale dans le canton de Tessin,* Berne, 1890).

development of Ticino. "The proposal," said the political editor of the *Revue Suisse*, "was altogether advantageous to the canton. To improve a great valley, to protect it against periodical floods, to bring into cultivation some very important land at a relatively small cost,[1] might have been expected to meet with the approval of all men." But politics interfered, and the Radicals voted to a man against the proposal. They very cleverly exploited the jealousy which the *Sotto Genere* felt towards the *Sopra Genere*, for whose advantage the improvement was undertaken. The result was that the law was rejected, and the State Council resigned.[2]

SECTION II.—THE REFERENDUM FROM THE SWISS POINT OF VIEW.

Tot capita, tot sensus. I came back from Switzerland with a large memorandum-book crammed full of notes, taken here, there, and everywhere, just as I happened to meet my informants, professors, deputies, journalists, public servants, popular leaders, Catholics, Socialists, and Radicals. In this curious collection, violent abuse and enthusiastic eulogies

---

[1] The Confederation paid fifty per cent. of the expense, the landowners interested thirty per cent., so that the canton was only called on for twenty per cent.

[2] In 1886 the Radicals collected 8000 signatures against a law which would have given the Church more independence in its dealings with the state. Fortunately, however, the law was passed on the 21st March 1880 by a small majority, the votes being 11,651 to 10,410. The year before, an excellent financial law was rejected without even a plausible reason being given, out of pure party spite.

mingle on every page. The referendum is an excellent thing, an incomparable institution : you turn a leaf, and this wonder is suddenly termed a reactionary measure, a clog and a hindrance to progress.

In order to spare the reader the sort of confusion I experienced during the first part of my stay in Switzerland under this flood of contradictory opinions, I will try and classify these criticisms, to some extent, according to the special point of view from which the different people whom I consulted regarded the referendum. It will help to explain the divergencies of opinion to a certain extent.

We will see, first of all, what the politicians think of "Monseigneur the Referendum," as M. Carteret expressed himself one day ; for they are the people who have the closest and longest acquaintance with his lordship.

I. "Parties," wrote a foreign observer, "judge the institution [the referendum] not according to its intrinsic value, but according to the services which it renders or is capable of rendering them. This explains why a further extension of the rights of the people is claimed by different parties in different cantons, in Basle by the Radicals, in St. Gall by the Ultramontanes."[1] This observation of Signor Brunialti is a just one.

Those devoted to active politics are utilitarians. With them it is a matter of calculating the gains and advantages that their party or their cause may hope

[1] Brunialti, *La legge e la libertà*, vol. i. p. 270.

to obtain from the referendum. It is not surprising, therefore, that the members of the government and the majority should speak ill of the referendum, or that the chiefs of the opposition should have no terms too flattering to apply to it. The former owe nothing to the institution, quite the contrary.

A great many of their laws, it is true, have obtained the sanction of the people, but how many others have been rejected after having been drafted with great labour, and defended clause by clause against the minority, and from which its supporters hoped for valuable results for the whole country, and espe cially for their party? The opposition does not experience these regrets. It considers the laws that it has succeeded in rejecting as so many acts of revenge, or as so many landmarks on the road to power. In its hands the referendum has become a weapon with which to do battle, and it has often proved victorious.

All politicians do not regard the referendum in this light. There are some rare exceptions. I have met men who struggled in their youth with all the energy of sincere conviction for the success of demo-cratic institutions. The fortune of elections has brought them into power, and the referendum has done them a bad turn. All the same they have remained faithful to it, and pardoned it with a good grace. I do not undertake to say whether this is the result of democratic conviction or *amour propre*. I simply state the fact as a somewhat exceptional one.

As a general rule, the opposition, whether it be Catholic or Liberal, is satisfied with the referendum.

The majority, on the contrary, whatever its political complexion, wishes to be rid of it. Signor Brunialti quotes two cantons as examples, and I would add those of Geneva, Fribourg, Berne, Lucerne, Aargau, the Grisons, and others. Fribourg is the most curious of all. The cantonal referendum is one of the planks of the Radical platform, and the government and the majority will not have it at any price. It has been said, therefore, that Fribourg is not a democratic canton. If, on the other hand, the eagerness with which the electors go to the ballot-box on voting days is any criterion of the intensity of the democratic opinion in that country, then Fribourg is one of the most democratic cantons in Switzerland. A considerable number of Fribourg voters, moreover, take part in each federal referendum.

What is true of the different cantons in particular is also true of the Confederation in general.

I will not prove the point by quoting the declarations that have been made to me by important members of the Federal Councils. It is only necessary to mention two facts in the parliamentary and political history of Switzerland which every one there knows. One of these is of recent date, and the other several years old.

The question of conferring on the electors the right of initiative afforded the Radical party on three occasions the opportunity of disclosing its enmity towards any measure which increased the legislative power of the people.

In the Assembly the "formulated" initiative, which was advocated by the Right, was resisted by nearly all the speakers on the side of the majority. The Right were successful, thanks to the support of the Socialists and the adhesion of a section of the Radical democrats. But the Federal resolution had still to obtain the sanction of the people, and with few exceptions the Radical newspapers recommended their readers to vote "No." In spite of their eloquence the resolution was adopted, and the result of the poll clearly showed who were the partisans and who the opponents of democracy.

The *Journal de Genève* contained the following paragraph on the day after the voting of the 5th of July 1891 : "Three cantons, Aargau, Thurgau, and Vaud, and two half cantons, Rural-Basle and Appenzell (Outer Rhodes), have been the only ones to vote 'No.' In all these states the majority is Radical. There are also very large minorities against the initiative in the Radical cantons of Berne, Schaffhausen, and Neuchâtel. If we except Basle-City, Solothurn, and Geneva, the largest majorities in favour of the resolution have been given in the Catholic cantons. We might say that the revision which has just been carried is the work of the opposition, supported by a section of the Radicals, who act consistently with the democratic principles which they profess." [1]

But the Radical majority had already shown on a previous occasion in the Chamber how little sympathy it had with the "rights of the people." That was in 1884, on the day after the referendum of the 11th of May, when the people rejected four laws at once.

On the 6th of June three members of the Right, MM. Zemp, Keel, and Pedrazzini, raised a demand in

[1] *Journal de Genève*, July 7, 1891.

the Chamber for constitutional revision, and specially claimed a larger extension of popular rights. There is nothing more instructive than to read the debates on this motion. I will only give two typical extracts. M. Zemp, in demanding the compulsory referendum and popular initiative, said: "Ten years ago we watched the introduction of the referendum into the constitution with considerable anxiety, but to-day our fears have been dissipated. As Federalists we were in doubt in 1874 as to the result of the exclusion of the vote by cantons. We were all labouring under a wrong impression at that time, and we have been taught by experience that the Swiss people are distinctly more Conservative than their representatives." [1]

M. Carteret answered M. Zemp, and did not try to conceal his opinion. "I should like," he said, "to see the referendum completely suppressed, and, above all, I want no compulsory referendum. As to the popular initiative, I dread it as a sort of legislative dynamite. In a word, the so-called rights of the people seem to me nothing more than democratic clap-trap. In the hands of the clerical party they are only used to impede progress." [2]

In less picturesque terms, most of the speakers of the majority expressed the same sentiments; and, some months after the discussion, M. Numa Droz re-echoed them in a long article in the *Revue Suisse*, which he devoted to an examination of the propositions of M. Zemp and his allies. [3]

---

[1] *Züricher Post* of 21st June 1884.

[2] *Züricher Post* of 23rd June 1884.

[3] Numa Droz, *La révision fédérale*, in the *Bibliothèque Universelle*, vol. xxv. It is interesting to compare this article by M. Droz with one he wrote three years later, which ended with the words:

Thus in ten years the attitude of the parties with regard to the federal referendum was completely changed. The Radicals, who introduced it in 1874, arrayed themselves against it; while the Conservatives, who were opposed to it at first, demanded that it should be made more complete, that its domain should be extended, and that it should be made easier in practice.

II. The political philosophers and jurists who judge the referendum from a more scientific standpoint, and to whom the immediate results or advantages of the system are not of paramount importance, nevertheless differ in their conclusions quite as widely as the politicians.

First of all, let us notice the opinion of M. Ernest Naville, who is an avowed adversary of the referendum, but who differs from other people in that he does not mind saying so openly :—

"Only the very unsophisticated could believe that each citizen, after mature consideration, forms a de-

"Switzerland is undoubtedly taking an unprecedented step in resigning the sovereign legislative power into the hands of a body of more than 600,000 electors. If we succeed, our descendants will be able to pride themselves on having been the first to make one of the greatest advances in civilisation and political progress. And I am convinced we are on the way to success" (Numa Droz, *La démocratie et son avenir*, in the *Bibliothèque Universelle*, vol. xvi.). [Writing in 1895, M. Droz says: "It seems to me that this institution, which is of a frankly Conservative character, has done more good than harm. Although I am a friend of progress, I do not desire that it should be hasty, inconsiderate, or turbulent. The democratic machine, like any other, has need of a counter-check, and for that reason I support it" (*La démocratie en Suisse, Études et portraits politiques*, p. 467). He is a most inveterate opponent of the popular initiative.]

cided opinion of his own on every law. In order that all the shepherds of the mountains, all the farmers of the valleys, and all the dwellers in the towns of Switzerland might have an intelligent personal opinion on the often very complicated laws, they would require an amount of culture and leisure which is at present, and always will be, beyond the reach of the great majority of the population."

"It is argued," wrote M. Naville further on, "that, since the laws are submitted to the people, nothing contrary to their wishes can be imposed upon them. That is true enough when the laws are clearly expressed, and are confined to one particular point. Such laws are, however, very exceptional. In the majority of cases the leaders of the political party in the majority in the councils have certain methods by which they induce the people to assent to the wishes of the party instead of asserting their own. One of these consists in incorporating several laws referring to different questions into one act, and submitting it as it stands to the popular vote. The second expedient is to make some slight alterations in a law that has been refused, and then it is submitted a second, and even a third time, if necessary.

"Independently of these considerations, the important fact which makes it impossible to attribute to the referendum the value in practice which it has in theory is, that such a large number do not vote at all. 'The people' who are said to have accepted or refused a law are too often only a very small part of the whole electorate.

"Legislation by the people, in the sense that every citizen is able to study the laws proposed, and is capable of criticising and of forming an independent judgment on their merits, is, and probably always will be, a chimera, in spite of free and compulsory education.

"The plebiscite is in its proper place when it is a question of voting on constitutions,[1] but, as far as law-making is concerned, the representative system is the only one capable of adequately expressing democracy under the conditions of modern society."[2]

The opinions of M. Wuarin, Professor of Sociology in the University of Geneva, are altogether different. Instead of wishing to restrict the right of the electors to votes in the revision of constitutions, he demands that the referendum should be extended to embrace a special domain from which it has hitherto been thought prudent to exclude it. In his book *Le Contribuable* (The Tax-payer), M. Wuarin enters upon an examination of the possible means by which the deterioration of public finance may be ameliorated or prevented; and an extension of popular rights to include a vote on the budgets and taxes is one of the remedies for which he expresses the strongest approval.

"The man who pays," he says, "ought to have the real control; and the public officials, who are only his

---

[1] Herr von Orelli also considers that the referendum ought to be confined to constitutional revisions. He adds that the vote should always be preceded by public meetings, in which the members could explain to their constituents the subjects they are expected to vote upon. —Von Orelli, *Das Staatsrecht der schweizerischen Eidgenossenschaft*, p. 107.

[2] E. Naville, *À propos du referendum*, in *Représentation proportionnelle*, April 1887. See, by the same author, *La question électorale*, Geneva, 1871, p. x. ; *La démocratie représentative*, Paris, 1881.

business agents, ought to be really dependent on him. In finance, as in everything else, the policy of the country should be directed by the country. The way to effect this is to put two levers into the hands of the people—the right of veto or the referendum, and the right of initiative." The referendum, according to M. Wuarin, should be extended in four respects :—

(1) The referendum as it now actually exists is more political than administrative, and it ought to be both.

As a matter of fact, financial decisions are among the questions on which the country can pronounce, but they have to assume a certain form, for the budgets, properly so called, are excepted from the popular control.

(2) The power of declaring a law to be urgent, by which it is removed from the sphere of the referendum, ought at least to be expressly restricted to a limited number of cases.

(3) The referendum ought to be compulsory.

(4) It ought also to be introduced for communal matters.[1]

M. Dubs, formerly one of the most formidable opponents of the referendum, recognises regretfully that it is now an accomplished fact.

"The *compulsory* referendum," he writes, "is the only form which gives due expression to the idea that the people must share directly in the work of legislation. But, on the other hand, it is impossible to deny that as soon as the state has

---

[1] [This has now been done in Geneva. There is also a referendum in the towns of Berne and Zürich. See Preface.]

increased in powers or in territory, this method of legislation becomes very burdensome and costly. Many laws have no great interest for the people in general; many have a special and technical character about which the great mass of the voters have not, and cannot have, any opinion. The people are forced to vote, with no wish to do so; they have a responsibility imposed upon them which they are not qualified to bear, while the council gets rid of a responsibility which is part of its duty.

"The *optional* referendum, by which the people do not participate in legislation, except on direct demand, seems to be open to none of these objections. But, as a matter of fact, the veto long ago rejected as undesirable, is there still, though under another name. The popular right of intervention has only been made exceptional. The agitation which necessarily precedes each popular voting in order to bring it about, paralyses the ordinary working of the political machinery, inflames the minds of the people, and leads to unnatural coalitions. More than all this, the idea of the regular co-operation of the sovereign people in legislation is definitely abandoned. Whatever be the form of the referendum, whether it be compulsory or optional, it is nevertheless but a poor substitute for a Landsgemeinde, owing to the fact that people are scattered at the time of voting, and that there is, as a rule, no previous discussion. The Landsgemeinde is the visible expression of the unity of the country, and the idea of this unity has a powerful and ennobling influence on the individual. No such feeling is aroused, however, by the mere fact of dropping a paper into the ballot-box, without anything approaching a discussion having preceded the mere writing of Yes or No on the ticket.

" The idea is in itself truly democratic, and it will be à task for future generations to evolve a method by which it may be better realised.

" It is still a new question, and experience will throw light on many points." [1]

M. Hilty, who defended the rights of the people against M. Dubs in '1868' has remained faithful to his original convictions. He published in 1887 a remarkable study of the Swiss referendum, in the *Archiv für öffentliches Recht*. While considering that the time had not come to pronounce a definite judgment, as Switzerland was only going through its apprenticeship to the system, he considers that the results of the referendum have not been discouraging. " It goes without saying," he concludes " that it would be unreasonable to propose the referendum in any country taken hap-hazard; but when the electorate possesses the essential qualities, the referendum is to be preferred to the representative system, for the four following reasons:—

" (1) Legislation acquires a doubly popular character. The people learn to understand the laws better, especially when they are accompanied by explanatory messages. On the other hand, the Chamber is obliged to draft laws that are short, simple, and intelligible to the majority.

" (2) The referendum encourages and strengthens patriotism, for government no longer appears the

[1] Dubs, *Le droit public de la Confédération Suisse*, Geneva, 1878, vol. i. p. 214.

privilege of an exclusive class. It develops also a feeling of responsibility in the electors, by calling upon them to make important decisions likely to influence the future of their country.

"(3) The great advantage of the referendum is to show on which side the majority lies, and to give a sharp and conclusive reply to the protests of the minority.

"(4) The referendum, finally, offers an inducement to the ruling classes to remain in permanent contact with the lower classes, and to take an active interest in their political education." [1]

III. It only remains for us to mention a very interesting discussion which has taken place during the last few years between the partisans of the

---

[1] Unlike M. Wuarin, M. Hilty, although he supports the referendum, would not think it prudent to submit financial questions to the vote (p. 416).

[M. Hilty, in his article in the *Revue de Droit internationale*, 1892, pp. 396–98, seems to consider that the optional form of the referendum is best at present, but that the compulsory referendum is the "system of the future," not only in the cantons, but in the Confederation. He says that the optional referendum, when put into force, is always an act of hostility against the government. The rejection of a law by the people is a censure, and a law accepted in spite of the opposition of a large minority has suffered a loss of prestige in public opinion. If the referendum were often demanded, the real direction of public affairs would pass into the hands of the popular coalitions, organised to collect the necessary number of votes and to direct this kind of political campaign. "On the other hand," M. Hilty continues, "the optional referendum, being less frequent than the compulsory, is a sort of apprenticeship in legislation which is by no means to be despised. The difficulty about the compulsory referendum is to define the exceptions, so as to withdraw from the popular vote unimportant administrative regulations, diplomatic matters, international treaties, and the decisions in case of peace and war."]

referendum and the partisans of proportional representation. An article by M. Numa Droz appeared in 1882 in the *Bibliothèque Universelle* which gave the adherents of electoral reform the opportunity of comparing their system with the referendum. M. Numa Droz, in mentioning the various advantages of the referendum, laid special stress on the fact that it made the question of proportional representation less acute.

"When Parliament can decide everything," he said, "the desire to be represented there is very strong; but when the people have the last word, the majority is less anxious to exclude the minorities, whose opinion may be so useful to the success of a law. The minorities, on the other hand, are less liable to be treated unjustly or to be excluded, because they can urge before the people themselves those ideas which they have not been able to express in the Council Chamber."[1]

Two years later, MM. Zemp, Keel, and Pedrazzini demanded the application of the principle of proportional representation in the case of the elections to the National Council. In the speech which he made to support his motion, M. Pedrazzini replied to the arguments of M. Droz. "It has been stated in the *Revue Suisse*," he said, "that minority representation is less necessary in our country because we possess the referendum. I cannot share that view. In its essence the referendum is only a machine for saying Aye or No to a law which has been already framed. It is of vital importance that

[1] Numa Droz, *La démocratie et son avenir*, in the *Bibliothèque Universelle*, vol. xvi. p. 411.

in Parliament, when the laws are discussed, every shade of opinion should find expression." [1]

M. de Laveleye reproduced the arguments of M. Numa Droz in an article on the referendum which appeared in the *Revue Internationale*, February 10, 1887. [2]

M. Ernest Naville answered him in the following month in the same review. [3] According to that eminent Genevan lawyer, the Swiss referendum, so far from diminishing the importance of electoral reform, is the indisputable proof of its necessity and urgency. The rejection of a large number of laws submitted to the people proves that there is a real divergency of opinion between the majority of the electors and the majority of the elected. This divergency, according to M. Naville, is only due to a bad electoral system, which leaves large bodies of electors without any representation.

" Proportional representation of all sections of the electors will, as far as institutions can effect it, make the majority of the representatives correspond to the majority of the electors. When this result has been brought about, the demand for a legislative plebiscite will only be justified in exceptional circumstances, and will become very rare."

As a matter of fact, M. Naville does not deny that the referendum may correct the injustices and defects

---

[1] Extract from an evidently incomplete report of M. Pedrazzini's arguments which appeared in the *Züricher Post* of 21st June 1884.

[2] The article by M. de Laveleye, first printed separately in Rome by Forzani, has been incorporated in his later work, *Le gouvernement dans la démocratie*, vol. ii. ch. 4.

[3] M. de Naville's article has been reprinted by the *Représentation proportionnelle*, April 1887.

of the existing electoral system; but the foregoing quotations show clearly that he attaches very little value to this palliative. He considers that it would be better policy to prevent the evil than to look exclusively for a remedy.

" To say that the referendum makes electoral reform less necessary and urgent, since the people are thereby enabled to give their opinion on the decisions of the councils, is much the same as reasoning in this way : We have doctors and medicines, so hygienic precautions to prevent illness have lost much of their importance." [1]

The ideas which M. Naville defends with so much talent and perseverance unfortunately still lack the weight of practical experience.[2]. Electoral reform is only making slow progress. Ticino and Neuchâtel have recently obtained proportional representation. Geneva and Basle-City have made many attempts to introduce it; in many other cantons the opposition, Catholic or Liberal, claims a fairer distribution of seats, but everywhere it encounters the same obstinate refusal on the part of the majority.[3] In the Con-

---

[1] M. Walras, Professor of Political Economy at the University of Lausanne, told me that he shared M. Naville's views on the referendum. But it is from the representation of interests that M. Walras expects to obtain the results which M. Naville hopes from proportional representation.

[2] See also an interesting article by M. Naville entitled, " M. Numa Droz's Views on Proportional Representation," in the *Bulletin de la Société Suisse pour la représentation proportionnelle*, August 1888.

[3] [Up to 1896 Ticino, Geneva, Neuchâtel, Zug, and Solothurn had adopted proportional representation for the election of the Great Councils. In Ticino, Geneva, and Zug the executive is also elected by the same method. It had been voted down by the people in St. Gall in 1893, and in Berne in 1896.]

federation, electoral reform now has many supporters among the Right; but on the day that a motion is brought forward from this quarter to obtain proportional elections for the National Council, the Radicals would immediately claim the revision of Article 80 of the Constitution. They would demand that each canton, instead of invariably sending two members to the Council of State, should enjoy a representation proportional to the number of its inhabitants. The prospect of so fundamental a change in the organisation of the Second Chamber will probably prevent, for a considerable time to come, any serious attempt that might be made to introduce the system of proportional representation in elections to the National Council.

CONCLUSION

THE referendum—the origin, forms, and results of which we have just studied—may in conclusion be considered from two directly opposite points of view. It can either be regarded as a complement to, and a corrective of, the abuses of a democratic representative system ; or, on the other hand, as an institution which inaugurates, in states of a certain size, government by direct legislation, which is incompatible with the representative system.

Representative government rests on the principle and practice of delegation of power. The nation, by means of the electoral body, periodically gives men in whom it has confidence a mandate to legislate for the general good. Whatever solution of the very difficult problem of representation is adopted, it is to be feared that an elected assembly, if left with the sole power, will not be able to escape the natural tendency to abuse its authority.

" That there should be in every polity a centre of resistance to the predominant power in the constitution I have already maintained, and I regard it as a fundamental maxim of government," says John Stuart Mill.[1] He thinks that the centre of resistance ought to be found in a Second Chamber. But in spite of

1 Stuart Mill, *Representative Government*, p. 242.

all precautions to ensure harmony between the repre-
tatives of the nation and the nation itself, it is impossible to prevent an occasional disagreement between
them.   Whenever a crisis of this sort occurs in the
course of a parliament, the difficulty can be overcome in two ways. 'If parliament has clearly lost
the confidence of the body of electors, there is no
resource but a dissolution.   If, without losing this
confidence, it has passed an unpopular measure, then
it is only necessary to prevent this measure being
carried into effect.

In a monarchy, the nation recognises in the king
the right of veto and the right to dissolve parliament.   In a republic, these prerogatives may belong
to a president elected by the people.   But when there
is neither king nor president, evidently the people,
in whom the sovereignty resides, must be invested
with the right of dissolution and the right of veto.
This is exactly what it has been necessary to do in
Switzerland.

After the French Revolution of 1830, when a representative democracy was substituted for aristocratic
republicanism, neither proportional representation
nor the representation of interests obtained any
recognition, and no acceptable basis could be found
for the institution of a Second Chamber.   When it
became necessary to put some check on the Great
Council, against the omnipotence of which no preventive measures had been taken, it was impossible
to consider the project of endowing the executive
with the right of veto, for it was nominated by the
Great Council as in the aristocratic constitution
before 1830.   To set against the elected assembly

there was only the power of the people, which had been proclaimed sovereign by all the constitutions.

It is no more derogatory to representative demo_cracy to arm this sovereign with the right of veto, and the power of dissolving the Chamber, than to give these prerogatives to a king in a constitutional monarchy. The system of representative democracy, as it is understood in the United States, is the delegation and not the abdication of power by the people.[1]

It is scarcely necessary to add that, regarded from this point of view, the referendum ought necessarily to take the optional form. *In practice*[2] the Chamber always remains invested with legislative power; it is only exceptionally that the people intervene directly to oppose the execution of laws which displease them.

As a form of popular veto, the referendum exists to-day in the Confederation and in a certain number of cantons. As we have seen, its method is defective and its results are questionable. No one denies that in the past there has been an absolute necessity for some such system, both in the cantons[3] and in the Confederation,[4] but to-day it is subject to the influence of two opposite tendencies: some wish to change it into

---

[1] In countries which have copied the main features of the English Constitution it would be paradoxical to suggest that the referendum is compatible with representative government, because the duty of electors is limited to choosing the members, while the veto is exercised by higher authorities. But in Switzerland, where representative government does not follow the classical model of England, the referendum has been found to fit in naturally with the rest of the body politic.

[2] *In principle* it is not so, as I have shown above (p. 177).

[3] See above, pp. 85–90.

[4] Pp. 93, 94, 100–102.

a compulsory referendum; others, without thinking of abolishing it, are seeking to make it of less frequent occurrence.

In this contest between democrats and parliamentarians, everything will depend on the tactics of the two parties. The compulsory referendum and proportional representation appear together in the programme of the opposition. In several cantons the leaders of the minority seem ready to let the question of the compulsory referendum alone, if they are given a number of seats in the Great Council proportional to the numerical strength of their party. They are generally of M. Naville's opinion, that electoral reform will make the referendum unnecessary. If proportional representation realises the hopes of its partisans, it will be the means of diminishing the number of plebiscites.

But there is another and perhaps more efficient method of attaining that result. Up till now it has been impossible to give the power of resistance to the Council of State (the executive authority), because it has been responsible to the Chamber; but now that its position has been altered so that in many cantons it is directly elected by the people, it might be possible to invest it, as in the United States, with the right of veto in the name of the people. In its hands the veto would run less risk of becoming a weapon of the opposition, which is the actual result of the referendum when parties are almost equal.

In the cantons where the minority is very small, it will find the veto of the executive power a more valuable protection than the referendum.

Finally, the veto will no longer be capriciously

exercised, or a law voted down for reasons which have no connection with the bill in question. Unlike the electors, the Council of State would be able to give the grounds of its refusal; it would know the faults and omissions of the laws better than any one else, since it gives advice to the Chamber on all legislative measures of any importance.[1]

Representative democracy, although it can work sometimes in harmony with the referendum, is, in the eyes of the Swiss democrats, a form of government which has had its day, and which is doomed to disappear. If one may believe them, the people will in future no longer delegate their sovereignty to elected representatives, but will exercise it directly themselves.

The type of government which most exactly corresponds to this idea is found in the Landsgemeinden of the cantons. There the people nominate the judge and the members of the executive. They have the right of initiative, and meet in a general assembly to discuss and pass the laws.

In larger states, legislation by the people has always been considered a utopia; but the Swiss democrats have openly defied the received opinion. They have aimed at proving practically, not theoretically, the futility of the objections brought against direct legislation. By the compulsory referendum—which is the first, though incomplete, realisation of their system—

[1] The Genevan State Council, which has been elective since 1847, has from that date had the right to temporarily suspend bills which have been drafted against its wish (Art. 54 of the Cantonal Constitution of Geneva). This may have been one of the reasons which prevented the introduction of the referendum in Geneva till 1879.

they have taken the final decision in legislation out of the hands of the Chamber to place it in those of the people.

We may ask whether their bold experiment has succeeded, and whether it would be possible to say from henceforward that direct legislation is a possible and practicable form of government even in great states. In my opinion, the experience in the cantons which enjoy the compulsory referendum is far from conclusive. It has not been possible, in the first place, to find a fairly satisfactory method of working the referendum. "We do not demand," the democrats said at first, "that the people should make the laws, but only that they should vote on them." [1]

Their claim had an importance which they did not seem to realise. The elector who writes Aye or No on his ballot-paper performs an act the apparent simplicity of which has attracted the democrats, but this act is, as a matter of fact, a very complex one. It requires that each voter should be able not only to understand why legislation is necessary, but also should be able to judge whether the law in question is adequate to meet the case. Nothing effectual has as yet been devised which would assist the elector in forming a personal opinion on such a subject. If the original supporters of the compulsory referendum really knew what they wanted, they are open to the reproach of having aimed at an end without considering the means, and with having made a start without even asking if there was any chance of arriving at the goal.

---

[1] Gengel, *Aphorismen über demokratisches Staatsrecht*, p. 25; *Die Erweiterung der Volksrechte*, p. 52.

The organisation of the compulsory referendum being so obviously defective, its partisans should have been satisfied with demanding the active co-operation of the electorate in legislation in a limited number of cases. On the contrary, however, they wished to begin on a large scale, and claimed that all legislative measures without exception should be submitted to the people. The result has only brought discredit on their system.

When we examine the statistics of the votings in the case of the compulsory referendum, we find that the first condition of success has been wanting. "The people have only to express their will," Herr Gengel said, "and direct legislation becomes an accomplished fact."[1] That is, however, exactly what the people will not do, and it is a little ridiculous to talk of legislation by the people when more than half the citizens refuse to exercise their legislative rights. An attempt is now being made to conceal this check by introducing the compulsory vote.[2] The tactics are bad, because the blank ballot-papers clearly demonstrate that though the elector may be forced to put a paper in the ballot-box, he does not necessarily vote when he does so.

The experiment of the democrats cannot be said to have met with success. If they wish to avoid complete failure they must do two things, and do them quickly. They must first find a better method

---

[1] Gengel, *Die Erweiterung der Volksrechte*, p. 59.

[2] "To establish true democracy it is necessary to be consistent, and when an election or a voting takes place the real sovereign must decide, and not only a section of the whole. Attendance at the polling-booth ought to be as compulsory as it is in the case of juries or military drill."—Wuarin, *Le Contribuable*, p. 282.

of direct legislation, and secondly, they must confine the referendum to a small number of laws. Then, perhaps, with a people as well prepared for direct government as the Swiss, they may succeed in proving that their system is not a mere Utopia, and that it is possible without any great danger under certain special circumstances.

There are indications to-day in different quarters that the referendum will not remain the monopoly of Switzerland, but that the question of its adoption will soon be considered in other countries.[1]

[1] [The referendum is recognised in all the states of the United States, except Delaware, for changes in the constitution. There is, moreover, a tendency to elaborate and add to the constitutions, so that they cover a great deal of ground, and the range of subjects controlled by the popular vote is a very wide one. See Bryce, *American Commonwealth* ; Oberholtzer, *The Referendum in America*, chap. ii.

Some of the constitutions also expressly provide for a popular vote on certain subjects not included in the constitution, such as the power of the Legislature to contract debts above a certain sum, the alienation of property, the expenditure of money beyond a certain amount, the creation of state banks, and the location of the state capital.

There is also a local referendum, "which has developed," says Mr. Oberholtzer, "until at this time there is not a state in the Union in which local questions of certain given classes are not submitted to the popular vote. In Iowa the advance has been almost to that point which the referendum has attained in Switzerland." See Oberholtzer, *The Referendum in America*.

The referendum has also been proposed in five of the Australasian parliaments, and a referendum on the education question was actually taken in South Australia in 1896. See article on the Referendum in Australia and New Zealand, *Contemporary Review*, August 1897.

The new Federal Constitution of Australasia was submitted to the popular vote in June 1898, and was rejected in New South Wales.

As to the question of its adoption into England, see the article by Professor Dicey, "Ought the Referendum to be introduced into England?" *Contemporary Review*, April 1890; also the discussion of the subject by various writers in the *National Review*, 1894. See also W. H. Lecky, *Democracy and Liberty*, vol. i. pp. 237-43.]

As early as September 1869, the question of direct legislation, by means of the compulsory referendum and popular initiative, was brought up at a congress held by the old *International* at Basle.[1] Legislation by the people has become since then one of the demands of international socialism. It appeared in the programme of Gotha in 1895, and last year it found a place in the programme of the Congress of Erfurt.

In Belgium, Article 1 of the programme of the workmen's party runs as follows: "Universal suffrage, direct legislation by the people — that is to say, popular sanction of, and initiative in, legislation— with secret and compulsory voting. Elections to take place on Sunday."[2]

[1] Burkli, *Direkte Gesetzgebung durch das Volk.*

[2] It has been proposed in some countries to leave the decision in all communal questions to the electors of the commune.

In 1880 a bill for a municipal referendum was presented in the Italian Chamber (*cf.* Crivellari, *Il referendum nella Svizzera e la sua introduzione nel diritto amministrativo Italiano*, in the *Archivio giuridico* of Serafini, vol. xxxiv. pp. 377–423 ; Brunialti, *La legge e la libertà*, pp. 283–286). A similar proposal has recently been made in France by M. de Mackau and some of the Bonapartists. The Chamber has not debated it. See *Journal officiel*, June 17, 1890, pp. 1083–89.

The subject of a communal referendum has not yet been discussed in the Belgian Chamber, but in several communes the people have already been consulted on local questions.

[M. Jean Signorel, in his book, *Le Referendum législatif*, devotes the second chapter of Book III. to giving an account of the eight different propositions with regard to the referendum which have been presented in the French Chamber of Deputies between 1881 and November 1895. In Book III., pp. 181–89, M. Signorel gives an account of some of the various referendum proposals made in Socialist journals and at Socialist congresses. The introduction of the municipal referendum in France is advocated by M. de la Sizeranne in a small book entitled *Le Referendum Communal*. M. Signorel gives, on p. 189, a list of French towns in which a referendum has been taken on questions of local importance.]

On the other hand, the referendum has been suggested as a means by which the sovereign in a constitutional monarchy could avoid having recourse to a dissolution of parliament. A Prussian statesman not long ago put forward and supported this idea in a pamphlet.[1] The idea was taken up by the Belgian Government, and the result was a proposal for the *royal referendum.*[2]

Whenever the referendum is discussed in the press or in the parliaments of other countries, its partisans and opponents will naturally turn their attention to Switzerland, and will ask what its effect has been there. This will be the surest means of never coming to an agreement. In 1872, when the referendum was discussed in the Federal Assembly, the various speakers dwelt on the results of the institution in the cantons. Some of them considered these votings excellent, whilst others characterised them as detestable.[3] A stranger would probably be equally at a loss, for there are so many different ways of regarding progress, and no two men regard it from the same standpoint.

The acceptance or rejection of laws which are at all complicated cannot be ascribed to either the good sense or the ignorance of the people; for, as the Swiss referendum is at present organised, the mass of the people has no opportunity of estimating the value of these laws. The actual result of a vote may be either good or bad, but it proves nothing for or against the

---

[1] Hoffmann, *Das Plebiscit als Correctiv der Wahlen,* Berlin, 1884.

[2] I have discussed this proposal in the *Revue générale* of December 1, 1891. (S. Deploige, *Le Referendum royal.*)

[3] Curti, *Geschichte der schweizerischen Volksgesetzgebung,* p. 254.

people as voters. The result of a vote may be fortunate or unfortunate, but it has been determined as a matter of fact by a thousand different influences, and to speak of it as the expression of a thoughtful and conscientious popular judgment is only to juggle with words.

It is, however, of considerable importance to determine the circumstances which make the direct interference of the Swiss people in legislation almost harmless. Some of the safeguards are as follows :—

(1) If the evolution of democracy in Switzerland is followed with attention, it is quite obvious that the referendum has not been introduced without due consideration, or merely to satisfy theorists. The popular veto, as we have seen, was a reform which was necessary on account of the unsatisfactory working of the·existing public bodies. The great expectations cherished by the authors of the compulsory referendum have been falsified by experience, but no reproach attaches to them for having believed in the possibility of success. The people in the cantons in which there is a compulsory referendum were better prepared than any other for the exercise of direct government. They had undergone a political education in the communes, and had been trained there in the discussion of public matters. There were many reasons for supposing that they were sufficiently advanced to be able to undertake cantonal legislation as well. One of the great faults of the democrats has been to wish to rush immediately to extremes, and to hurry on the people too fast.

(2) The popular initiative, which has followed the referendum by a natural evolution, may, it is true, excite some apprehensions. But first of all it must be noticed, that for legislative purposes it only exists as yet in a few cantons. Further, as M. Droz very cogently observed, " The citizens can no doubt demand what they like, but if they exceed the limits of cantonal sovereignty, there is above them the federal sovereignty, which has power to make them keep within bounds. For instance, some years ago a proposal was brought before the people of Zürich by means of the popular initiative, the object of which was to establish a monopoly in the issue of bank notes. The proposal was adopted, but the Federal Council quashed the law, as contrary to Article 39 of the Federal Constitution. The Federal Tribunal has more than once declared the laws or resolutions of the cantons to be invalid, and contrary to the constitution of the cantons as guaranteed by the Constitution." [1]

(3) Federal and cantonal laws have frequently been rejected by means of the referendum, yet these decisions of the electorate have never been taken as an order of dismissal to the legislative assembly. Could this be so in a country where the parliamentary system has a different meaning to what it has in Switzerland ? nor are Ministerial crises known in Switzerland ; the government does not invite the formation of another Cabinet by resigning. If it is impossible to come to an amicable solution of the difference by mutual concessions, they are content to postpone

[1] Numa Droz, *La révision fédérale*, in the *Bibliothèque Universelle*, vol. xxv. p. 29.

the settlement of the question to a more suitable time.

(4) Owing to the limitations of the federal power, the Swiss people as a whole do not often have the opportunity of giving a vote. The cantons are still sovereign states, which have only handed over to the central power duties which concern the whole population. Their sovereignty has remained intact within a very extended sphere—the civil law of persons, the law of real property, criminal law,[1] civil and criminal procedure, cantonal and local police, the organisation of the communes, public works, the organisation of education of all grades, &c.

Even within the narrow limits of the federal authority, restrictions and obstacles have been placed in the way of the direct interference of the people. The Federal Assembly, by its power of declaring urgency, can remove federal resolutions out of the reach of the referendum. There are, moreover, certain classes of laws which are never made the subject of an appeal to the people, such as international treaties, budget laws, estimates, &c.

(5) Finally, the federal referendum could never become an instrument of systematic opposition, or paralyse the ordinary progress of government. Switzerland is divided into twenty-five autonomous states, differing in language, in religion, and in traditions, all of which are insurmountable barriers to the creation of strong currents of opinion. There are

---

1 [The Federal Council sent a message to the Assembly in 1897 suggesting that the civil and criminal law should be codified. The constitutional amendment giving them the power to do this will probably be voted upon this year, 1898.]

no two great political parties in Switzerland. The Radical party, which is in a majority, is as united as ever when measures are being taken hostile to the Church, but it splits up when cantonal sovereignty is the question. On the other hand, no opposition group is sufficiently strong in itself to decide the result of a vote. Coalitions are always necessary to secure the rejection of a law, and these coalitions are difficult to form, because they require compromise and mutual sacrifices which are unpopular with the leaders of a party.

These, then, are some of the peculiar circumstances which explain the history, the development, and the results of the referendum. It is important to bring them out into strong relief, because they are very important. If they are altered in Switzerland, the referendum and the popular initiative will in their turn be fundamentally affected. If they are not found in a foreign country which desires to transplant the system of popular consultations, then the result can only be a succession of surprises.

APPENDIX

I

THE POPULAR INITIATIVE IN THE FEDERAL CONSTITUTION

THE popular initiative, as at present organised in the Swiss Confederation, is a very important innovation. The right of initiating laws now belongs to an indeterminate body who are as important as the Government and Legislature put together. When 50,000 citizens use their right of initiative and bring forward a complete bill, it goes to the people as it stands, just as a law would do which has passed the two houses of the Federal Assembly. Thus any chance combination of citizens unknown, and perhaps unskilled, possess the drafting powers of the Federal Council and the legislative powers of the National Council and the Council of States.

By the amendment of 1891, these 50,000 citizens have the right of demanding that a new constitutional article be inserted or an old one altered or abolished. But a constitutional article is nowhere defined. Any proposition of whatever nature may now be submitted to the people if only it be called a constitutional article.

"By means of the initiative," says M. Jacques Berney, Professor in the Lausanne Faculty of Law, "the Swiss people may govern themselves freely in every domain. They may enact laws, adopt a penal code, naturalise foreigners, grant amnesties, contract loans, convert the public debt, grant subsidies, conclude or reject treaties, declare war, make peace, frame a revenue tariff, abolish duties, try cases, pronounce judgments, annul sentences of the court, condemn citizens to death, &c. They may do anything they will, upon the sole condition that they inscribe it in the constitution." This is, of course, an extreme statement, but it brings out very forcibly the scope of the new initiative amendment. Thus, under cover of a constituent power, the people have secured an important legislative right subject to none of the limitations of ordinary legislation which must move in the groove prescribed by the constitution. There is no existing power in the constitution which can restrict the exercise of the new right to any particular subject, or which can quash any law brought forward by the initiative as unconstitutional.

The right of thus initiating laws or constitutional changes is a very different thing from the right of petition, as M. Deploige has already pointed out. The initiative is an appeal to the people; a petition is a suggestion to the Government. The former must be attended to within the prescribed time and in the specified way, even against the wishes of the Government; the fate of the latter is entirely in the hands of the Government. Any number of people may sign a petition without any formalities and within any time. A petition, moreover, is not submitted to the popular vote. An initiative demand must be signed by 50,000 citizens, *i.e.* by one-fourteenth of the present voting population, and its fate rests with the sovereign people.

There is, however, a certain superficial similarity between the initiative and the optional referendum, which only takes place when 30,000 citizens demand that a law shall be referred to the people. The resemblance lies in the fact that both are the spontaneous movement of a certain number of citizens to determine the vote of the people. The sphere of the optional referendum is, however, confined to the decisions of the legislative authority, and, as the activity of the State cannot rest for ever in suspense, a certain time is fixed within which action must be taken. After ninety days the people in Switzerland are powerless. They have thus to pronounce on laws before they can esti. mate their effect. By means of the initiative, however, a law can be repealed at any time.

Again, the referendum places the people in the same position 'as a sovereign in a monarchy. Their sanction, which may be express or tacit, is a necessary part of the constitutional machinery, and no law can come into force without it. The people invested with the right of initiat. ing laws do not ordinarily co-operate in legislation. They only intervene accidentally, exceptionally, and on extraordi. nary occasions.

In the federal domain only "laws and decrees of a gene- ral character, and which are not urgent, are subjects for the referendum. It has been possible for the Federal Assembly to treat certain decrees as "urgent," or not general in character, and so withdraw them from the popular vote. Treaties and the budget are also outside the scope of the referendum.

By means of the initiative the people are able to obtain a decision on any question whether qualified as "urgent" or "not general," whether it be a treaty or the Federal Budget. Its domain is therefore much wider than the referendum. The initiative can do all that the optional referendum can do, and a great deal more. The optional referendum is therefore practically unnecessary in a State that has the popular initiative.

The organisation of the initiative is much the same as that of the optional referendum. There are the same regulations as to personal signature and attestation. In the demand by initiative each list of signatures must contain the text of the demand, so that each person may know what he is signing; and if this formality be omitted, all the signatures on that paper are null and void. The signatures have to be collected within six months, or they are not counted in the total.

The demand when ready is sent in to the Federal Council. They examine it and lay it before the Assembly at the next session, with their report on the subject, dealing with both the form and the matter of the demand. The Assembly must decide upon its attitude within a year. If the proposal be by general motion, they decide whether they agree with the proposal, in which case they can practically take their own time in framing the law ; or they may decide against the petition, and consult the people as to whether a revision in this sense shall be undertaken. If the answer be in the affirmative they proceed to draft the law. All they are bound to do, however, is to determine on one course or another within a year. If the formulated initiative be used, they have to decide within a year whether they will accept or reject the popular law, or whether they will present a counter proposal. If they decide on a counter proposal, it has to be ready within the year. The formulated initiative is therefore more expeditious, and it also ensures that the Assembly does not misinterpret the wishes of the people.

The organisation of the voting in the case of the Federal Assembly presenting a counter project, gave rise to a great deal of discussion. The Federal Council proposed to submit the two schemes to the popular vote, and then have a second voting, in which the proposal which obtained the majority should be submitted as opposed to the *status quo*. Another system proposed was that three questions should be stamped on the voting papers : (1) Is there any necessity for a revision ? (2) If so, do you approve the proposal of the initiants ? (3) Do you approve the proposal of the Assembly ?[1] The proposal finally adopted was that of the

[1] These proposals are discussed by M. Jacques Berney, *L'Initiative populaire*, p. 19.

National Council, and the result is that two questions are to be stamped on the voting papers—

I. Do you approve the proposal of the Assembly?

II. Do you approve the proposal of the petitioners?

The voters may put a NO against either of them, or a NO against one and a YES against the other. If, however, YES be placed against both, the vote is invalid. This system is favourable to the *status quo* for two reasons : (1) The partisans of the *status quo* possess two votes, the partisans of a reform only one. Those who vote against one proposal because they prefer the other are in reality voting for the *status quo* in preference to the proposal they have vetoed, whereas, as a matter of fact, they might prefer that proposal to no reform at all. They cannot place them in order of merit. Should the proposal they have voted for be rejected, they are in the same position as if they had voted against any change.

(2) It is possible for the Federal Assembly to present a proposal differing but slightly from the popular proposal. This would split the votes of those who wished for a reform, and play into the hands of those who wished for no change. This was brought out very clearly in 1845, when the Great Council of Vaud was discussing the question of the introduction of the initiative. The deputies were pretty generally agreed on the advisability of introducing the initiative, but as each voted for his own system of working it, none of the proposals gained a majority, and the temporary result was no initiative at all.

When the Assembly does not present a counter proposal, it merely advises that the law drawn up by the initiants be " accepted " or that it be " rejected," and the law is printed and sent round to the electors with the voting-ticket, in the same way as a constitutional law which has passed both houses. The elector writes his "Yes" or "No" on the ticket which contains the title of the law, and it is adopted if there is a double majority in its favour—a majority of the people and a majority of the cantons. If either a majority of the people or a majority of the cantons pronounce against the law, it means that the partisans of reform have failed. The opponents of a constitutional law need only the one majority, the reformers need two.

In theory, of course, the initiative is a logical consequence of the referendum. If you allow the people to say, " We don't want this," you cannot deny that it would be only sensible to let them say what they do want. The actual legislative results of the method have accordingly been described when we discussed the legislative results of the referendum. We saw that between 1893 and 1894 there were three initiative demands, each of which was presented in the form of a " complete bill." In each case the Assembly advised the rejection of the proposed measure. One was eventually carried, and two were voted down. I would merely reproduce here some of the criticisms of the initiative given by writers on the Swiss Constitution.

M. Borgeaud points out that the initiative by bill and not by general motion has greatly increased the power of two factors in public life, viz., political clubs and the press : No one citizen would conceive the idea of drawing up a law all by himself and going round and getting 50,000 others to sign ; it would be impossible. A question must either be taken up by the press or by some political association. The evil is that in this case a law proceeds from powers that are anonymous and irresponsible. The article which may one day become an integral part of the constitution of the land, which will stand as a model for future legislation, which judges will have to apply and jurists to expound and interpret according to the intention of the framers—this law may be drawn up behind closed doors, or around the council board of some committee, who are then of as much importance as the regular Government. As soon as there are two signatures the law is unalterable, and goes forth to challenge the suffrages of the Swiss people. There is no room for compromise, or debate, or mutual concession. (Borgeaud, *op. cit.*, p. 325.)

The same opinion has been expressed very forcibly by M. Droz: "It is now generally agreed," he says, "that the popular initiative might at any time place the country in very considerable danger. From the moment that the regular representatives of the people have no more to say in the matter than an irresponsible committee drawing up articles in a bar parlour, it is clear that the limits of sound democracy have been passed and that the reign of demagogy has begun. The shaping of a wise constitution must always be a matter of weighing and balancing. It cannot be permitted that the gravest decisions should be the work of impulse or surprise. The generally adopted system of two Chambers and of two or three readings for every bill, is a recognition of this fact. It cannot be denied that the Swiss people have shown a want of wisdom in adopting a system of initiative which places all our institutions at the mercy of any daring attempt instigated by the demagogue, and favoured by precisely such circumstances as should rather incline us to take time for reflection." (*Contemporary Review*, p. 342, Nov. 1895.)

Both these objections are levelled against the system of initiative by completed bill. Mr. Lowell has pointed out that the differences between the initiative by completed bill and by general motion are not always so great as one would suppose, and that when the article is simple the same results would probably be brought about by either method. See p. 289.

The whole of the Federal Constitution is a carefully elaborated compromise, the aim of which was to reconcile opposing interests of canton and Confederation. By the initiative they are now placed at the mercy of any chance majority. The way is opened to both capricious legislation and clumsy legislation. The people, only interfering accidentally in public affairs and on exceptional occasions, cannot take account as well as the legislative body of the binding character of the engagements entered into by the latter in the name of the state. They cannot perceive the harmony which ought to exist between the different parts of the edifice, or the necessary inter-connection of laws. There is a danger that, by means of the initiative, encroachments may be made upon the rights acquired against the state by other states or by individuals. There is no supreme court, as in America, to quash a law of this kind, and no person or state injured has any redress. When the cantons overstep their limits they can be checked by the federal authorities, but there is no constitutional check except the people in the Swiss Confederation.

M. Droz looks upon the popular initiative as destined to accomplish a work of disintegration and destruction. He considers that whereas democracy ought to rest on a solid basis, it is now put in peril at every moment, and he suggests a total revision by which the representative Assembly may be strengthened, and the whole question put on a more solid basis.

M. Hilty, writing in 1892, says, "The initiative is a two-edged sword, and one does not know against whom it will first be turned." The unfavourable criticisms have been borne out by the results of the initiative in practice. For further criticisms see M. Numa Droz's articles in the *Contemporary Review*, March 1895, in his *Études et Portraits politiques, La Démocratie en Suisse et l'Initiative populaire*, and *La Suisse jugée par un Américain*. Also Borgeaud, *Adoption and Amendment of Constitutions*, pp. 306–332; Signorel, *Le Referendum législatif*, pp. 80–85; Hilty, *Le Referendum en Suisse et l'Initiative populaire*, in the *Revue de Droit International*, 1892, No. 5, 484–489; Berney, *L'Initiative populaire en Droit public fédéral*, and Lowell, *Governments and Parties in Continental Europe*, pp. 280–292. See also *Progressive Review*, July 1897, "The Latest Phase of Direct Legislation," by L. Tomn, and "Some Recent Political Experiments in Switzerland," by L. Waurin, in the *Annals of the American Academy*, Nov. 1895.

II

CONSTITUTIONAL REVISION IN THE CANTONS

I. Every constitution recognises the right of the citizens to demand a revision of the constitution,[2] and fixes the statutory number of signatures necessary to make such a demand valid.

The numbers are as follows :—

1 person in Glarus (8276 electors)[3] and in Appenzell, Inner Rhodes (3111).
1 person, with support of one-third of the council, in Zürich.
50 in Uri (4178).
70 in Appenzell, Outer Rhodes (12,314).
500 in Obwalden (3643).
400 in Nidwalden (2933).
1000 in Zug (5746), City Basle (12,450), and Schaffhausen (8123).
1500 in Rural Basle (11,516).
2000 in Schwyz (12,500 *cir.*).
2500 in Thurgau (24,030), and Geneva (18,909).

---

[1] See Stüssi, *Referendum und Initiativ in den Schweizer cantonen.*

[2] In Geneva the people are consulted on the question of a total revision every fifteen years. No provision is made by which they can demand a total revision during the interval. Article 152 says that "all projects of amendment"—which would seem to mean partial revisions—"shall be deliberated according to the form prescribed for ordinary laws." In 1891 a constitutional amendment was passed by which 2500 citizens could demand any ordinary law by means of a general motion or by bill. It would seem, therefore, as if the constitution now recognised the right of the people to initiate a partial revision. M. Arnoult (*La Révision des Constitutions*) seems to be of this opinion (see pp. 690–691), but M. Borgeaud (*Adoption and Amendment of Constitutions*) is doubtful. The new law does not in any way refer to Article 152, and the identification of ordinary and constitutional laws, M. Borgeaud thinks, is contrary to the spirit of the constitution.

[3] These figures in brackets are the number of registered electors according to the census of 1891.

U

3000 in Solothurn (18,374) and Neuchâtel (25,407).
5000 in Zürich (80,317), Lucerne (30,212), the Grisons (21,865), and Aargau (39,475).
6000 in Fribourg (28,733), Vaud (61,258), and Valais (27,414).
7000 in Ticino (29,500).
10,000 in St. Gall (51,639).
15,000 in Berne (112,269).

II. Every constitution, with perhaps the exception of Geneva, distinguishes in some way between partial and total revisions, and allows its citizens to demand either one or the other.

In the case of a total revision the right of the citizens seems to be limited to presenting a general request for a revision, which is carried out by the Legislature. No canton expressly recognises the right of the people to draft a total revision themselves.[1] In every canton, when a total revision is demanded by a certain number of electors, the people are first of all consulted on the general principle, and are asked, "Do you wish for a total revision?" This preliminary question is not always necessary when a total revision is proposed by the Legislature.

In the case of partial revisions two methods of procedure are recognised. In every canton the statutory number of citizens may present a general motion or request for a revision (*einfache Anregung*). In certain cantons they may, if they choose, demand the change by means of a bill on the subject drafted by themselves (*ausgearbeiter Entwurf*).

(i.) The procedure in the case of a general motion is as follows :—

(*a*) The partial revision proposed by the statutory number of citizens is laid before the people at once in Glarus, Fribourg, Rural Basle, Appenzell (Outer Rhodes), Obwalden, Nidwalden, St. Gall, the Grisons, Thurgau, Vaud, Valais,

---

[1] The canton of Appenzell (Inner Rhodes) leaves the matter doubtful : "Any citizen may propose to the Landsgemeinde either the total or partial revision of the constitution."

Neuchâtel, and Zug. In some of these cantons the Legis-lature reports for or against the popular proposal.

(*b*) In certain cantons, should the Great Council agree to the popular proposal, they draft the article without more ado ; but should they not agree with the reform demanded, they can consult the people. These cantons are Zürich, Berne, Aargau, Lucerne, Basle City, and Solo-thurn. In the case of an affirmative answer they must carry out the revision.

(*c*) In Schwyz, Ticino, and in Schaffhausen the Great Council must undertake the revision at once, whether they approve or no, and carry it out in the sense of the peti-tioners. It comes before the people to be voted on in its final shape.

(ii.) The initiative by bill is only recognised in certain cantons. They are Zürich, Schaffhausen, the Grisons, Ticino, Berne, Solothurn, and probably Geneva. In Schaffhausen, Zürich, and Berne, it it is expressly stated that partial revisions may be carried out like ordinary legislation, which may be initiated either by motion or bill. In Geneva the same identification of ordinary and constitutional laws is implied.

In every case the popular bill is voted on as it stands. The Legislature may present a counter proposal in Zürich, Schaffhausen, the Grisons, Ticino, and Solothurn. In Berne the popular proposal must be accompanied by a Government message explaining the views held by the Legislature one way or the other.

III. In many of the cantons the people do not merely decide on the revision of the constitution when they vote; they also decide by what body it shall be undertaken.

(*a*) In the following cantons the people, when they vote on any revision, total or partial, determine also whether it shall be undertaken by a constituent assembly or by the ordinary legislature : they are Nidwald, Obwald, City Basle and Rural Basle, St. Gall, Thurgau, Vaud, Valais, and Neuchâtel.

(*b*) In the case of a total revision only do the people in the following cantons decide whether the revision shall be undertaken by the Great Council or by a constituent assembly—partial revisions are undertaken by the Great Council—they are Berne, Schaffhausen, Appenzell (Outer Rhodes), Zug, Ticino, Glarus, and Grisons.

(*c*) The constitution provides that a total revision shall be undertaken by a constituent assembly, a partial one by the ordinary legislature, in the following cantons— Fribourg, Aargau, Solothurn, Geneva, Lucerne, Uri, and Schwyz.

(*d*) In Zürich, in the case of a total revision, the Great Council has to be renewed for the purpose of carrying out the contemplated change.

IV. Provision is made in the constitutions of many of the cantons that the initiative demands shall receive due attention from the Legislature, and not be put on one side. In many cases a month is given for the Great Council to decide on its course. In other cases the Great Council has to go into the matter "without delay." Should it be decided that the revision is to take place by means of a constituent assembly, it is often directed that the election of its members must be proceded with at once. In Zug the maximum time during which the Great Council can consider the demand, the maximum time during which they must appoint a constituent assembly, and the maximum time in which that assembly must have finished the revision, are all fixed. We find various provisions to guard against unwarrantable delays in Zürich, Berne, Lucerne, Solothurn, Zug, St. Gall, Aargau, and Ticino. In the Landsgemeinde cantons the proposals must be laid before the next Landsgemeinde.

V. The Great Councils have also the right to propose revisions either with or without consulting the people.

(*a*) The Great Councils may undertake a partial or a

total revision on their own authority in Zürich, Zug, Valais, Thurgau, the Grisons, Solothurn, and Appenzell (Inner Rhodes). In the Grisons the councils may, if they prefer it, consult the people first ; and in Zug the council must consult the people on the question of revision, if it be only decided on by a relative majority of the members, not by an absolute majority of all the members. The result is, that in every canton, except those just mentioned, the people are always asked, "Do you wish for a total revision ?" whenever a total revision is proposed, whether it be proposed by the Legislature or by a certain statutory number of citizens.

(*b*) The councils cannot undertake either a partial or a total revision without first asking the people, "Do you wish for a revision ?" in the following cantons—Fribourg, Obwald, Nidwald, Basle (Rural), and Neuchâtel. Ticino may be classed with the group. The Executive, which is a body of five, chosen directly by the people, can propose either a total revision or a partial revision, but the people must first of all be consulted. In the case of an affirmative answer the revision is carried out by the Legislature if they agree with the proposed revision ; if they disapprove, by a constituent assembly. The Legislature has no initiative for a partial revision, only for a total revision, and in that case the people must first be consulted.

(*c*) In City Basle the council has to consult the people on the question of a total revision, should it wish to undertake it. A partial revision may, however, be resolved on without an appeal to the people ; and the council may decide, moreover, whether it will undertake it itself or appoint a constituent assembly. The resolution on the subject is, however, submitted to the referendum upon demand.

(*d*) A fourth group give the legislative council the power to initiate and carry through partial revisions, but a total revision needs a consultation of the people : these are

Berne, Schwyz, Glarus, Schaffhausen, Appenzell (Outer Rhodes), St. Gall, and Aargau.

(*e*) In Geneva the Great Council seems to be able to undertake and carry through partial revisions, but does not seem to have any power to bring about a total one.

VI. Certain cantons provide special regulations for the passing of the proposed revision, whether it be undertaken in consequence of a demand by the people, or in consequence of a resolution of the Legislature.

In Berne the constitutional amendment must obtain a two-thirds majority of those voting. In Schwyz, Aargau, and Ticino, the proposal for a total revision needs an absolute majority of the members; in Zug an absolute majority is necessary for either partial or total revisions; and in St. Gall, for partial revisions. In Fribourg six months must elapse between the first and second reading of the revision bill. Valais, Solothurn, St. Gall, Aargau, Berne, Lucerne, Zug, Thurgau, and Zürich, all fix a certain statutory interval between the two readings.

VII. In some of the cantons it is expressly stated, that if a partial revision of the constitution bears on several points, they are to be voted on by the people separately: these are Ticino, Lucerne, Aargau, and Solothurn. St. Gall, however, provides that a total revision shall be voted on *en bloc*, and a partial one according to the articles revised. Zug directs that the constitutional amendments may be presented in groups (*gruppenweise*) or *en bloc*. The different provisions are sometimes separated in practice by a resolution of the Great Council.

VIII. In either the preliminary or the final voting, it is the absolute majority of the electors voting who decide whether the constitution or the amendment shall be accepted or not. Every constitutional change in its final form must be voted on by the people before it can come into force.

IX. If a constitution or a constitutional amendment

be rejected, several constitutions expressly state that the old one remains in force. When it is not expressed, it is understood, unless something else is determined upon. In Obwald and Nidwald the Landsgemeinde decides whether the revision shall again be undertaken or not, and by what body. In Glarus the proposal may be sent back to the Landrath for further consideration.

In Solothurn and Fribourg a second scheme has to be worked out after the first is rejected. If this is again re. jected, the people are asked if the revision shall take place. If so, a new assembly is chosen. In Rural Basle, Berne, Zug, a second project is elaborated, and if that is rejected, the old constitution remains in force.

In Schaffhausen the constituent assembly must go on drawing up new schemes until it either satisfies the citizens, or a demand has been made by 1000 voters for its dissolution. It may also itself refer the question of its own dissolution to the people. In Aargau the people are consulted on the question of going on with the revision when the first draft is rejected, and if they still wish a revision, they are asked whether it shall be undertaken by a new or by the old constituent assembly.

X. Many constitutions provide that after a total revision has been accepted, the Great Council is *ipso facto* dissolved, and fresh elections must take place. This is the case in Schaffhausen and Thurgau. The Constitutions of Lucerne, Zug, and Solothurn declare a renewal of the Legislature to be necessary only when the revision has been demanded by the people. The Constitutions of Thurgau and Solothurn not only provide for a renewal of the Great Council, but declare that all officials must be re-elected. The temporary provisions of a new constitution often contain some such provision.[1]

---

[1] See Constitution of Zug, 1894. Such a clause was incorporated into the last Constitution of Rural Basle, and omitted in the present one of 1893.

M. Borgeaud, in his book on the Amendment and Adoption of Constitutions, distinguishes between the popular and the plural initiative in constitutional matters. The distinction has been adopted by M. Arnoult in his book on the Revision of Constitutions (Paris, 1896).

The popular initiative is said to be exercised when the people decide as a necessary preliminary that a constitutional revision shall take place. The popular initiative may be invoked by a certain number of citizens or by a specified authority; but when no body is competent to undertake a revision unless commanded to do so by the majority of the people (in practice the majority of those voting), then the initiative may be said to belong to the people.

The plural initiative is exercised when a certain specified number, not a majority of the whole, are sufficient to bring about a revision without any preliminary popular consultation.

There are practically four steps in bringing about a revision by means of the popular initiative :—

(1) A preliminary demand by a certain number of citizens, or by a certain body, that the majority will exercise their right.

(2) The exercise of the right by the majority of those voting.

(3) The drafting of the scheme proposed.

(4) The final voting of the people on the scheme drawn up.

In the case of the plural initiative—

(1) A bill is drafted by one or more persons.

(2) A certain specified number of citizens sign it.

(3) It is sent to the council, who forward it to the people as it stands, and until it comes before the people in this way for final acceptance or rejection they have no voice in the matter.

The plural initiative may, however, be exercised in another way.

(1) A certain number of citizens demand a revision.

(2) The drafting is done by the council upon the petition of this certain number. The council has not the option of refusing to comply with their demand, but must draw up the scheme required.

(3) The scheme is voted on by the people.

The Swiss Constitutions themselves do not seem to grasp or express the significance of the distinction in many cases. There is, nevertheless, a fundamental difference. In the one case the people are the starting-point for the revision; in the other, a fraction of the whole people.

The initiative may be said to belong to the Legislature when the council may decide on a revision on its own authority (*von sich aus*), and carry it through without any popular consultation, only submitting the finished scheme to the people for their acceptance or rejection.

We find in the twenty-five Swiss cantons examples of all three forms. They have been classified by M. Arnoult as follows :—

(1) In certain cantons the initiative in the case of a partial or total revision belongs either to the Legislature or to the people. These cantons are Thurgau and Valais.

(2) The initiative in the case of a partial revision belongs either to the people or the Legislature. The initiative in the case of a *total* revision belongs to the people alone. These cantons are Lucerne, Aargau, St. Gall, Basle City, and Schwyz.

This means that in the case of a total revision there *must* always be a popular consultation. In the case of a partial revision there *may* be a popular consultation.

The great feature of groups 1 and 2 is that the initiative in matters of revision does not belong exclusively to the people; it is shared with the council.

(3) The popular initiative is compulsory in every case in certain cantons. The council can undertake no revision, whether partial or total, without first consulting the people. These cantons are Fribourg, Rural Basle, Neuchâtel,

Vaud, Unterwalden (Obwald and Nidwald). Either the council or a certain number of citizens can provoke the popular initiative by a demand for a total revision.

(4) Certain cantons recognise the popular initiative, the plural initiative, and the initiative of the Legislature.

(i.) They recognise the popular initiative and the legislative initiative in both partial and total revisions.

(ii.) They recognise the plural initiative in partial revisions as well. The plural initiative is exercised by a bill drafted by the electors themselves. Neither the majority of the people nor the Legislature play any part in determining whether the revision shall or shall not be undertaken. The revision comes before the people in its final shape. These cantons are Zürich, the Grisons, Berne, Zug, Solothurn, and probably Geneva.

(5) The fifth group of cantons do not recognise the popular initiative in partial revisions at all; only the initiative of the Legislature and the plural initiative. These cantons are the Grisons, Uri, Appenzell (Outer Rhodes), Schaffhausen, and Schwyz. There is no preliminary consultation whether the initiative be by bill or motion. If the initiative be by motion, the council has no option, but must draft the law demanded.

(6) A revision, whether total or partial, may be proposed by any one single person, and laid before the whole body of electors, in Glarus and Inner Rhodes, and also in Zürich if the demand be supported by one-third of the council. This is the individual initiative group.

BIBLIOGRAPHY

ADAMS (Sir Francis Ottiwell), and C. D. Cunningham. "*The Swiss Confederation.*" The French edition, by H. G. Loumeyer.

"*Annuaire de la législation étrangère,*" from 1872.

ARNAUD. "*La révision belge.*" Paris, 1893.

ARNOULT. "*Révision des Constitutions.*" Paris, 1896.

BANDELIER. "*Du referendum au point de vue jurassien.*" Porentruy, 1869.

BAUMGARTNER. "*Geschichte des schweizerischen Freistaats und Kantons St. Gallen.*"

BÉCHAUX. "*Le referendum,*" in the "*Correspondant*" of the 25th April 1892, p. 247.

—— "*Une démocratie modèle l'Unterwald.*" Paris, 1888.

BENOIST. "*Une démocratie historique, la Suisse,*" in the "*Revue des deux mondes.*" January 15, 1895.

BERNET. "*Nach zwanzig Jahren.*" 1868.

BERNEY, Professor J "*L'initiative populaire en Droit public fédéral.*" Lausanne, 1893.

BLUMER. "*Staats und Rechtsgeschichte der schweizerischen Demokratien.*" St. Gall, 1850–58.

—— "*Handbuch des schweizerischen Bundesstaatsrechtes.*" Basel, 1891.

BLUNTSCHLI. "*Lehre vom modernen Staat.*"

—— "*Geschichte des schweizerischen Bundesrechtes.*" 1875. 2 vols.

BONAPARTE (Prince Roland). "*Assemblées démocratiques en Suisse*," in the "*Figaro*" of the 28th May 1890.

BOREL. "*Étude sur la souveraineté de l'État fédératif.*" 1886.

BORGEAUD. "*Histoire du plébiscite.*" 1887.

—— "*Adoption and Amendment of Constitutions.*" 1895.

BRISSAUD. "*Le referendum en Suisse*," in the "*Revue générale du droit de la législation et de la jurisprudence.*" 1888.

BRUNIALTI. "*La legge e la libertà.*"

BRYCE. "*The American Commonwealth.*"

BURKLI. "*Directe Gesetzgebung durch das Volk.*" 1869.

CANOVAS DEL CASTILLO. "*Problemas contemporaneos, Discurso del Ateneo, La democratia pura en Suiza,*" p. 45.

CHATELANAT. "*Die Wirkungen des Referendums im Kanton Bern,*" in the "*Zeitschrift für schweizerische Statistik.*" 1877.

—— "*Die schweizerische Demokratie in ihrer Fortentwicklung.*" 1879.

CHERBULIEZ. "*De la Démocratie en Suisse.*" 1843.

COOLIDGE "*The Early History of the Referendum,*" in the "*English Historical Review.*" October 1891.

CRIVELLARI (Galileo). "*Il referendum nella Svizzera,*" in "*Serafinis Archivio Giuridico.*" Vol. xxxiv.

CURTI (TH.). "*Geschichte der schweizerischen Volksgesetzgebung.*" Zürich, 1885.

—— "*Zur Geschichte der Volksrechte.*" Zürich, 1881.

—— "*Die Volksabstimmung in der Schweizergesetzgebung.*" 1886.

—— "*Le referendum suisse,*" in the "*Revue politique et parlementaire,*" for August 1897.

DAENDLICKER. "*Histoire du peuple suisse.*" Paris, 1879.

DARESTE. "*Constitutions modernes.*"

DEPLOIGE. "*Le vote obligatoire en Suisse,*" in the "*Revue générale.*" Brussels, March 1893.

—— "*Le referendum royal,*" in the "*Revue générale.*" December 1891.

DESCHWANDEN. "*Die Entwicklung der Landsgemeinde in Nidwalden als gesetzgebende Gewalt,*" in the "*Zeitschrift für schweizerisches Recht.*" Vol. vi.

DESJARDINS. "*De la liberté politique dans l'État moderne.*" Paris, 1894.

DICEY. "*Ought the Referendum to be introduced into England?*" in the "*Contemporary Review,*" April 1890. See also the "*National Review,*" March 1894.

DROZ (Numa). "*Études et Portraits politiques.*" 1895.

—— "*The Referendum in Switzerland,*" in the "*Contemporary Review,*" March 1895; also articles in the "*Revue politique et parlementaire,*" in June and December, from 1894 to 97.

"*Direct Legislation Record,*" published in Newark. Editor, Eltweed Pomeroy. Quarterly.

DUBS. "*Die schweizerische Demokratie in ihrer Fortentwicklung.*" 1865.

—— "*Le droit public de la Confédération Suisse.*" 1878.

DUNAND (A.). "*La Législation par le peuple en Suisse.*" Geneva, 1894.

DUPRIEZ. "*Les ministres dans les principaux pays d'Europe et d'Amérique.*" Paris, 1893. 2 vols.

DUVERGIER DE HAURANNE. "*La Suisse et la révision de sa constitution,*" in the "*Revue des deux mondes.*" 1873.

ELLERO. "*La sovranità popolare.*" 1886.

ERNST. "*Die Volksrechte im eidgenössischen Bunde,*" in the "*Monat Rosen.*" 1883–84.

ESMEIN. "*Deux formes de gouvernement,*" in the "*Revue du Droit public.*" January and February 1894.

FAVRE (E.). "*La Confédération des huit Cantons.*" Geneva, 1879.

FREEMAN. "*The Growth of the English Constitution*" (description of Landsgemeinde).

FULD. "*Die versuchte Einführung des Referendums in Belgien,*" in the "*Archiv für öffentliches Recht,*" pp. 558, &c. 1893.

FÜRRER. "Histoire du Valais."

GAMOND. "*De la révision constitutionnelle en Belgique,*" in the "*Belgique judiciaire.*" 1893.

GANZONI. "*Beiträge zur Kenntniss des bündnerischen Referendums.*" Zürich, 1890.

—— "*Das Referendum im schweizerischen Staatsrecht,*" in the "*Archiv für öffentliches Recht.*" Vol. i.

GAVARD. "*Les formes nouvelles de la démocratie—Le referendum et l'initiative populaire en Suisse,*" in the "*Nouvelle Revue.*" March 15, 1892.

GENGEL. "*Aphorismen über Demokratisches Staatsrecht.*" Berne, 1864.

—— "*Die Erweiterung der Volksrechte.*" Berne, 1868.

GROTE. "*Seven Letters from Switzerland.*" 1847.

HENNE AMRHYN. "Histoire du peuple suisse." 3 vols. 1865.

HEPWORTH DIXON (W.). "*The Switzers.*" 1872.

HERZOG. "*Das Referendum in der Schweiz.*" Berlin, 1885.

—— "*Öffentliche Vorlesungen über die Helvetik.*"

HILTY. "*Das Referendum im schweizerischen Staatsrecht, Arch. für öffentliches Recht.*" Vol. ii.

—— "*Theoretiker und Idealisten der Demokratie.*" Berne, 1868.

—— "*Die Bundesverfassungen der schweizerischen Eidgenossenschaft.*" 1891.

HILTY. " *Le referendum et l'initiative en Suisse*," in the " *Revue de Droit international*," pp. 384–405, 476–489. 1892.

—— " *Politisches Jahrbuch der schweizerischen Eidgenossenschaft.*" Annual from 1886.

HOFFMANN. " *Das Plebiscit als Correctiv der Wahlen.*" Berlin, 1884.

HYMANS. " *Le Referendum dans la Constitution Suisse*," in the "*Revue de Belgique.*" January 1892.

HAULEVILLE. " *Le Referendum royal.*"

KELLER. " *Das Volksinitiativrecht nach den schweizerischen Kantonsverfassungen.*" Zürich, 1889.

LAFITTE. " *Lettres d'un parlementaire.*" Paris, 1894.

LAVELEYE. " *Le gouvernement dans la démocratie.*" Paris, 1891. Vol. ii.

LECKY. " *Democracy and Liberty.*" Vol. i.

LEFÈVRE-PONTALIS. " *Les assemblées plénières en Suisse.*" Paris, 1895.

LORAND. " *Le Referendum.*" Brussels, 1890.

LOWELL (A. L.). " *Governments and Parties in Continental Europe.*" Vol. ii. 1896.

—— " *The Referendum and Initiative : their Relation to the Interests of Labour in Switzerland and America,*" in the " *International Journal of Ethics.*" Vol. vi. October 1895.

MAINE. " *Popular Government.*" 1885.

MARSAUCHE. " *La Confédération Helvétique.*" Neuchâtel, 1891.

MACCRACKAN. " *How to introduce the Referendum and Initiative in the* 'Arena.'" Vol. vii. p. 676.

—— " *Swiss Referendum,*" in the " *Cosmopolitan,*" p. 329. 1893.

MacCrackan. "*A President of No Importance,*" in the "*North American Review,*" p. 118. 1896.

Naville. "*Apropos du referendum,*" in the "*Représentation proportionnelle.*" April 1887.

—— "*La démocratie représentative.*" Paris, 1881.

—— "*La question électorale.*" Geneva, 1871.

Nimal. "*Représentation proportionnelle et referendum,*" in the "*Journal des tribunaux.*" No. 879.

Oberholtzer (E. P.). "*The Referendum in America.*" 1893.

Orelli. "*Das Staatsrecht der schweizerischen Eidgenossenschaft, Marquardsens Handbuch des öffentlichen Rechtes.*" Vol. iv. Fribourg, 1884.

Raggio. "*La révision constitutionnelle,*" in the "*Revue socialiste.*" October 1889.

Ramalho. "*Étude historique sur le referendum,*" in the "*Revue générale d'administration.*" October and November 1892.

Rambert. "*Les Landsgemeinde de la Suisse,*" in "*Les Alpes suisse.*" Lausanne, 1889.

"Revue de droit public." September and October 1896. "*Les constitutions cantonales de la Suisse et leur révision. Le referendum législatif.*"

Rittinghausen. "*La législation directe par le peuple et ses adversaires.* Brussels, 1852.

Ross. "*The Referendum and the Plebiscite,*" in the "*Canadian Magazine.*" August 1895.

Saleilles. "*Criticism and Summary of 'The Referendum in America,' by E. P. Oberholtzer,*" in the "*Revue du Droit public,*" p. 345. September and October 1894.

Salis. "*Le droit fédéral suisse.*" 1892.

Segesser (Von). "*Sammlung kleiner Schriften.*"

Shickler. "*Schweizerisches Verfassungsbüchlein.*"

"*Sammlung der Bundesverfassungen und die in Kraft bestehenden Kantonsverfassungen,*" with yearly supplements published by the Federal Chancery.

Signorel. "*Étude de législation comparée sur le referendum législatif.*" 1896.

Sismonde de Sismondi. "*Études sur les constitution des peuples libres.*" Paris, 1836.

Sizeranne (R. de la). "*Le referendum communal.*"

"*Spectator*" (*The*), *passim.*

Sturler "*Die Volksanfragen im alten Berne.*" Berne, 1869.

Stüssi. "*Referendum und Initiativ im Kanton Zürich.*"

—— "*Referendum und Initiativ in den schweizerischen Kantonsverfassungen.*" 1893.

Sullivan (T. W.). "*Direct Legislation by the People.*" New York, 1893.

Un Progressiste. "*Le referendum en France et le futur du parti progressiste,*" in the "*Revue politique et parlementaire.*" November 1897.

Vincent (T. M.). "*State and Federal Government of Switzerland.*" Baltimore, 1891.

Vogt (G.). "*Referendum, Veto und Initiativ* in the *Zeitschrift für die gesammte Staatswissenschaft.*" Tubingen, 1873.

Wolf (P.). "*Die schweizerische Bundesgesetzgebung.*" 2 vols. Basle, 1890–91.

Wuarin. "*Le contribuable. L'evolution de la démocratie en Suisse,*" in the "*Revue des deux mondes.*" August 1, 1891.

—— "*Le referendum belge,*" in the "*Revue des deux mondes.*" August 1891.

WUARIN.   "*The Swiss Referendum,*" in the "*Progressive Review.*"   July 1897.

—— "*Some Recent Political Experiments in the Swiss Democracy,*" in the Annals of the "*American Academy of Political Science.*"   Vol. vi.   November 1895.

"*Zeitschrift für schweizerisches Recht,*" from 1892–97 (No. 3).

ZELLWEGER.   "*Geschichte des appenzellischen Volks.*" Trogen, 1830–70.

INDEX

INDEX

AARAU, 52 *n.* I
Aargau, viii *n.*, xviii, 81, 83,
88 *n.* I, 116, 123, 137, 142, 143,
154 *n.* 2, 174 *n.* I, 176, 178,
179 *n.* I, 180 *n.* I, 181 *n.* I,
184, 186, 187, 188 *n.* I, 193
n. I, 195, 197, 198, 212 *n.* I,
221, 235, 259, 270, 307, 308,
310, 311, 313
Act of Mediation, 20, 58, 59, 60,
62, 64
Age of Political Majority, 4, 45,
165
Allgemeine Tage, 52 *n.* I
Allied Powers, 61
Ambassadors, 33
America, United States of, vi,
285, 286, 290 *n.* I, 304
Amman, 72
Amnesty, 146 *n.* 2, 151 *n.* I
Anderwert, M., 105
Annemasse, 262
Anti-Semitism, 235, 236
Appenzell, xiv *n.* 2, 3, 4 *n.* 2,
5 *n.* I, 7 *n.* I, 15
—— (Inner Rhodes), 5 *n.* 2,
9 *n.* I, 22 *n.* 3, 65 *n.* I, 117,
137 *n.* 3, 212 *n.* I, 213, 221
n. I, 305, 309, 314
—— (Outer Rhodes), 9 *n.* I, 22
n. 3, 25 *n.* 2, 116, 123, 137 *n.* 3,
212 *n.* I, 270, 305, 306, 308,
310, 314
Army, control of, 111, 146 *n.* 2,
241

Army, discipline in, 242
Attestation of signatures, 156,
160
Athenian democracy, 257
Ausschreiben auf die Gemeinden,
29
Aussersihl, 254
Australasia, v, 290 *n.* I

BADEN, 12 *n.* 2, 52 *n.* I
Bailiff, 4 *n.* I, 9 *et seq.*
Bailiwicks, 6, 52 *n.* I
Bankruptcy, 114, 170, 230
Bankrupts, 4 *n.* 3, 165, 217
Basle, xiv *n.* 2, 51 *n.* 3, 60 *n.* 5,
66 *n.* 3, 213, 267
—— City, xxxiii, 85, 116, 137,
140, 143, 148 *n.* I, 154 *n.* 2,
171, 173, 188 *n.* I, 195, 197
n. 2, 201 *n.* I, 212 *n.* I, 281,
305, 307, 309, 313
—— Rural, 72, 75, 83, 88 *n.* I,
116, 123, 137, 139, 142, 175,
176, 180 *n.* I, 186, 187, 188
n. I, 195, 196, 197, 198, 201
n. I, 212 *n.* I, 259, 270, 305,
306, 309, 311, 313
Basler Volksblatt, 234 *n.* 2.
Beitag, 30 *n.* I
Belgium, proposed referendum in,
v, xxxix *et seq.*
Belgian Communes, 291 *n.* 2
Berne, x *n.* I, xv, xviii, xxii,
44 *et seq.*, 51 *n.* I, 60 *n.* 5, 76,
83, 88 *n.* I, 93, 94, 104, 116,

Office, plurality of, 263
—— tenure of, xxiii, xxviii, 7 *n.* 3
Officials, removal of public, 65
—— salaries of, xxiii, 146, 235
Ohio, 139 *n.* 1
Old Catholics, 114, 258
Opposition in Federal Assembly, the, 215, 222, 286

PARDON, right of, xxiii, 146 *n.* 2
Parish meetings, xii
Party system, absence of, xxv *et seq.*, 296
Patents, decree concerning, 222
Patrician families, 44, 48, 49, 54, 61, 63, 64, 65, 90 *n.* 1, 165
Paupers, 165, 215, 217
Peace, conclusion of, 33, 46, 62, 108, 146 *n.* 2
Pedrazzini, M., 270, 279
Pensions, 232, 256 *n.* 1
Petition, definition of, 298
—— right of, 67, 110, 191
Places of burial, 115
Police, 32, 52 *n.* 1, 172, 295
Political societies, influence of, 106, 302
Poor law, 179 *n.* 1
Population, ix, xxxiii, 25 *n.* 2
Postulat, xxiv
Prefectures, 55
President of the confederation, xxiv
"Presiding canton," 60 *n.* 5
Press, freedom of, 65, 67, 102
—— influence of, 85, 106, 163, 302; foreign, 247
Priests, 112
Primary assemblies, 75
Privileges, abolition of, 59, 62, 158 *n.* 1, 263
Projet Girondin of 1793, 57 *n.* 2
Proletariat, absence of, xxxiii, 247
Property, law of real, 295

Proportional representation, xv *n.* 9, xviii, xxi, 60, 67, 122, 234, 256 *n.* 1, 279, 280, 281, 286
Proudhon, 35
Proxy vote, 186, 256
Prussia, King of, 66
Publication of laws, 153, 173
Publicity, 160 *n.* 2
Public meeting, right of, 102
—— works, 295
Python, M., 151 *n.* 1

RADICALS, xxv, 72, 78, 83, 93, 108, 113, 115, 123, 141, 221, 223, 225, 227, 264, 266, 269, 270, 272, 296
Radical measures, popular dislike of, 247, 250 *n.* 2
Railway, Jura Simplon, 244
—— St. Gothard, 153 *n.* 1, 245
—— Swiss Central, 233
Railways, 82, 83, 111, 233, 244 5, 256 *n.* 1, 262
—— accounts demanded, 242
—— Alpine, 220
—— funicular, 245
Referendary delay, cantonal, 173; federal, 154, 299
Referendum, v, 3, 29 *n.* 2, 76, 117 *n.* 1, 150, 190, 193, 226, 268, 285
—— at the option of the Legislature, 174 *et seq.*
Referendum in cantonal affairs, 29 *et seq.*, 38, 42, 45 *et seq.*, 49 *n.* 1, 60, 63, 75, 76, 81 *et seq.*, 89; compulsory, 45, 75, 84, 137, 140, 141, 142, 176 *et seq.*, 188, 262, 278 *n.* 1, 287; optional, 45, 76 *n.* 2, 171 *et seq.*, 183, 192, 278 *n.* 1
Referendum in federal affairs, 52, 56, 101 *et seq.*, 147 *et seq.*, 295; compulsory, xvi, 125 *et seq.*

Printed by BALLANTYNE, HANSON & Co.
Edinburgh & London

Other Works by the same Authors.

Lightning Source UK Ltd.
Milton Keynes UK
UKOW06f2100200617

303778UK00012B/649/P